Couture BRIDALWEAR

Pattern Layout and Design

by Margot Arendse

BT Batsford · London

First published 2000

Illustrations by Margot Arendse

Front cover: Clifton Hill House, University of Bristol
Photograph by Paul Phillips

ISBN 0 7134 8473 X

A CIP catalogue record for this book is available from the British Library.

Printed in Spain
for the publishers,
B. T. Batsford Ltd,
9 Blenheim Court,
Brewery Road,
London N7 9NT

A member of the Chrysalis Group plc

Contents

Acknowledgements

To Ann Kay, editor, who gave me such good advice and encouragement.

To Peter Hawkins, University of Bristol, and a supportive husband, without whom this book would have been impossible.

To Dawn Cloake, author of fashion textbooks and retired lecturer at the London College of Fashion, who shared some of her experiences with me.

To Maureen Goodwin, retired lecturer and pattern cutting specialist at the London College of Fashion, who gave me the chance to teach and supported this idea.

To Nottingham Laces and Trimmings, who provided all the fabric examples.

To Paul Phillips, my photographer, who diligently came at a moment's notice to provide me with the shots I needed.

Last but not least, the help and support from B.T. Batsford and a special thanks to Martina Stansbie who gave me this opportunity in the first instance.

Margot Arendse

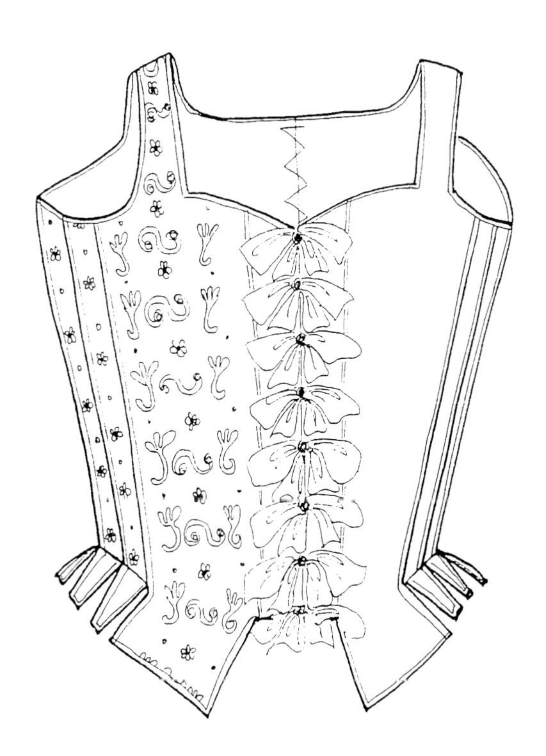

Introduction

When I came to do bridalwear, having worked as a designer in women's fashion for many years, I realised how much satisfaction it gave me. The more complicated the dress became, the better I felt. Then when I began teaching it as a subject, I learnt to appreciate the extent to which students, whether full time or part time, wanted to know more about the concept and creation of the dress.

This book is aimed at reaching students who do not have specific training in this area when they leave college *and* for those who want to know more about how a dress pattern is achieved from beginning to end. The expansion of the wedding market in recent times has meant that more students are keen to broaden their profile in this direction.

I have tried to give coverage to both basic and intricate shapes, and to take you through all aspects of the dress from the design stage through to make-up. The influx of costume drama on our screens has meant that period styling has increased, from the empire line to bustles and boned bodices. Here I've illustrated how these shapes come about, with the hope that these examples will enable you to do similar things. I have included a certain amount of material about the origin of these styles, as some students like to learn about their history.

There are many books on *pattern cutting* which provide a more comprehensive study for general use and for the drafting of blocks. I've tried to tailor this book down to the most popular shapes in bridalwear and to show how these shapes unfold from a flat pattern to a three dimensional shape. It's possible to combine the flat pattern method with draping, especially on collars, some necklines and skirt styles, and here making a *toile* is important. A *bought pattern* that fits your measurements can be used and readjusted to a style or styles that suits you, even if you don't have a college block or a block to your personal measurements, to work from.

A brief history of the bridal gown

The origin of the bridal gown is not clearly defined but wedding ceremonies do date back to the Middle Ages and beyond. It was an honour for the father to find a suitable husband for his daughter and for the family to celebrate the occasion. Then, the head-dress worn as a *garland* and the hair length of the wearer symbolised purity and played an important role in the discipline of the church. Later on, the wearing of a *veil* replaced this practice.

The *white wedding*, a tradition celebrated for centuries, was galvanised by the Victorians. This period saw the most elaborate changes in the bridal gown. An important feature of the dress of this period was the extreme fullness of the skirt. In the later half of the 19th century, there had been a colour change from white to cream and subtle changes to the dress began to occur. Sleeve shapes, like the *leg o'mutton sleeve* and draped train became important. Veils were long and bustles replaced the full crinoline skirt. Extravagant embroidery and lace applications to designs meant that manufacturing skills and output made Britain a leading influence in this field. Stiff silk satins and taffetas were some of the popular fabrics worn at the time. The *Empire line* in the Edwardian and Georgian period was soft and flowing with chiffons trimmed with rich embroidery: with result that lace makers found themselves in work for a long time. The *aristocracy* led the way in fashion and after a royal wedding, simulated versions would flood the market. The upper-class influence is still relevant to style today.

Ivory is still the main colour worn in contemporary bridal wear. However, experimentation in the design of the bridal gown has set a new agenda for the future. Rich shades of gold and bronze and other baroque features are becoming popular. Veils are being replaced by *hats* and *ornate coronets*. Ceremonies can be performed almost anywhere today, making the modern wedding day a less formal occasion.

Measurements

PART 1

The size chart is loosely based on the British Standard measurements. It's a guide line to use when taking your own. The chart deals with four basic sizes, in both *metric and imperial measurements.* Check these sizes against your block or bought pattern as it will be useful for alterations when using them for different people or styles. *No two figures of the same size will be identical.* Do not make assumptions with regard to what your measurements ought to be. They will be personal to each individual and therefore it is important to take them accurately for a perfect fit. The height and girth of the individual may or may not be in proportion and so proceed with caution when one allows tolerance in some areas and not in others for different shaped figures.

SIZE	10(38)		12(40)		14(42)		16(44)		
Bust	83	32½″	88	34½″	93	36½″	98	38½″	99
Waist	61	24″	66	26″	71	28″	76	30″	85
High Hip	80	31½″	85	33½″	90	35½″	95	37½″	102
Hip	90	35½″	95	37½″	100	39½″	105	41½″	104
Across back	32	12½″	34	13¼″	36	14″	38	14¾″	42
Across chest	31	12¼″	33	13″	35	13¾″	37	14½″	36
Neck	36	14″	37	14½″	38	15″	39	15½″	
Shoulder	11.5	4½″	11.8	4⅝″	12.1	4¾″	12.4	4⅞″	9
Nape to back waist	39.5	15½″	41	16¼″	41.6	16½″	42.2	16¾″	36
Nape to hip	60	23¾″	69	27¼″	78	30¾″	87	34¼″	54
Front neck to waist	33	13″	34	13 ⅜″	35	13¾″	36	14⅛″	47
Upperarm girth	25.5	10″	27	10½″	28.5	11¼″	30	12″	
Elbow girth	24	9½″	25.5	10″	27	10½″	28.5	11¼″	
Wrist	15.2	6″	16	6¼″	16.8	6½″	17.6	6¾″	
Overarm length	57	22½″	58.5	23″	60	23½″	61.5	24″	
Underarm length	45	17¾″	46	18⅛″	47	18½″	48	18⅞″	
Armhole depth	17.5	6¾″	18.3	17¼″	19.1	7½″	19.9	7¾″	
Nape to knee	96.5	38″	98	38⅝″	99.5	39⅛″	101	39¾″	
Nape to floor	137.2	54″	139.2	54¾″	141.2	55½″	143.2	56¼″	
Height	160	63″	162.5	64″	165	65″	167.5	66″	

Figure assessment

Figs 1 - 2 illustrate the measurements taken for the essential parts of the body that would determine the fit of the garment. For bridalwear, it's important to have the design of the garment in mind or even with you, when measuring a client, since there will be a some measurements that will not be available on the chart.

Fig 1: Front ***Fig 2: Back***

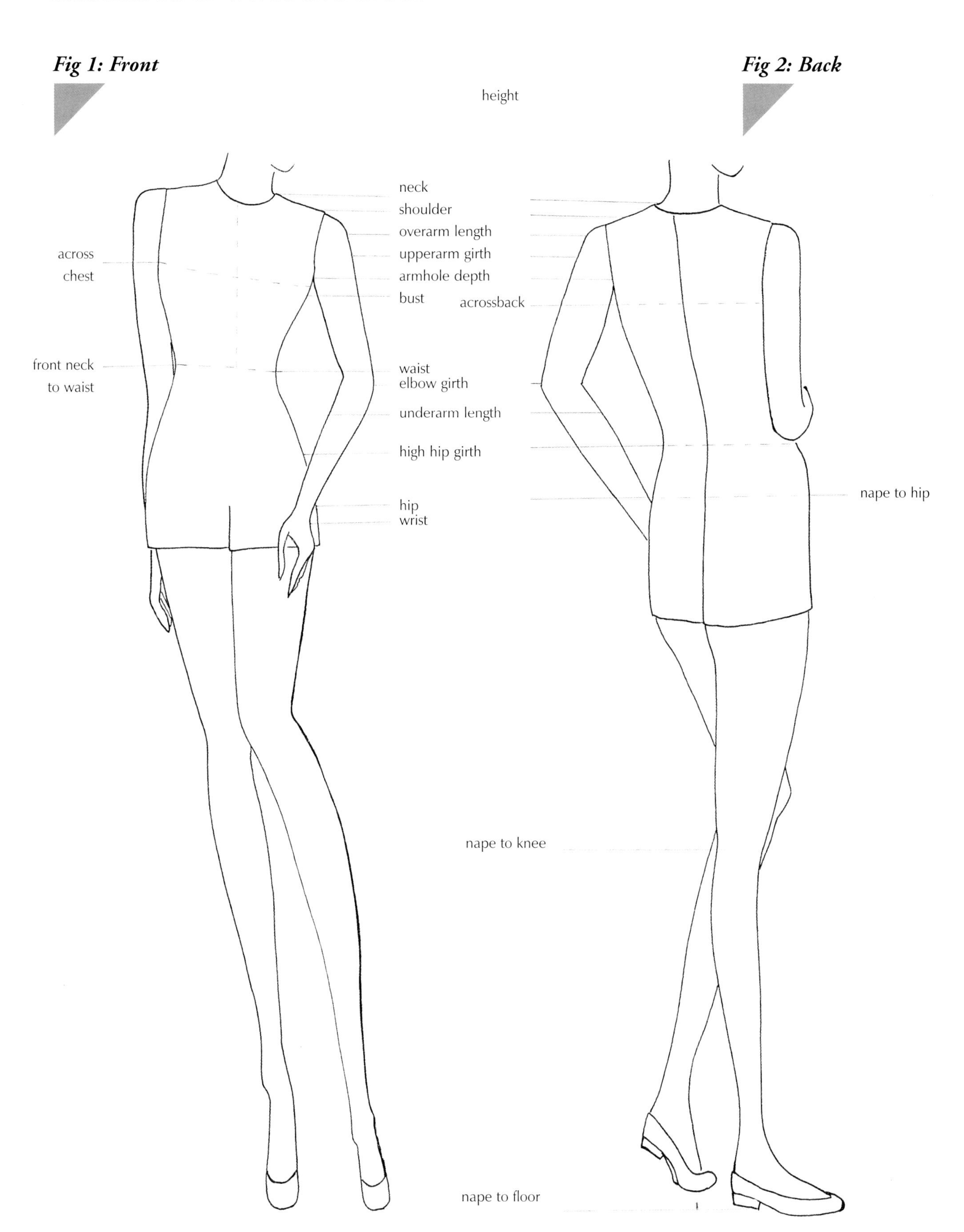

Taking measurements

- Ensure that the person wears similar underwear to that which will be worn with the dress she has planned, when taking her measurements. Surfaces with dimensions should be removed, such as belts and buckles, heavy clothing etc.

- Note down on your personal chart, alternative or extra measurements your might need for different styling, or when applying more ease or less ease in some places. Also include special measurements such as:

  a. From the side front waist to the CF point on most bodices.

  b. Train lengths.

  c. Off the shoulder necklines.

  d. The head circumference for veils and head dresses.

- The section under part two *(Fig.27)* and part six (boned bodices) are good examples where this matter applies. Here, a variety of styles are altered from the measurements of the basic block.

- Tape or string can be used on the waist and base of neck when taking measurements so that the distance from nape to waist or waist to hip can be judged more accurately.

- The nape to waist measurement is taken from the bone at the back of the neck (which can be felt with a finger, when tilting the neck forward slightly) down to the waist.

- The shoulder measurement is taken from the base of the neck (where the neck has been taped), to the bone at the end of the shoulder line.

- Measurements that are taken across the bodice for the back and chest for boned bodices or off the shoulder styles, may need to be pinned onto a foundation garment. A leotard or a stretch body will be suitable.

- Place the tape over the fullest part of the bust. Remember to have the bra or a replica of the one (if worn) on the figure, to achieve an accurate measurement.

- The bust, waist and some hip measurements for bridalwear, are taken without ease. However, the hip measurement will usually have some ease, especially on bridesmaids' dresses. For some styles, however, which include boned bodices, they are taken quite tightly.

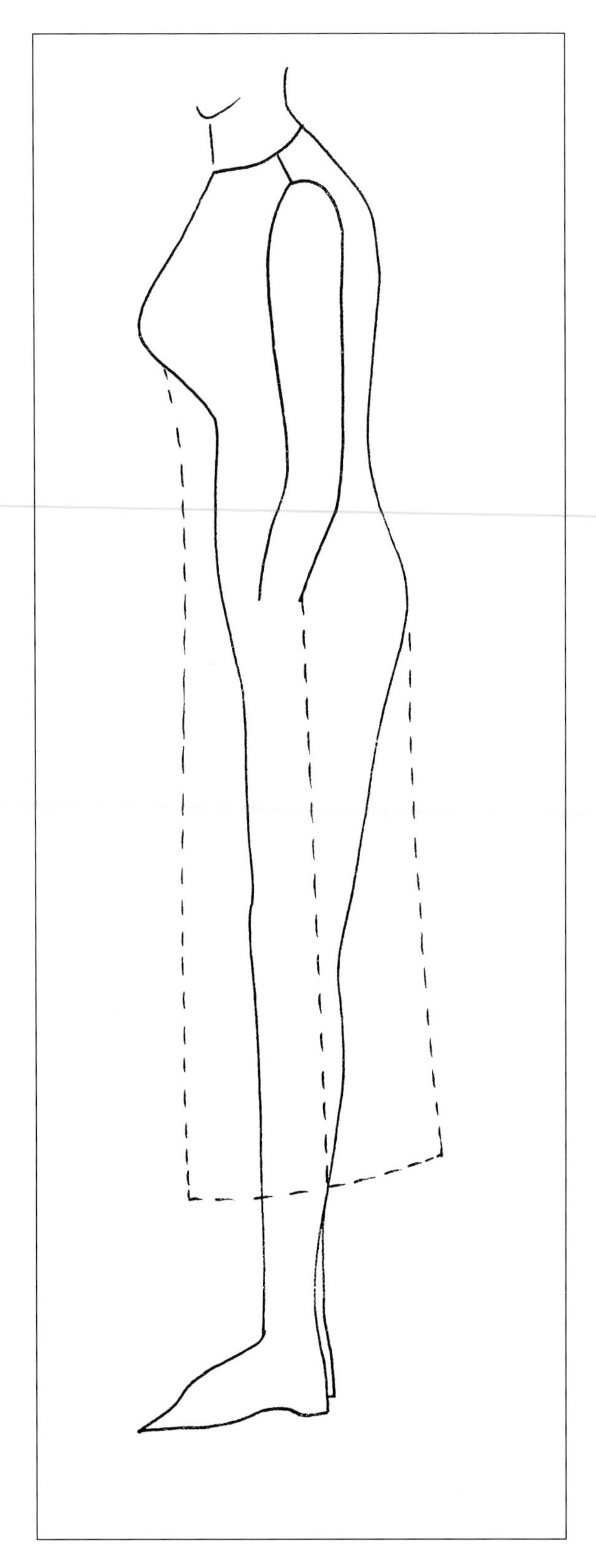

Fig. 3: Slouching posture

- The high hip measurement is taken approximately 10cm (4") down from the narrowest part of the waist. Mark with a pin or chalk and then measure down to the hip (over the widest part of that area).

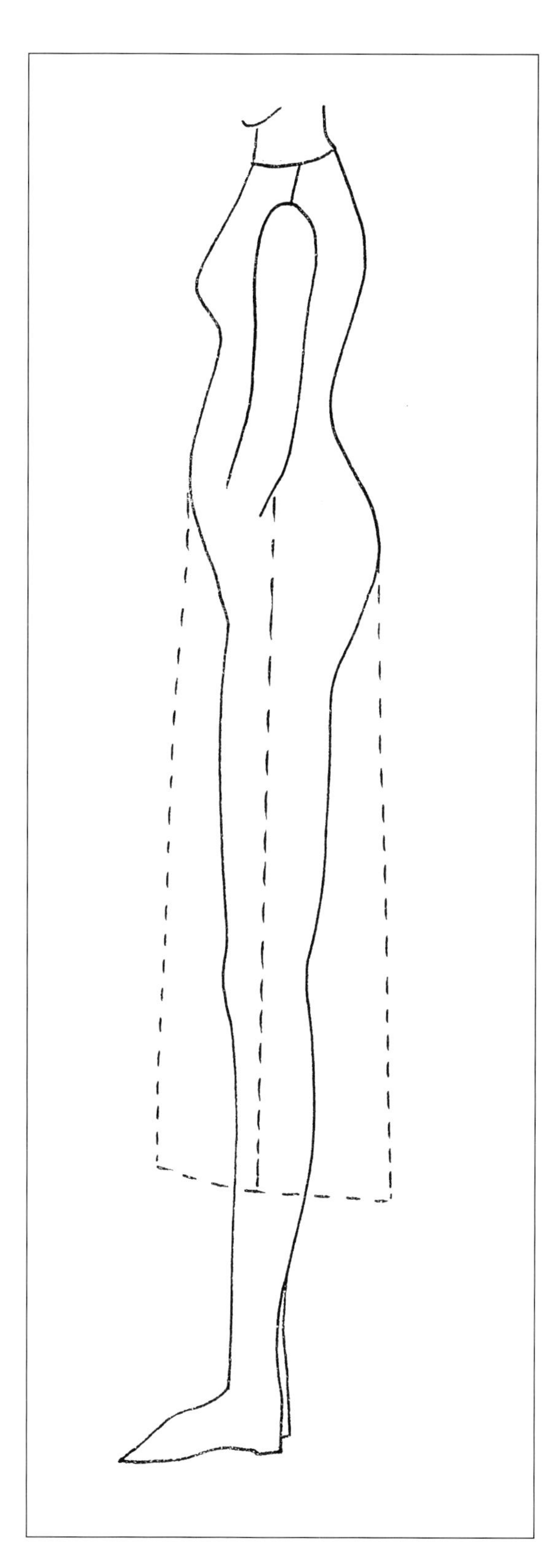

Fig. 4: Large bust and round shoulders

- Taking the sleeve measurements, the arm should be at a slight angle bending inwards at the elbow, with the wrist positioned towards the hip. The armhole depth is determined by the style of the garment as there is no tangible measurement to take.

- The upperarm girth is taken on the widest part of the arm with the tape positioned closely under the arm. The circumference on the upper and lower arms should have some ease especially at the elbow.

- The wrist measurement can vary depending on the shape produced. For styles with pointed CF sleeve edges, the wrist measurement is taken quite tightly, if there is an opening.

- The outer sleeve is taken with the tape positioned on the shoulder bone and brought down over the elbow and stops at the wrist bone. Allow some ease (0.5cm-¼″).

- The underarm length is taken close to the hollow of the underarm and stops at the wrist bone.

- The height of the figure is taken from the top of the head to ground level at the back of the ankle (after shoes have been removed).

Garment balance: Figs 3-4

In the two illustrations shown here we see the importance of the garment balance which affects garments that hang loosely, more so than those which fit the bodice. With the help of these fundamental points, the balance can be evened out.

- Sound judgements have to be made where the contour and stance of the body shape is not in proportion to the height of the figure. A large bust on narrow hips tends to produce round shoulders and may induce the swing of the garment (*Fig.3*). This also applies to a slouching posture, where the stomach protrudes in front and the bottom sticks out at the back (*Fig.4*).

- The examples given can determine the swing from the shoulder. The shoulder line, therefore, has to be adhered to as it is crucial for the fit of the garment and hemline.

- In order to counterbalance the swing, the drafting of the pattern may in some cases alter the shape of the block. For instance, a fraction more on the front shoulder, and less on the back, may be required to produce an even hemline. This would also change the position of the side seams.

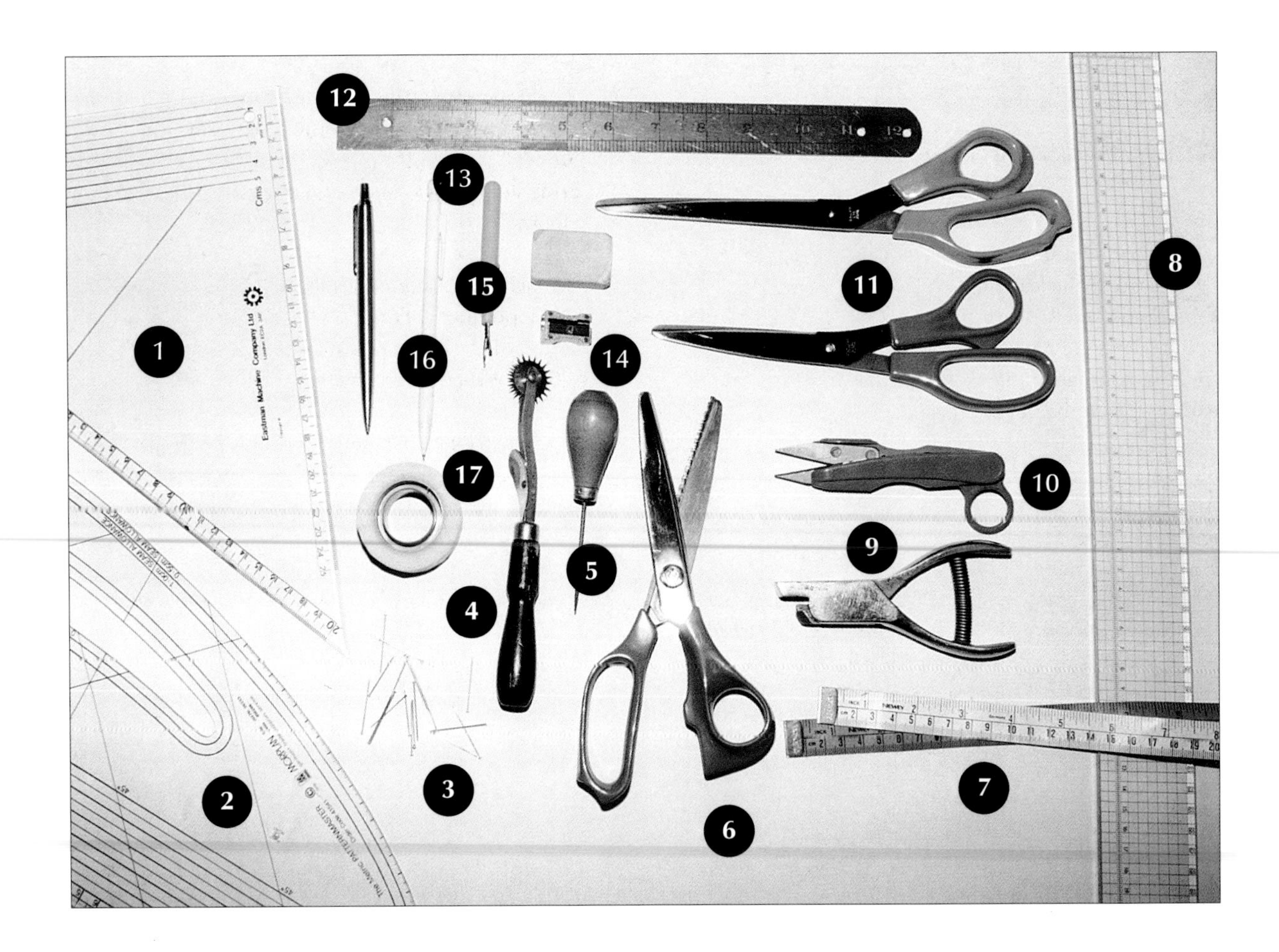

Equipment

- Tools for pattern cutting and measuring.
- Some of these tools are essential.
- The ones marked * are optional.

1 *Set square*
2 *Pattern master**
3 *Pins*
4 *Tracing wheel*
5 *Bradawl**
6 *Pinking shears*
7 *Tape measure*
8 *Metre or yard stick*
9 *Notches*
10 *Paper shears*
11 *Fabric shears*
12 *Ruler*
13 *Rubber*
14 *Pencil sharpener*
15 *Unpicker*
*Pinking shears**
Pattern paper (can be obtained through specialist shops or brown paper at any stationers or post office)
16 *Pen and pencil*
17 *Sellotape*

Darts and their function

PART 2

A basic bodice normally has two darts: for the front block there is one on the shoulder line and one at the waistline *(Fig. 1)*. The back bodice darts are narrower and the shoulder dart is small in comparison to the waist dart, which is long and reaches to below the shoulder blades *(Fig. 2)*.

Shoulder darts on the bodice for both the front and back block are seldom used in bridalwear because most necklines are low and styled without them. For the front bodice, however, the shoulder dart, when used, is placed into the waist dart or elsewhere, except in *shoulder panelled seams and tailored jackets,* where these darts are important. As for the back shoulder dart, when not in use, remove it *(Fig. 2/A)* or ignore it. The chest line and the bust line are usually marked on patterns. Sometimes, near the bust point, smaller darts extend into the armhole and towards the centre front; they are there for ease in the bodice or they may be suppressed and put into the main darts when a more structured silhouette is required.

a. Cut through to dart point and fold up shoulder dart.
b. Make the closed dart the same width at the shoulder seam.
c. There is a small amount of ease along the seam line of the shoulder.
d. Fill in the amount lost at armhole from slash line at (a) to shoulder point

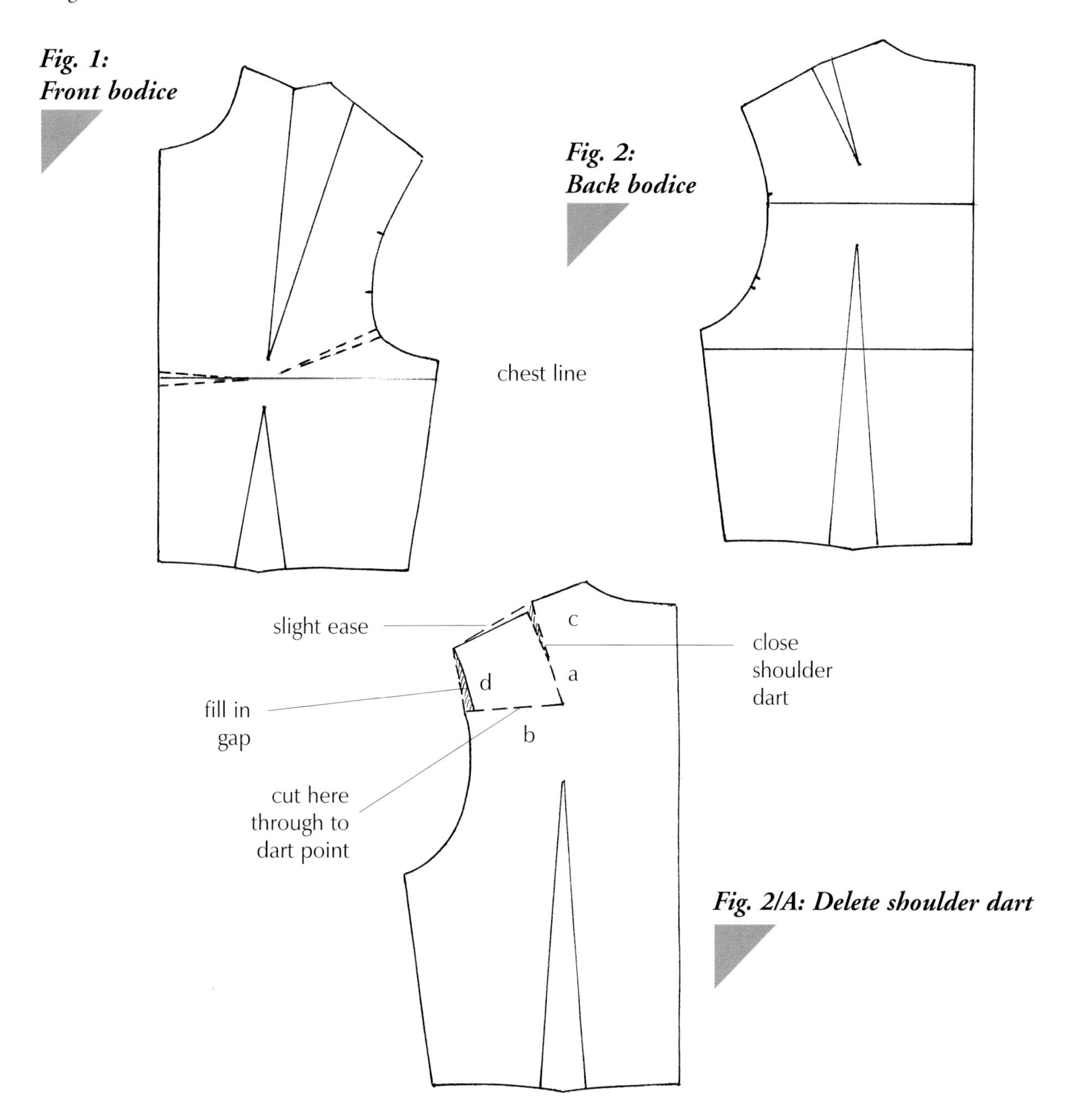

Fig. 1: ***Front bodice***

Fig. 2: ***Back bodice***

Fig. 2/A: Delete shoulder dart

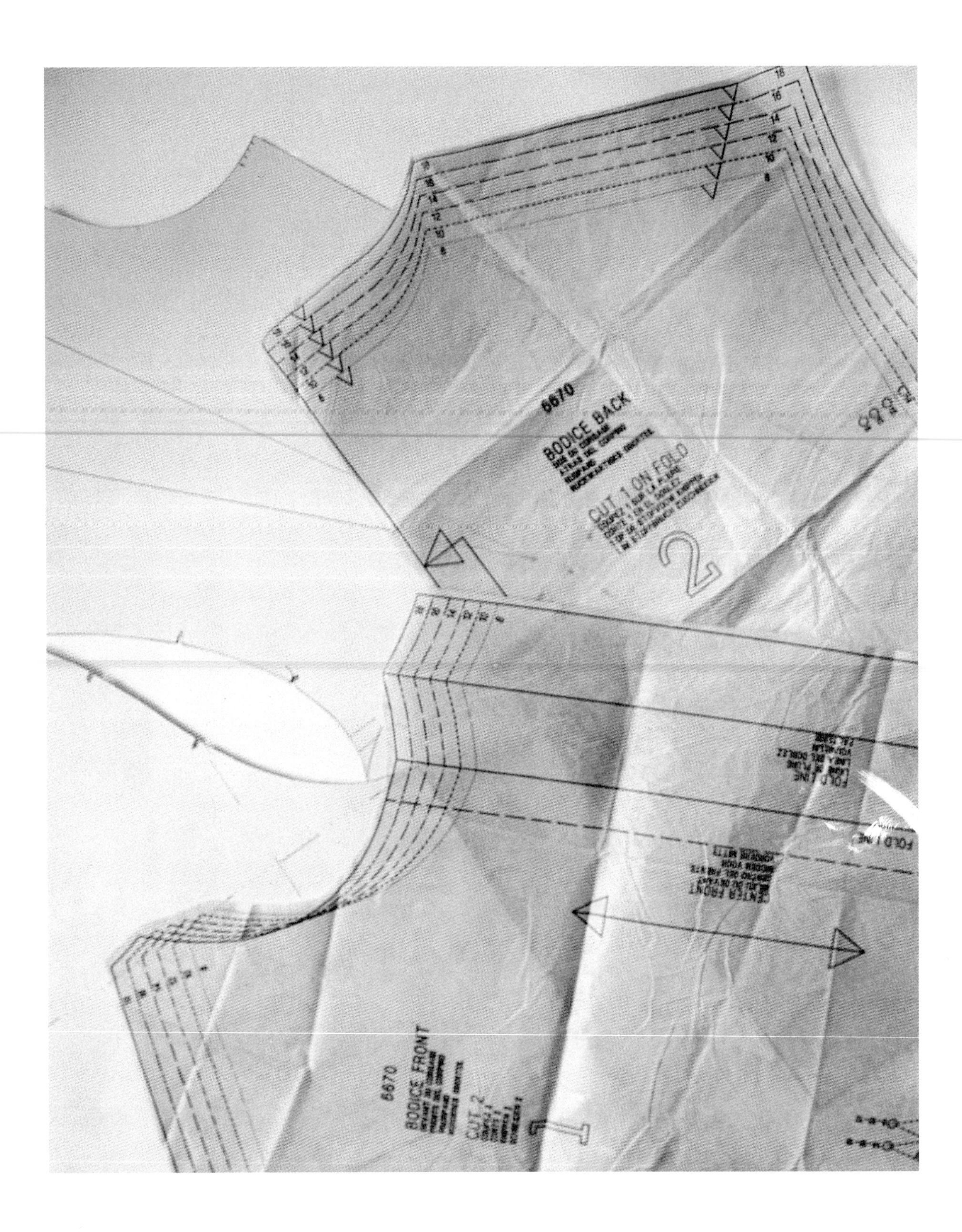

Bought patterns: Fig. 3

If a college block is not available then there are several bought patterns one can use for creating one's own bodice. ***Fig. 3***: *Bought patterns* require a side or waist dart or princess line seams. When choosing a style with a fitted bodice, make sure the bust size matches your full bust measurement. Other important measurements are the waist line and hip measurements. To be accurate, let someone else take your measurements. *Bridal patterns* are less easy to adapt into something new, unless the styles are quite simple. Unlike college blocks, some patterns will already have seam allowances on them (1.5cm-⅝" normally) so be sure to take this into account before adapting your pattern into a new shape. To avoid confusion, re-style your new shape without seams. These can be put in later.

Finding a new dart position: Fig. 4

A new dart position is found:

- When the style line is changed i.e. when the existing dart(s) are to be replaced by new ones and the basic bodice neckline and armholes are altered *(Fig. 4)*.
- To do this, you close it by *folding up* the old dart and *opening up* where the new dart(s)are to be (*Fig. 4/A*).
- Or by *pivoting* to create the darts as illustrated on *Fig. 5*. This method is used by the more experienced pattern cutter. However, either way, the fit will be achieved. Pivot the pattern by using a sharp pencil or a pivot pin through the bust point of both the darts as seen on ***Fig. 5/A***. As the shoulder dart line **(A)** closes to the neck edge, swing your block pattern clockwise to **(B)** and mark in pattern. The dart at the waist remains the same. From **(B)** mark in pattern to **(C)** where the new dart is to be.

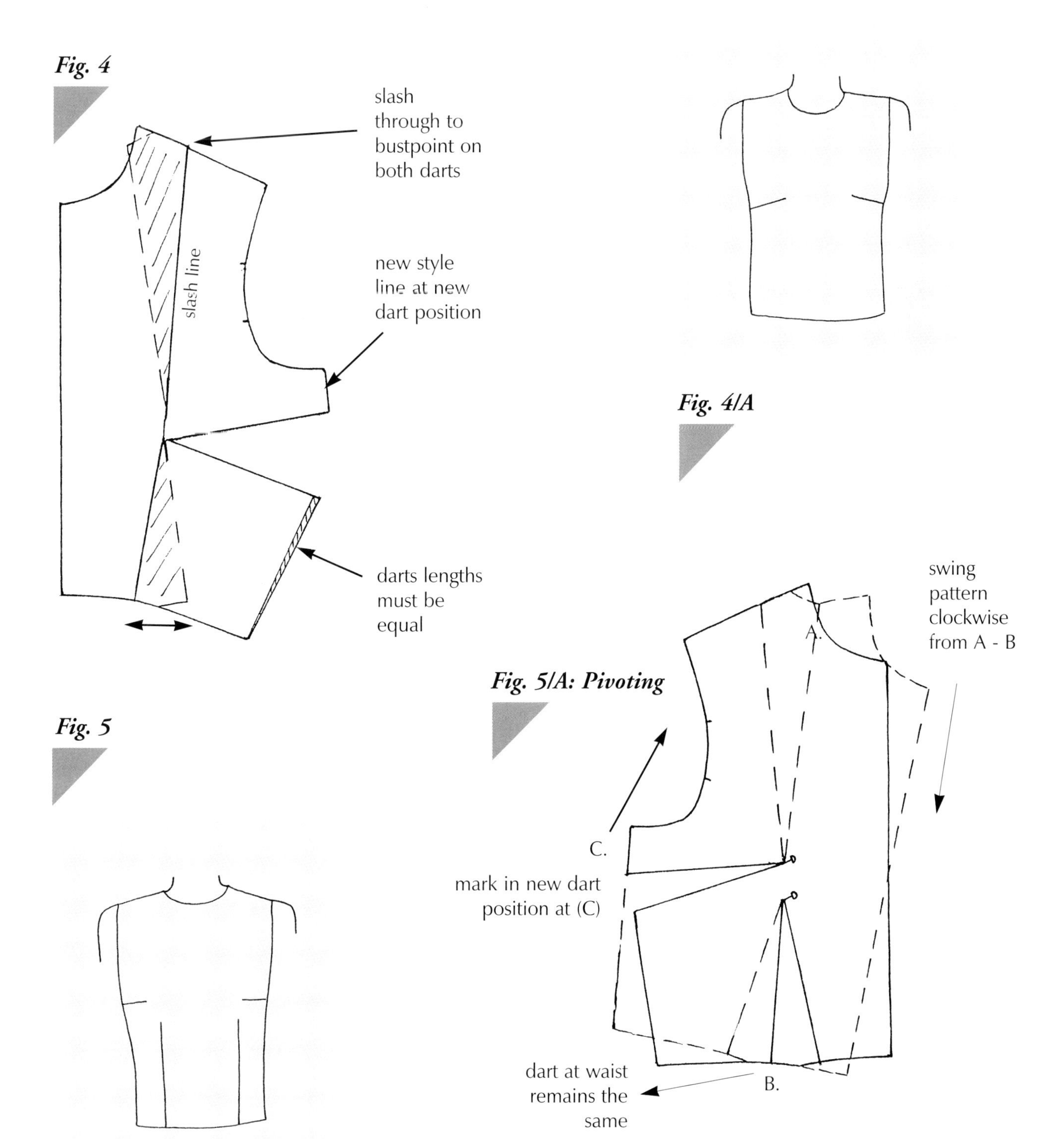

The folding of darts: Figs 6-9

The folding of darts is important and needs to be accurate for the following reasons:

a. When *folding dart seams together* see that the seams are the *same length*, so that they do not work against each other (***Fig. 6***).

b. When stitching *darts into other seams* make sure that they don't pull. This happens when the dart lengths are not the same (***Fig. 7***).

c. Before you change the position of your dart, it's worth *joining up* your shoulder and waist darts through your bust point. It becomes easier when you slash through these darts and open up where your new style line is to be (***Fig. 8***). Some ease is lost across the bust point but can be restored when you create your new shape.

d. Straight darts are *not stitched to the bust point* because they distort the bust shape (***Fig. 9***). The finished dart should be stitched about 1.5cm (5/8") away from the bust point. *Measure down to bust point from shoulder and at CF between bust points.

e. The **bust point** always remains the same *unless the bust size and shape have altered.* When this happens move the bust point away from its position by between 1.5 and 2cm. It's worth making up a toile to establish its accuracy, before creating a new style.

Fig. 6

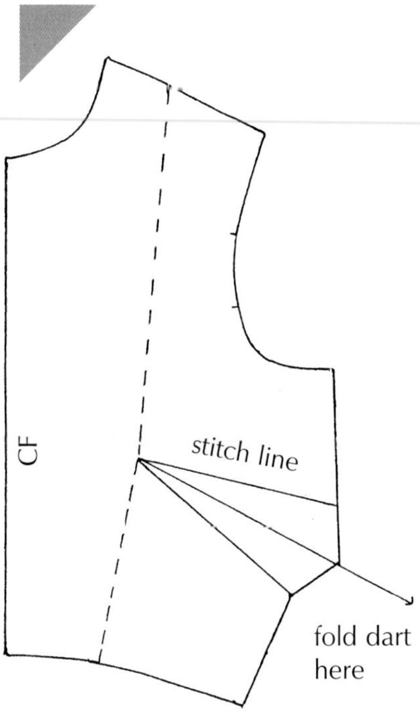

CF
stitch line
fold dart here

Fig. 7

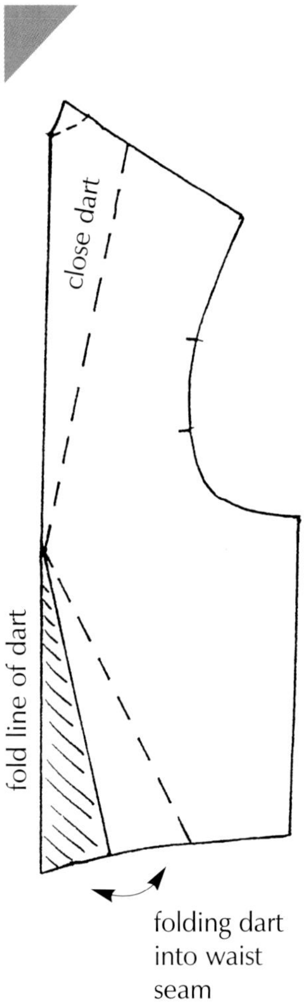

close dart
fold line of dart
folding dart into waist seam

Fig. 8: Joining up of darts:

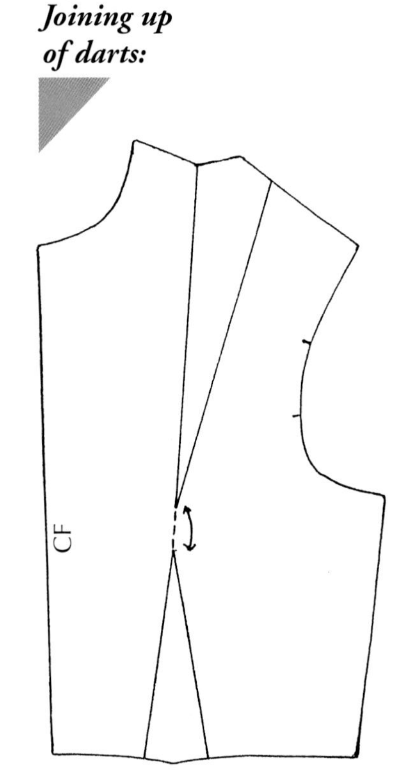

Fig. 9: Stitch away from bust point

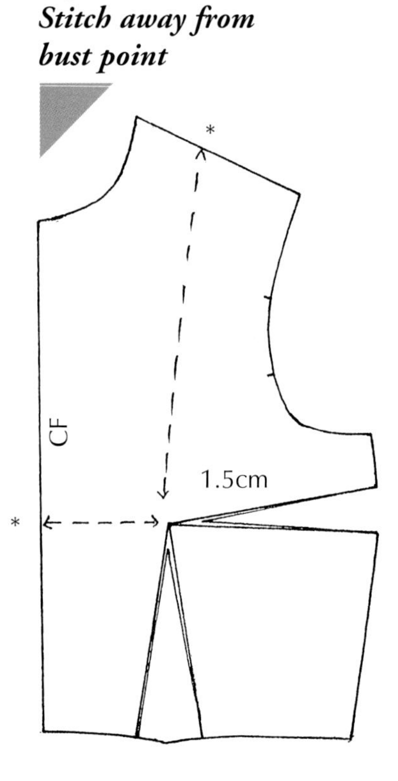

Grain lines and notches: Fig. 10

Grain lines and **notches** (*Figs 10 - 10/A*), are as important to the fit of the bodice and sleeves as are new style lines, especially on panelled seams and bias cut patterned pieces, where all too often front and back panels can get mixed up. *Fabric textures* vary from natural fibres through to synthetic ones. The *warp threads* run down the length of the fabric. Position your grain line onto the warp and use the selvedge of your fabric as your guide to a straight grain. Grain lines help to *prevent shading* especially on raised surfaces such as velvet or on silks with shots of colour in them. They help when marking in pattern pieces to fit into the width of one's cloth for costing purposes and to match up stripes and checks. *Notches* at the armholes (***Fig. 10/B***) should correspond with those on the sleeve crown. Extra ones are put in for gathers and tucks. On bought patterns these are clearly marked.

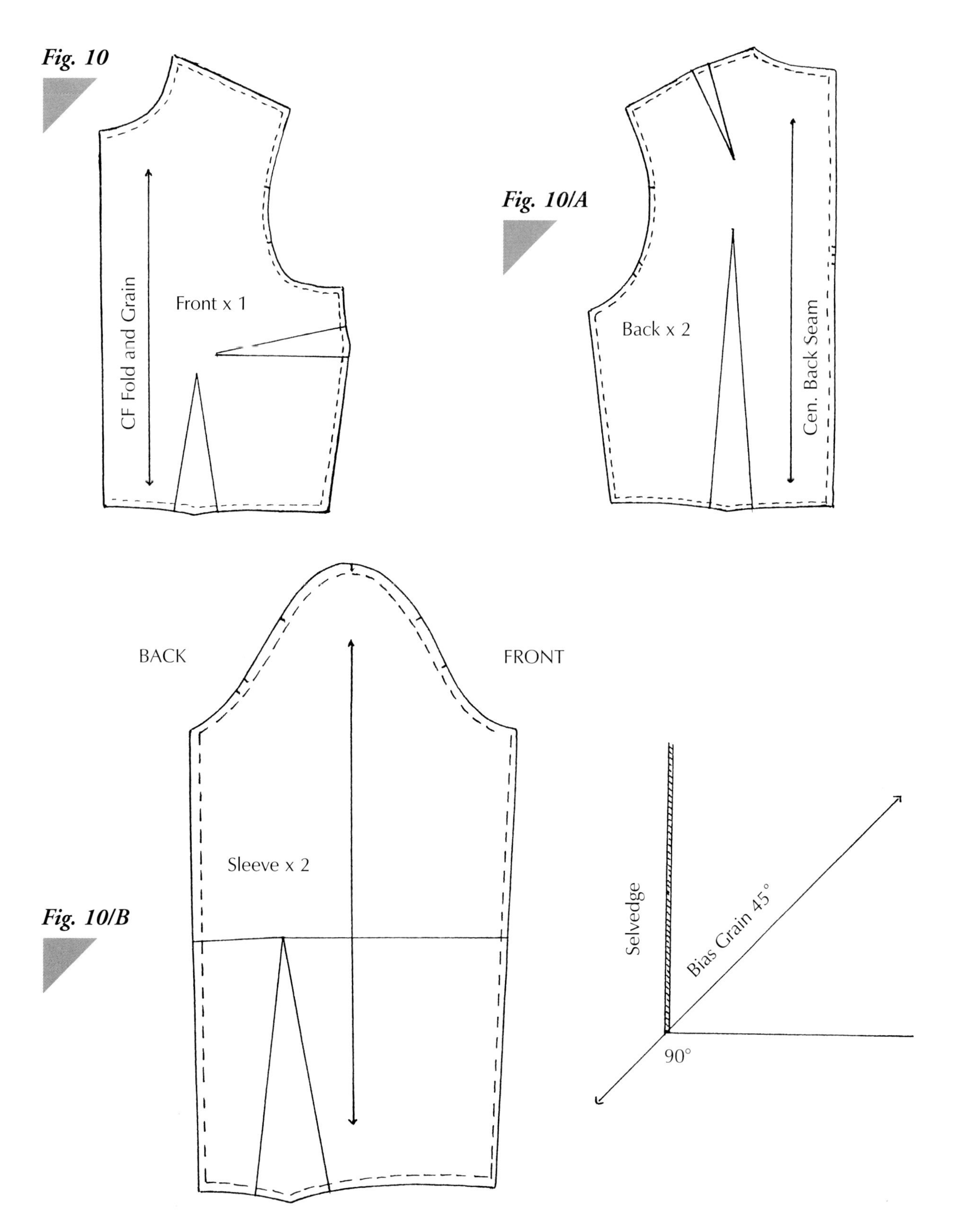

Dart shapes

In the shapes we see illustrated in this chapter, the bodice darts are either straight or curved, or they are long or short. The aim of the dart(s) is to shape the figure according to the style you want to achieve. By moving the dart(s) from one position to another on the flat pattern method, you control the shape of the design and give the fabric dimension when it comes to fitting it on a body or a stand. This activity is called *dart manipulation*. Many dart shapes in contemporary bridal wear are straightforward. These examples are but a few *basic dart shapes* which are commonly used: *Figs 11-12* are short darts for bodices with under-bust seams or those placed at the armhole. *Figs 13-14* are longer straight darts starting below the bust point and finishing at the waist seam. Panelled seams start either from the shoulder line or from the armhole (*Figs 15-16*).

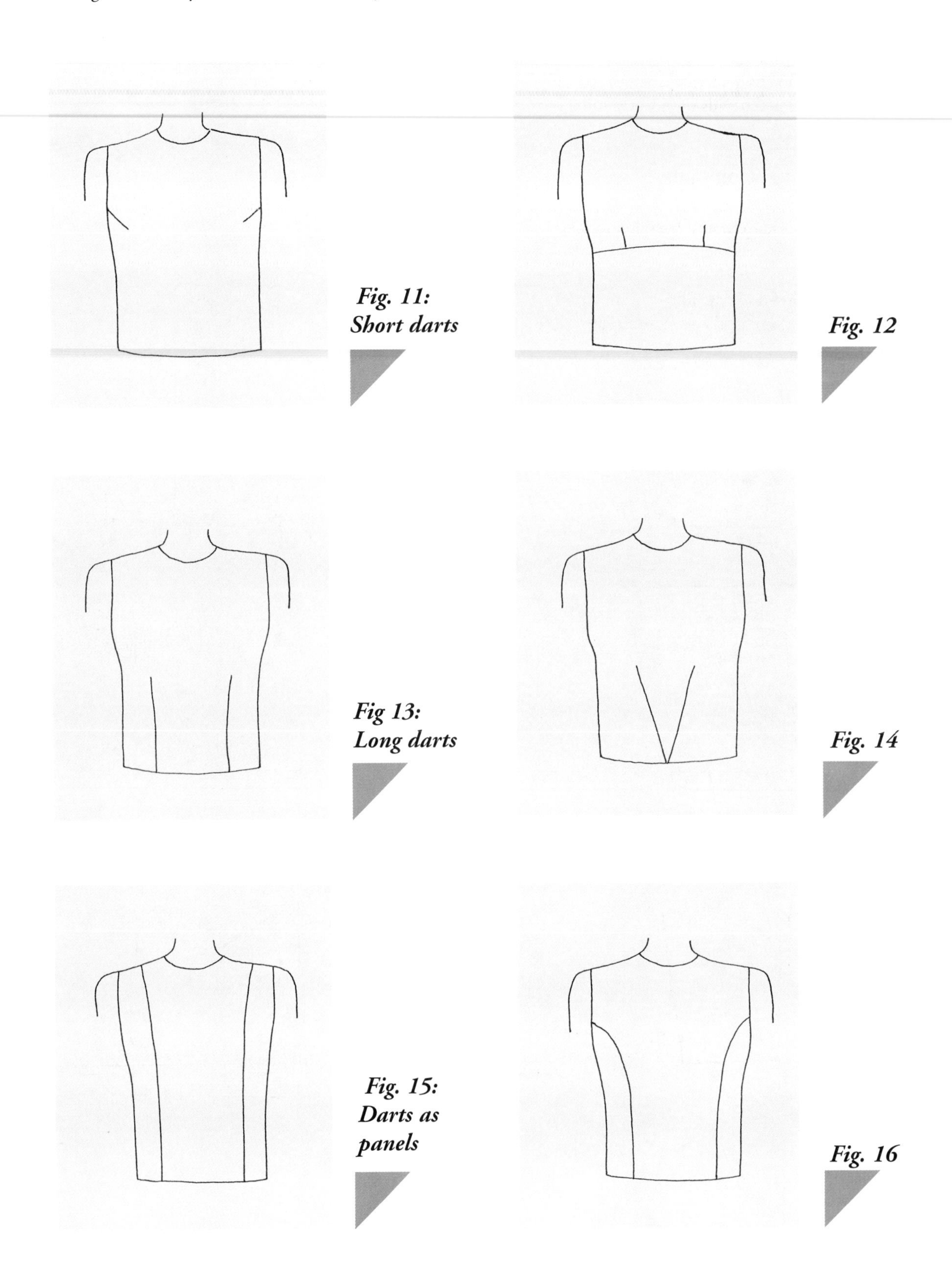

Fig. 11: Short darts

Fig. 12

Fig 13: Long darts

Fig. 14

Fig. 15: Darts as panels

Fig. 16

Dart manipulation

The following points demonstrate the function of dart manipulation on the shapes illustrated above.

The *equipment* needed for pattern layout is the following: paper shears, a tape measure, sharp pencils, a rubber, set square and tracing wheel. Any paper can be used to draw a pattern, providing the width is wide enough to prepare each pattern piece.

It is always worth keeping the *draft* of your design layout as a reference for any changes and minor alterations you do. Tracing paper is useful for tracing off the more complicated details on bodices for instance.

To draw out a pattern on paper: Fig. 17

a. *Fig. 17/A*: Place the front and back block onto paper and mark around them.
b. The centre front and back is on the straight grain and the CF is placed on the fold of paper.
c. Leave sufficient room at the bottom of the pattern pieces, especially when dropping the waist line.
d. Mark in darts, the bust point, grain lines and notches.
e. Draw in your style lines.
f. Cut on line at new position through to bust point.
g. *Fig. 17/B*: Close and fold up unwanted dart(s).
h. The new dart opens up (where the line has been cut through).
i. Now add seam allowance to the new pattern shape.
j. *Fig. 17/C*: Cut out new pattern and remember to fold dart up so that the lines are equal on both sides and cut away excess fabric to prevent puckering on curved seam.

Fig. 17/A

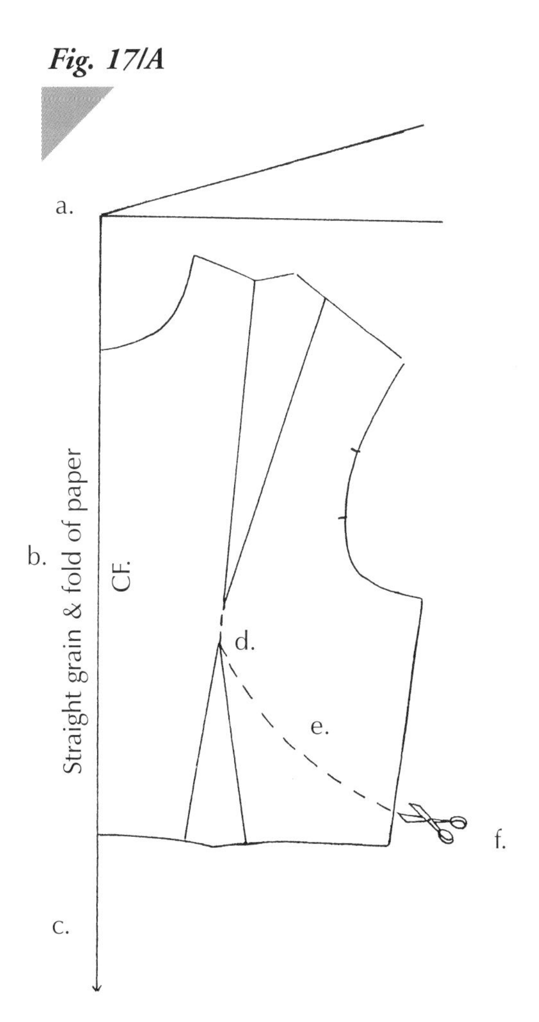

Fig. 17/B

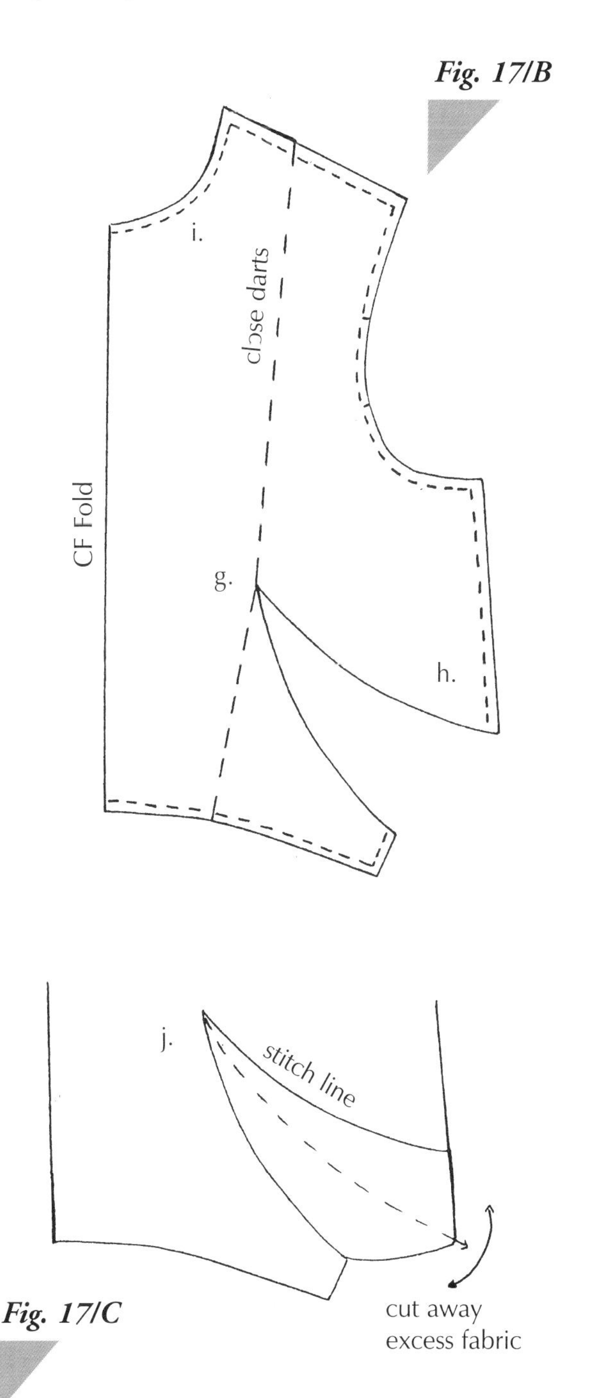

Fig. 17/C

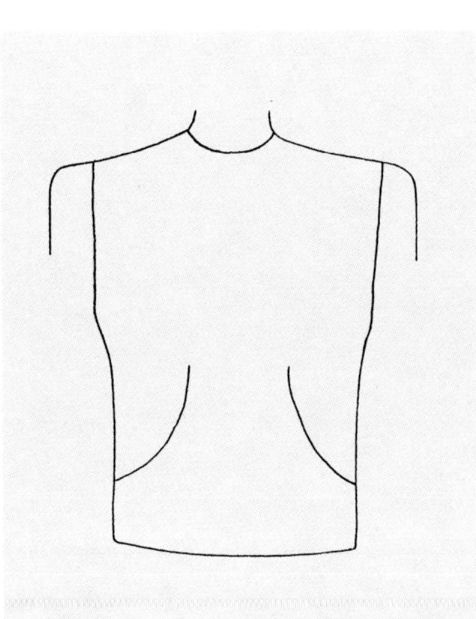

Fig. 17

Seam Allowances vary according to fabric types:

- Medium and heavyweight fabrics like raw silks, linens, satins, brocades, allow 1.5cm (⅝").
- Lightweight fabrics such as fine cottons, fluid silks and polyester satins: allow 1cm (⅜").
- Knitted and stretch fabrics need only 1cm-0.5cm (⅜"-¼").

Fig. 18 : **Short darts: example 1**

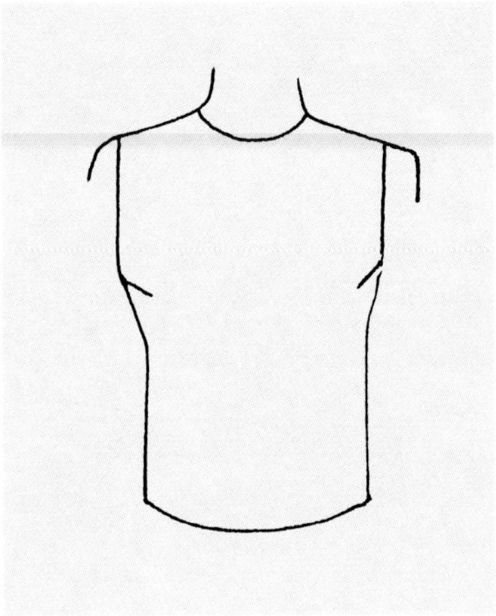

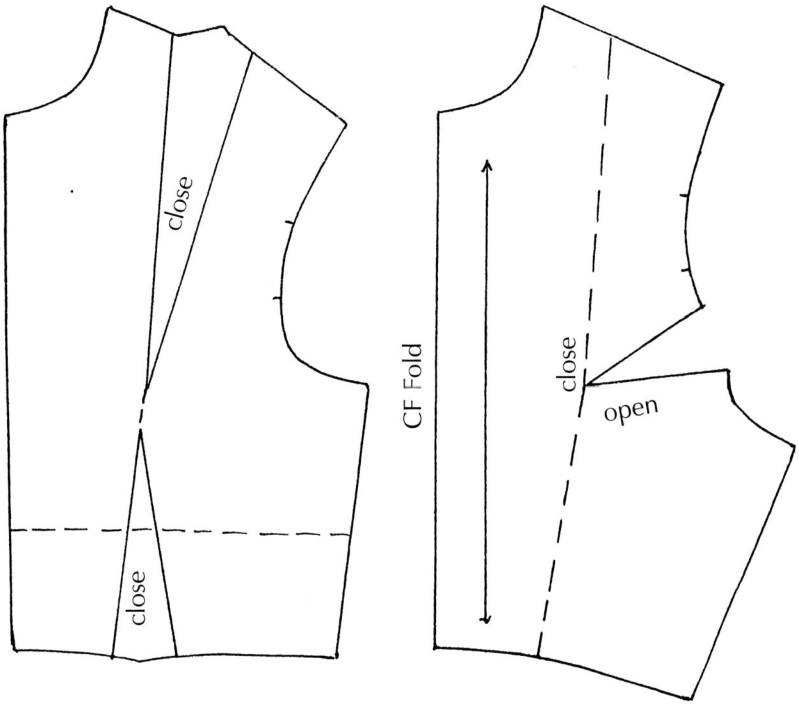

Fig. 19

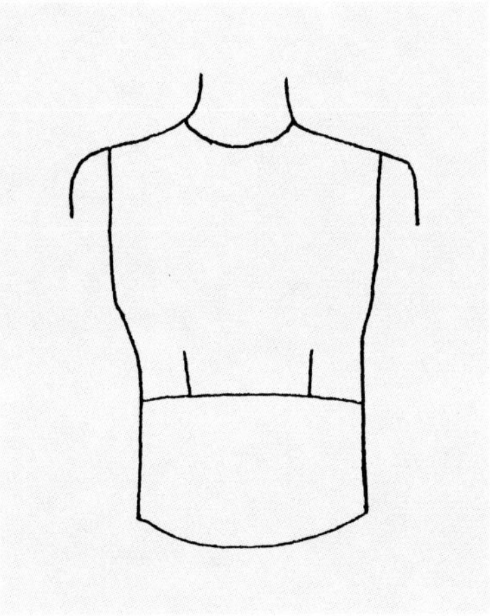

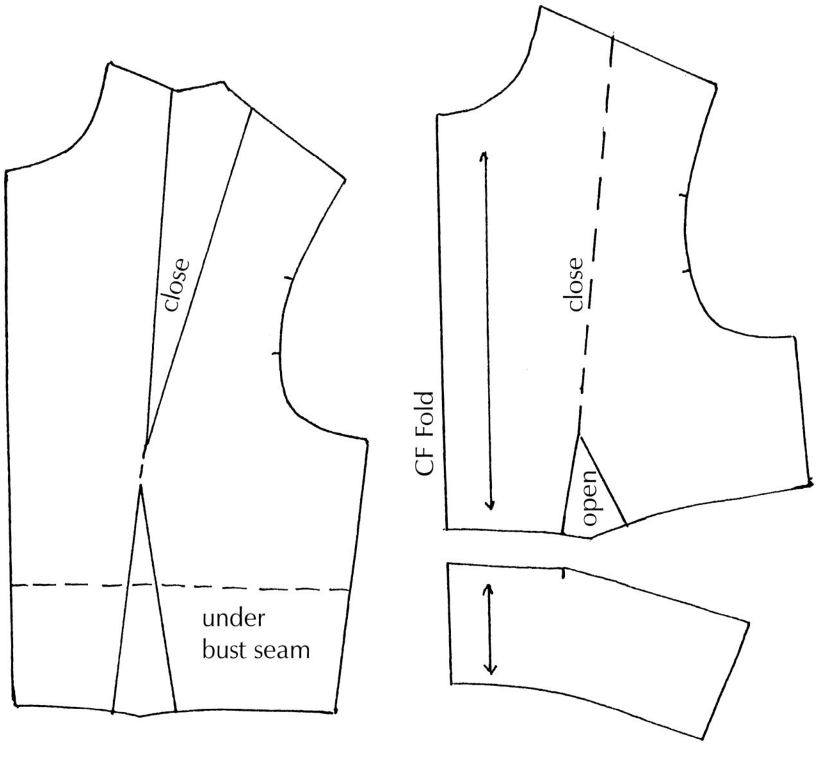

Long darts: example 2. Figs 20 - 21.

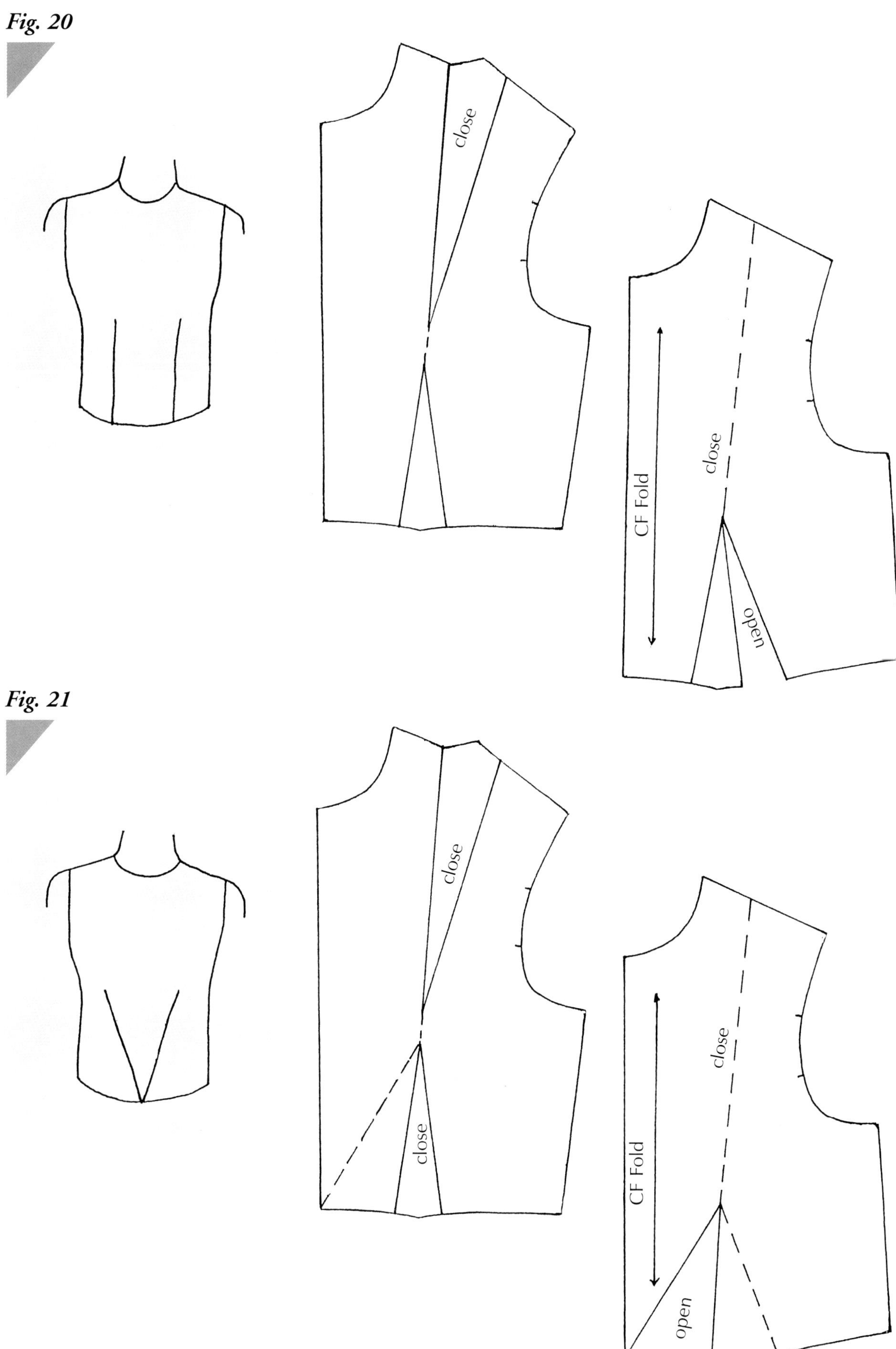

Panelled seams: example 3.
Curved panels: Fig. 22

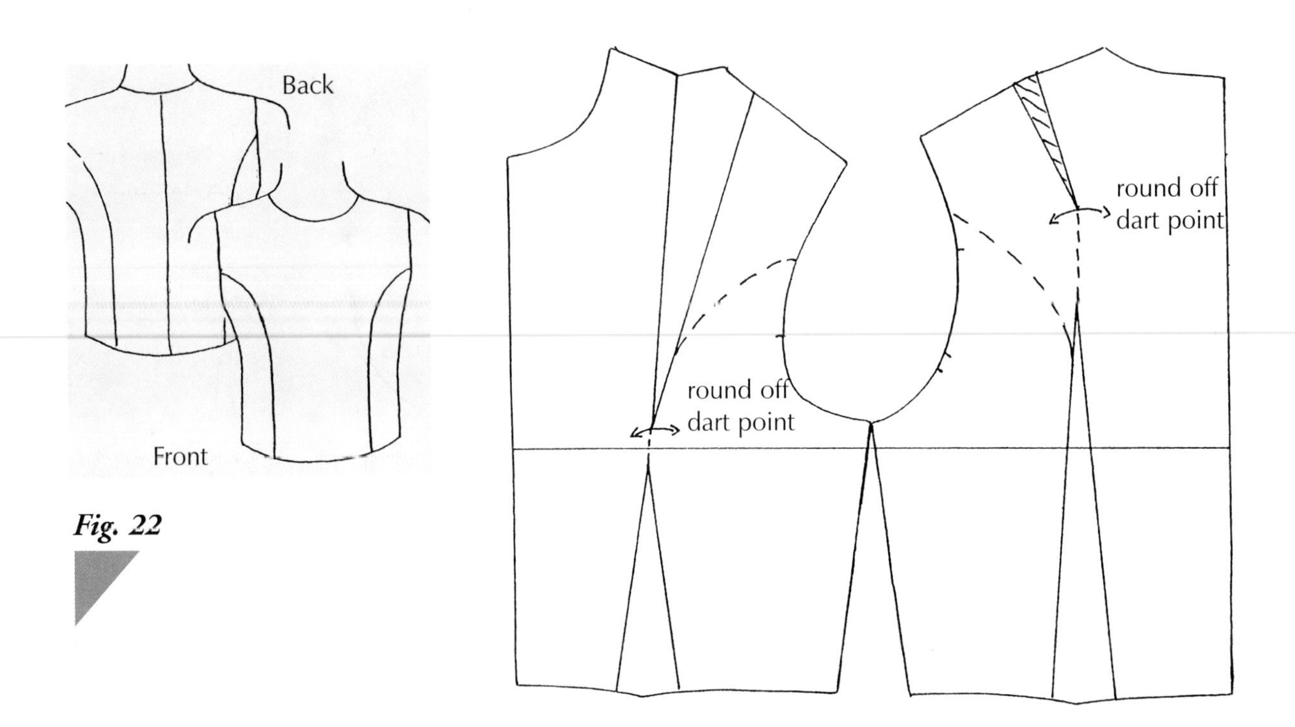

Fig. 22

Fig. 22/A

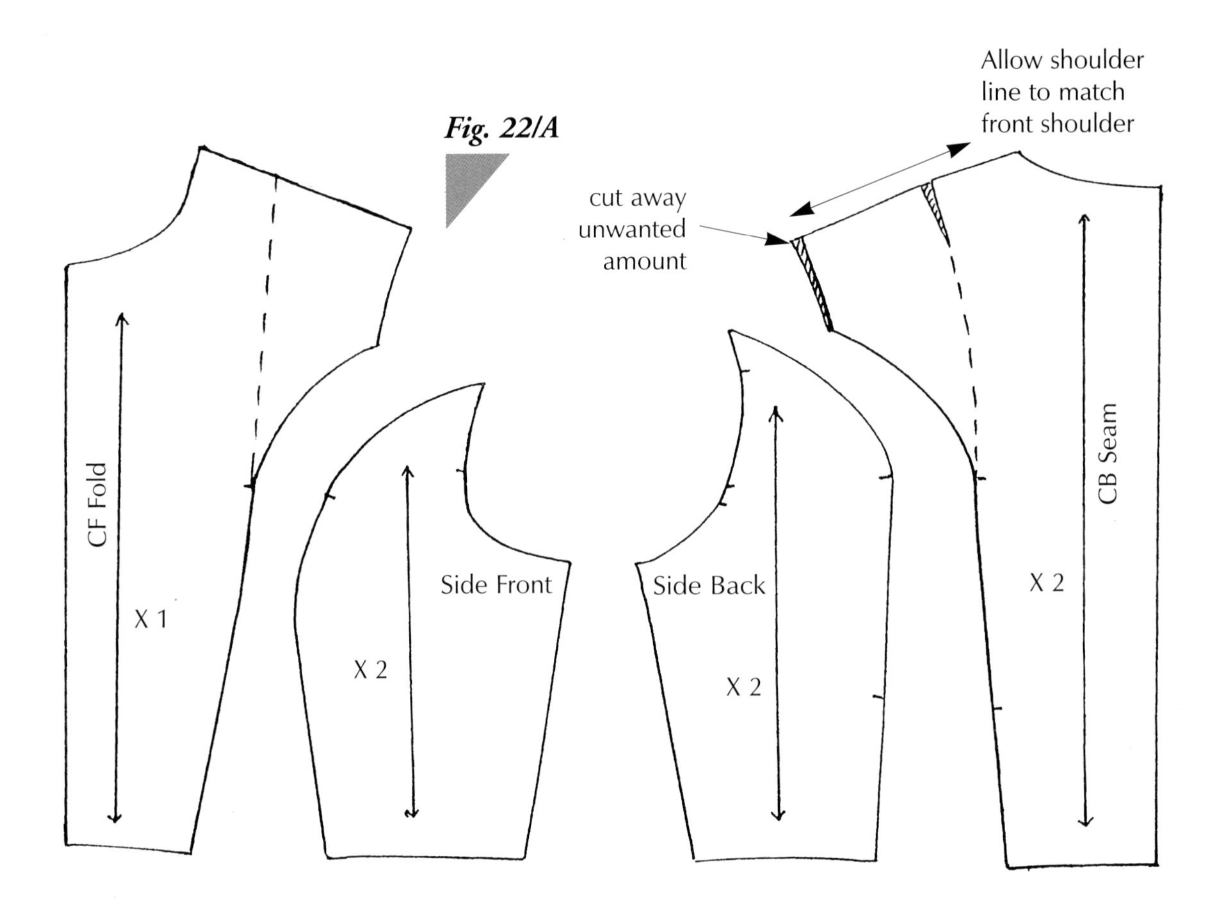

Straight panels: Fig. 23

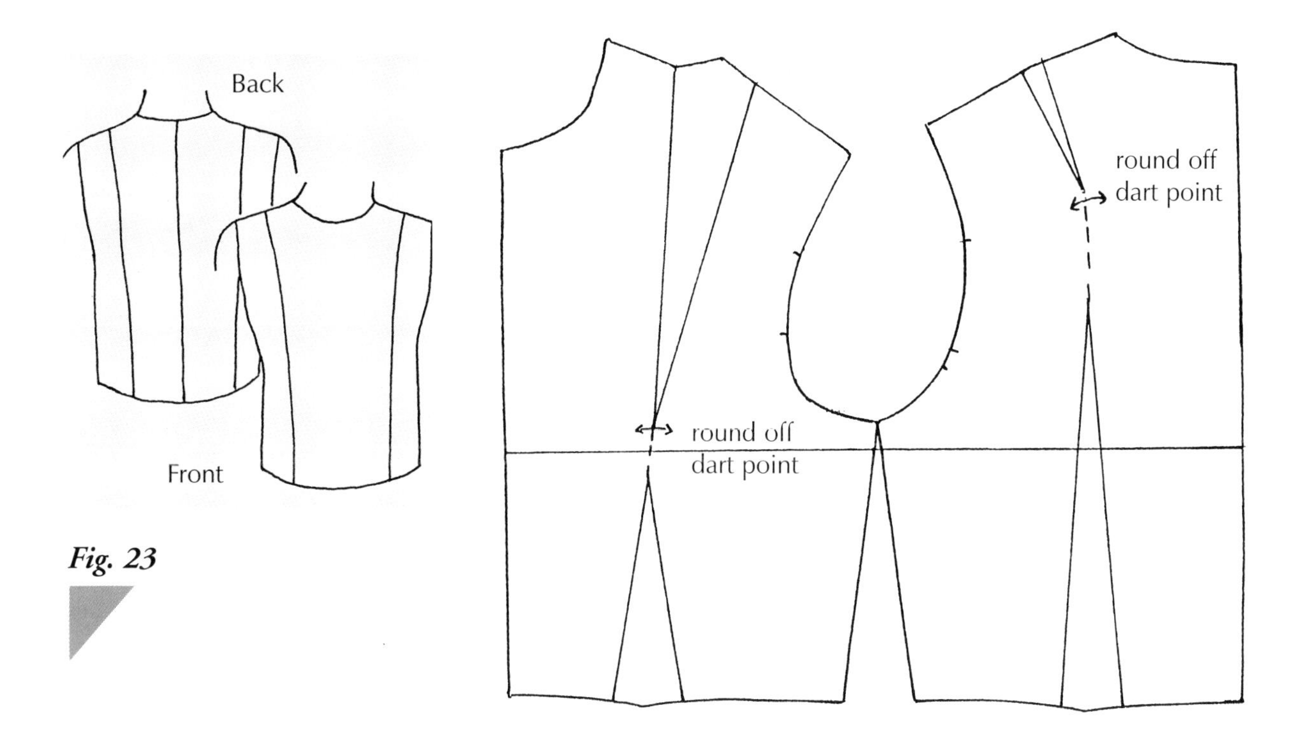

Fig. 23

Fig. 23/A

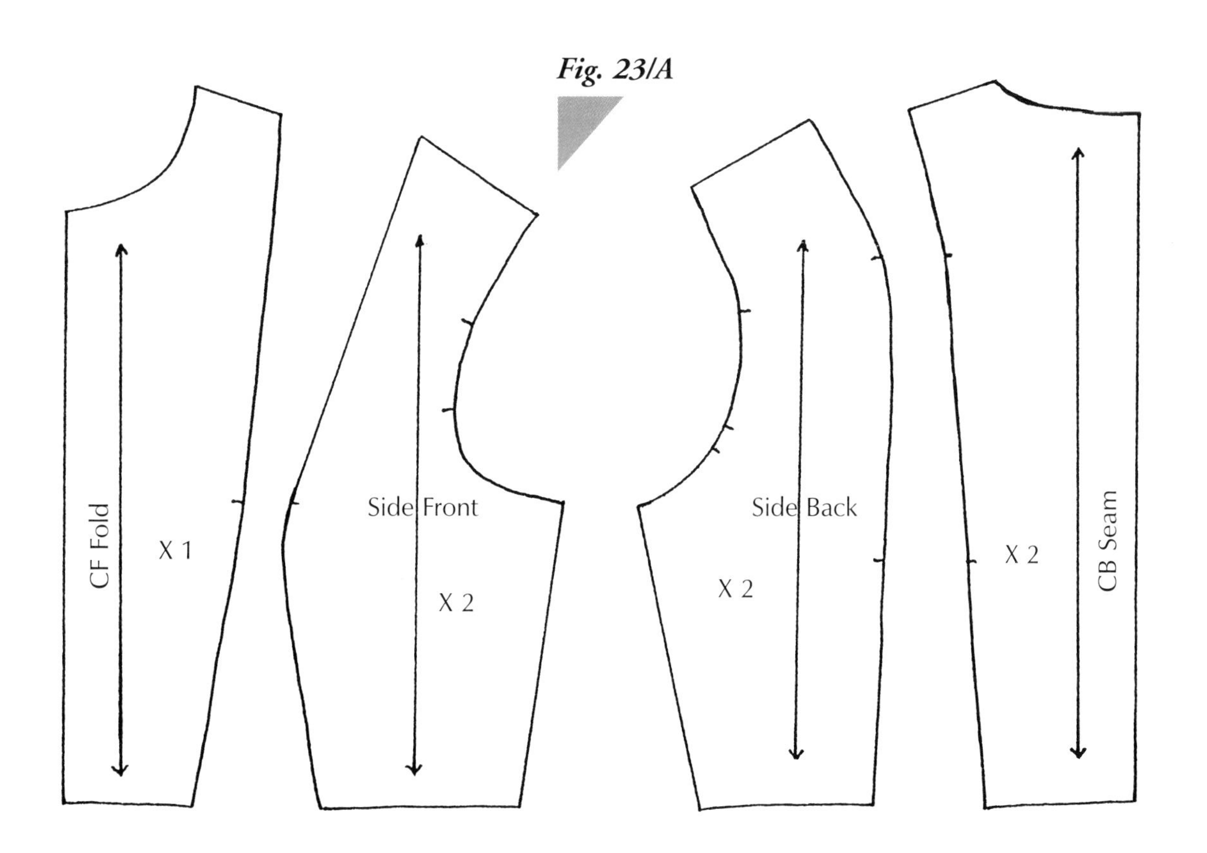

Bodice shapes, necklines and neck facings

Bodice shapes

Most brides want to look slim and elegant, so a well-fitted bodice has very little tolerance in it. As I've mentioned under 'Fittings', allow for loss of weight in these circumstances (up to four weeks before the wedding).

These are crucial times for many brides. Nervous energy makes some lose weight without even trying. Any alteration can easily be remedied on the back opening of the dress. Elegance is embodied in the way you wear the dress and what you choose to wear no matter what shape you are! Whatever style you choose to do, the silhouette should be *well cut and fitted.* To achieve this it's important to make a toile first.

The bodice is incorporated into the whole appearance of the dress and this includes how the neck is shaped and sleeves are sewn in. The shapes as seen below are examples of styles where all the features tie in as a whole. **Using the same examples as before**, we see the difference a **styled neckline and armholes** can make to alter the appearance of the silhouette.

The *empire line* (***Fig. 24***) is popular and is used in many different ways. It can show off a nice cleavage or simply be used to enhance the bodice shape as seen in ***Figs 25-26.*** Using long darts as before (***Figs 27-28***) these new style lines indicate how it can transform the silhouette. *Panelled seams* are by far the most popular shape used for the bodice (***Figs 29-30***)**.** They enhance the shape of the garment and breathe life into the figure.

Very few bodices in bridalwear have *gathers or yoke* design details featured on them. But that's not to say they don't exist. Here are two examples of how one can use gathers to their best advantage. ***Fig. 31*** has some fulness under the bust with a sweetheart-shaped neckline, often worn on bridesmaids' dresses. ***Fig. 32*** shows that *ruching and draping* parts of the bodice is applied where the fulness is required; the volume of the front waist darts are opened into that area and extra fullness is put into the shoulder darts where they are gathered into the shoulder seam. ***Fig. 33*** is a more complicated and structured bodice.

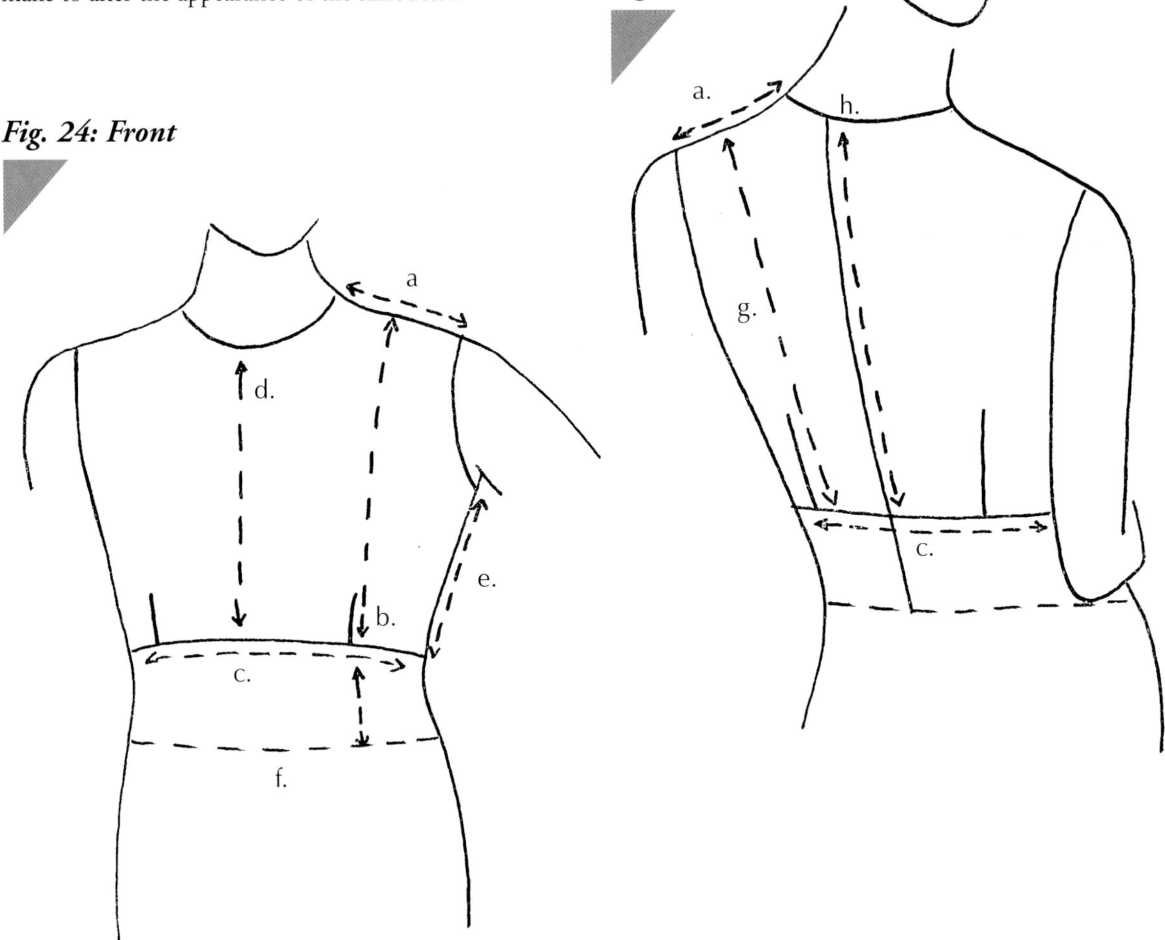

Fig. 24: Front

Fig. 24A: Back

How to measure the empire line on the fitted bodice: (Figs 24 - 24/A)

1. From centre shoulder at **a**, measure down to below bust point at **b** *and* from **a-g** at centre shoulder to new back seam.
2. Your dart will be approximately 7.5cm (3") long for a small bust and up to 10.5cm (4 ¼") for a large bust. It would depend on how close you want the seam to be under your bust to achieve this measurement.
3. The measurement at **c** is taken on the round and has very little ease.
4. Take further measurements from **d-c** *and* **e-c** *and* **h-c**. The front and back neck and under-arm measurements are determined by the *style lines* you want to achieve on your pattern. The neckline could be more scooped, for instance.
5. From **f-c** at the waist seam to the under bust seam on your pattern, allow this measurement to correspond with that of the centre back seamline. It helps to achieve a straight hemline.

Short darts: (with new stylelines)

Fig. 25/A Close shoulder and waist darts and slash open new position so that both darts are now in the armhole. Reshape the armhole by curving the style line from the dart seam towards the neck edge, making the shoulder width narrow by about 5cm (2") to form a *halter neck.* The waist seam is raised as shown above.

Fig. 25

Fig. 25/A

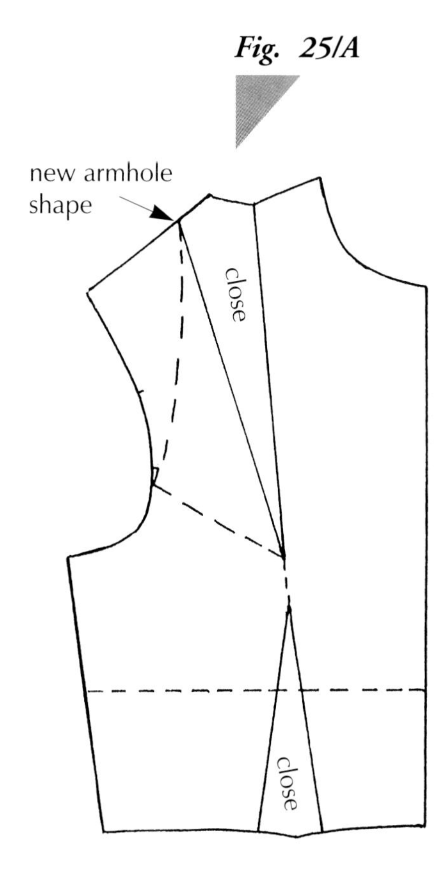

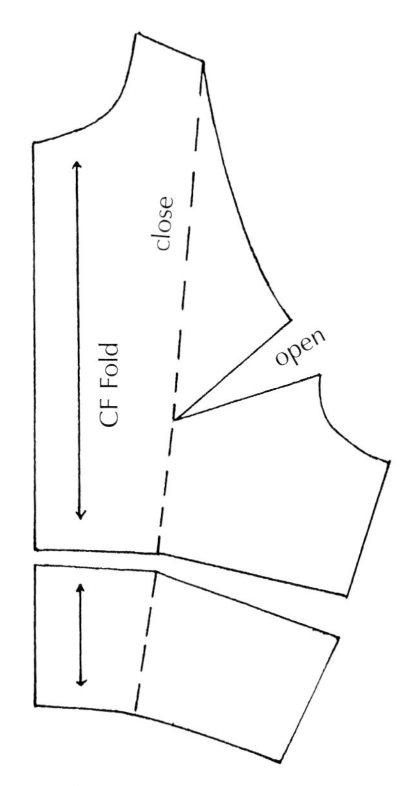

Fig. 26: A scooped neck shape alters the empire bodice which is held in place by a *neck band* or *yoke*. **A.** Close the shoulder dart and open it into the waist dart. **B.** Mark in the neck yoke for front and back, starting from the edge of the shoulder to a width of approximately 5cm (2") using the same dimensions throughout. **C.** The waist seam is raised as above on back and front bodices. Find a suitable position on yoke to reshape back and front armhole, and notch it. The yoke can be *with or without* a shoulder seam. **D.** Fold out any fulness that may occur along the neck edge of yoke and reshape. Bias cut the yoke(s). The facing is cut to the foundation pattern.

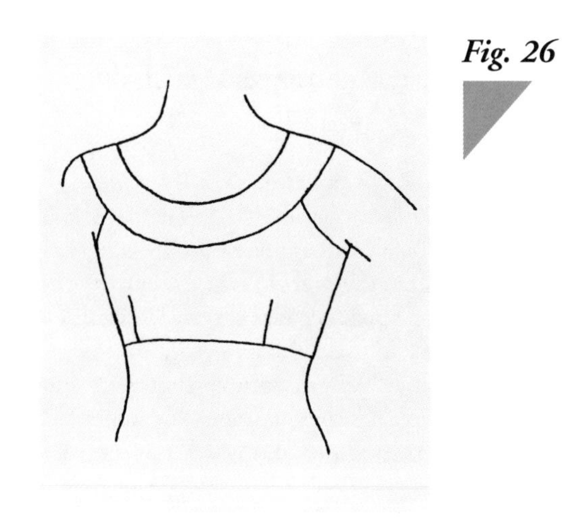

Fig. 26

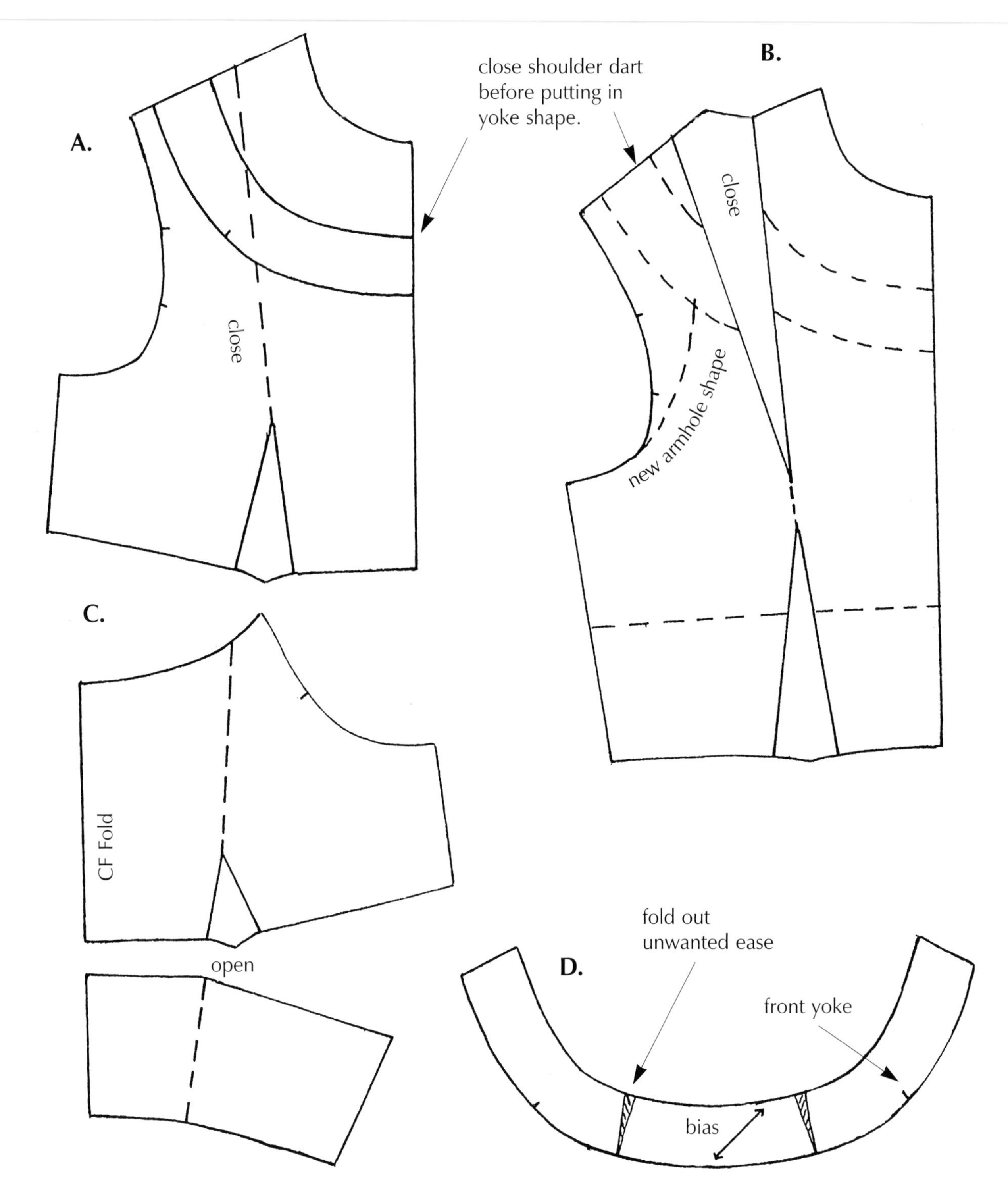

Long darts (with more exaggerated styling):

Fig. 27: The neckshape includes a short cap sleeve, with armhole seams taken out. The shoulder dart is closed and moved into the waist dart. **A.** The shoulder line is then reshaped to accommodate ease for arm movement. **B.** Measure down from centre front neck to where bodice shape begins and draw in style line. Mark in new *wide neck shape.* **C.** Close waist dart to reshape waistline where it dips at centre front. Cut into bodice at centre front and open up dart. The bodice hugs the bust accentuating the contours of the figure, so taking out fulness at the side seams may be necessary. Leave in darts for the back bodice.

Fig. 27

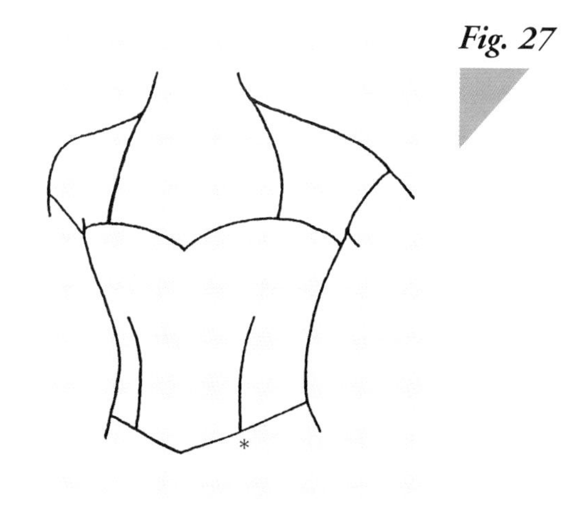

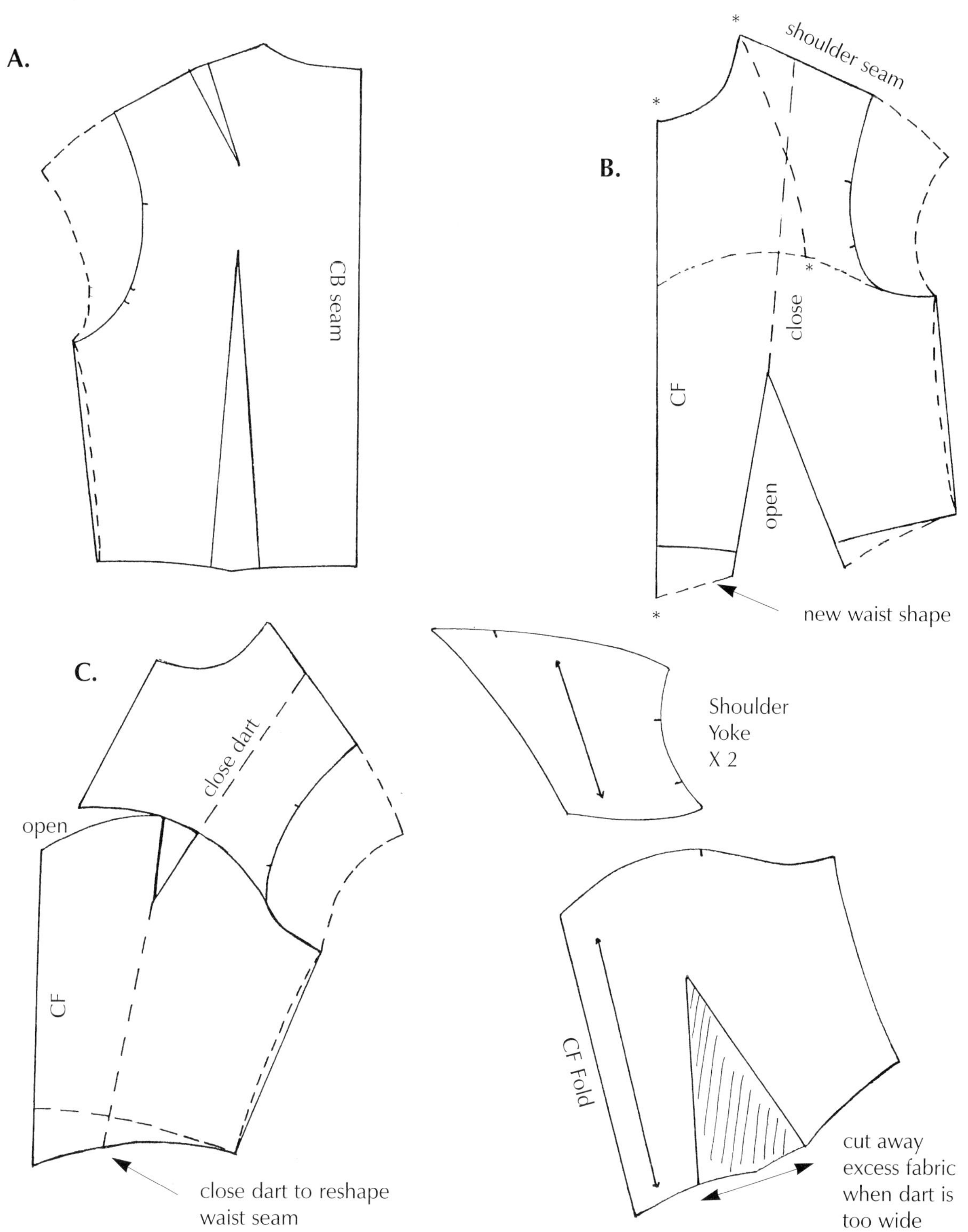

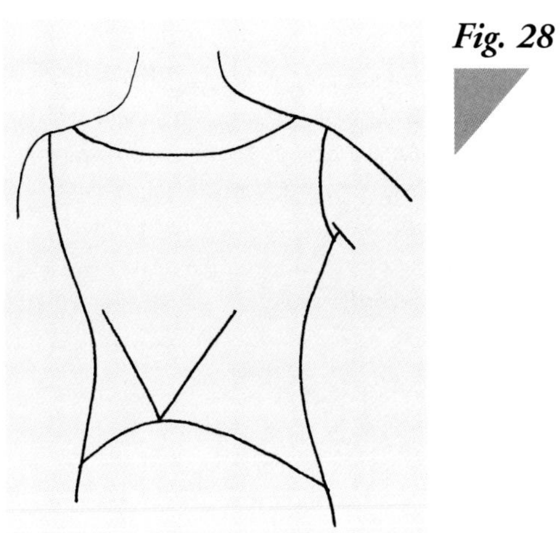

Fig. 28

Fig 28: The shoulder dart is closed and opened into the waist dart. Mark in neck shape from the shoulder's edge (to a depth of about 5cm [2"] for shoulder width) towards 1.5cm (5/8")at the base of the centre front neck to form a *boat shaped* neckline. A new dart position is marked from centre waist seam through to below bust point and the old position is closed. Measure down from waist seam to high hip and curve downwards from centre front towards the high hip line, forming a new bodice shape at waist seam.

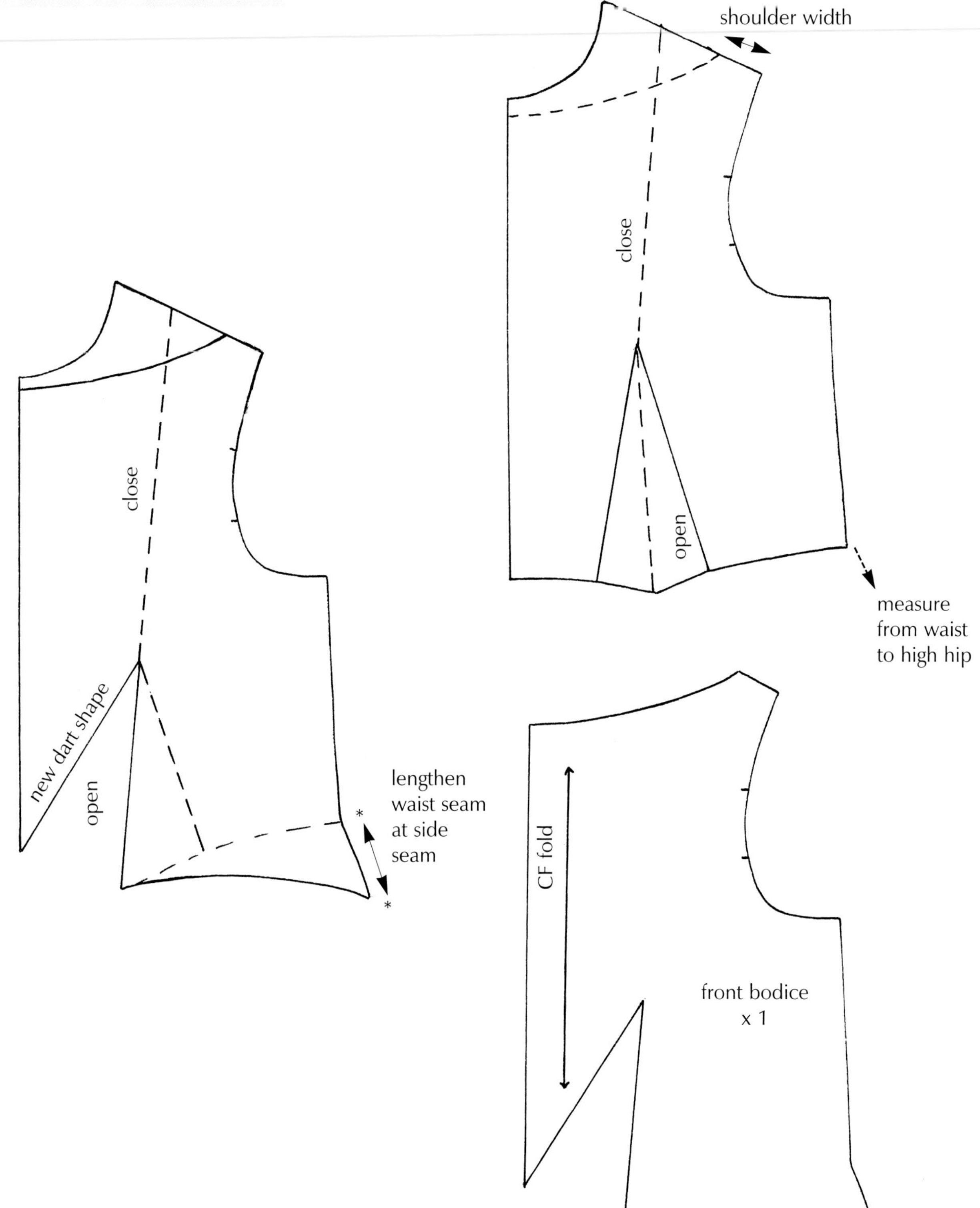

Fig. 29: A *structured panelled bodice* with *straight seams* through the bust darts. Make sure that the front and back bodice is lined up on the *chestline* measurements. Close shoulder dart and open it into the waist dart. Ignore dart on back shoulder. Mark in new front bodice shape by *taking the measurement from hollow at centre front neck down to cleavage and *from centre shoulder to panel seam. When satisfied with shape, open shoulder dart once more, and close waist dart to *reshape waistline*. The waist seam is dropped onto the high hip measurement. Ensure that this measurement fits comfortably over the high hip position. Mark in *grainlines* and *notches*. This bodice would normally be boned.

Fig. 29: Structured panels

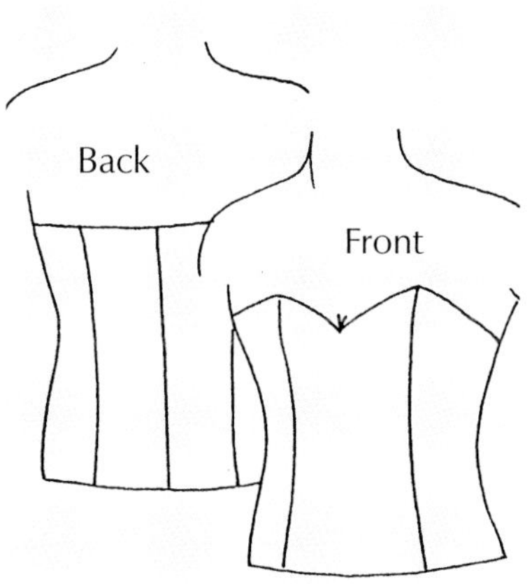

Back
Front

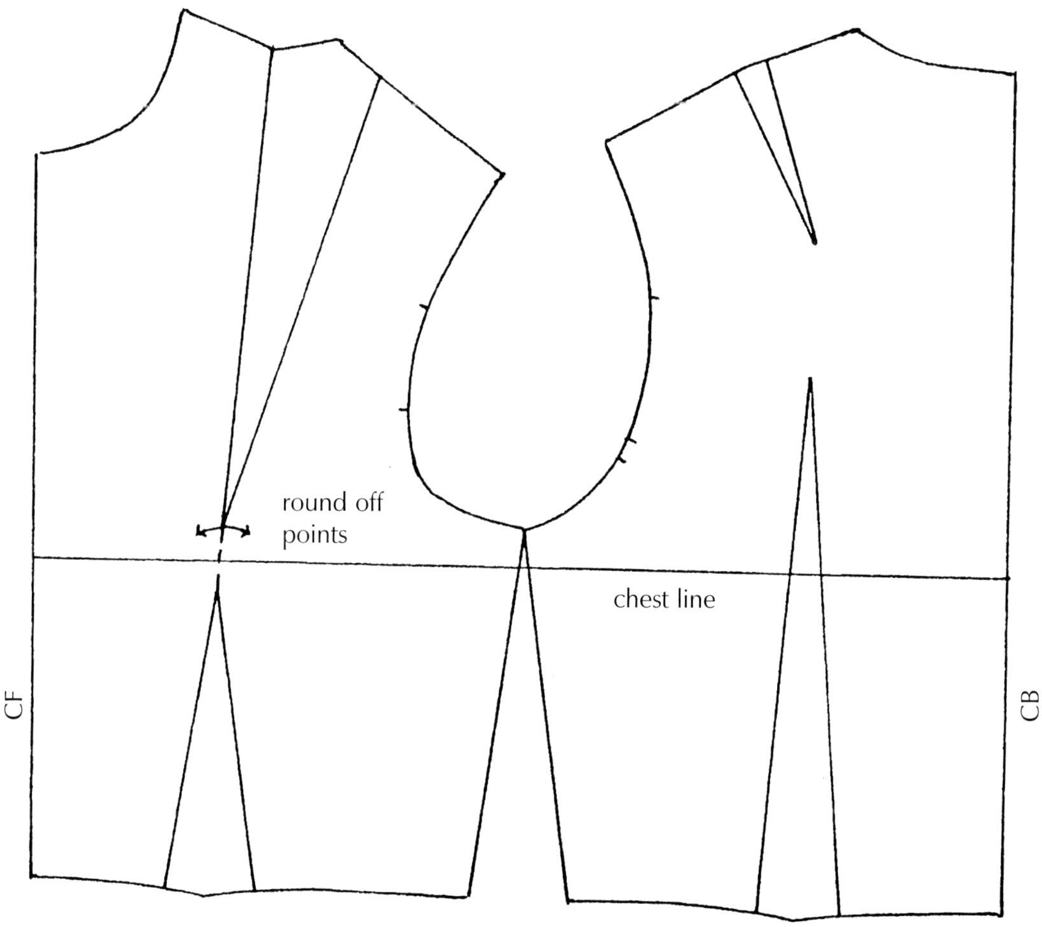

round off
points

chest line

CF

CB

Fig. 29/A: Front bodice

Fig. 29/B: Back bodice

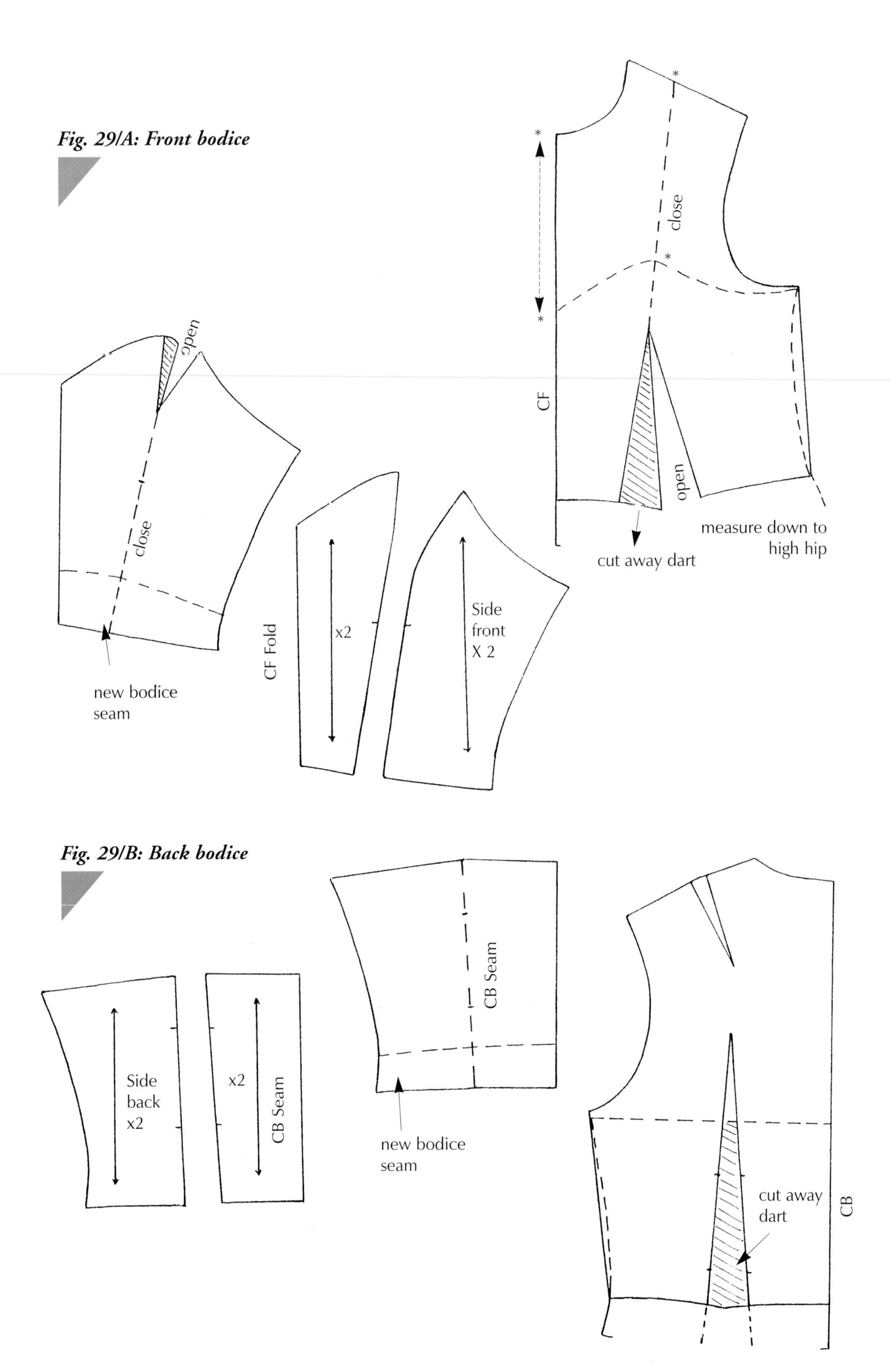

Fig. 30: This *panelled* bodice has *curved seams* with the centre front and back panels forming a cap sleeve over the edge of the shoulder. Close the shoulder dart and open it into the waist dart. The *neck shape is scooped* low across the chest. Mark in new style line: *from hollow at centre front neck down to where the new neck edge will be * and 1.5cm ($\frac{5}{8}$") inwards from edge of shoulder then out towards upper arm by 5cm (2") making cap sleeve measurement 6.5cm (2"+ $\frac{5}{8}$"). Do the same for the back panels as seen on ***Fig. 30/A.*** Curve the sleeve shape through to bust point and down towards waist seam. Find a comfortable position to move back and front armhole into and notch. Drop the waistline at centre front to a point about 5cm (2") and curve towards waist at side seam. Close dart at CB from the dart point to where new neckline is and reshape panel.

Back Bodice

Front Bodice

Fig. 30: Front bodice

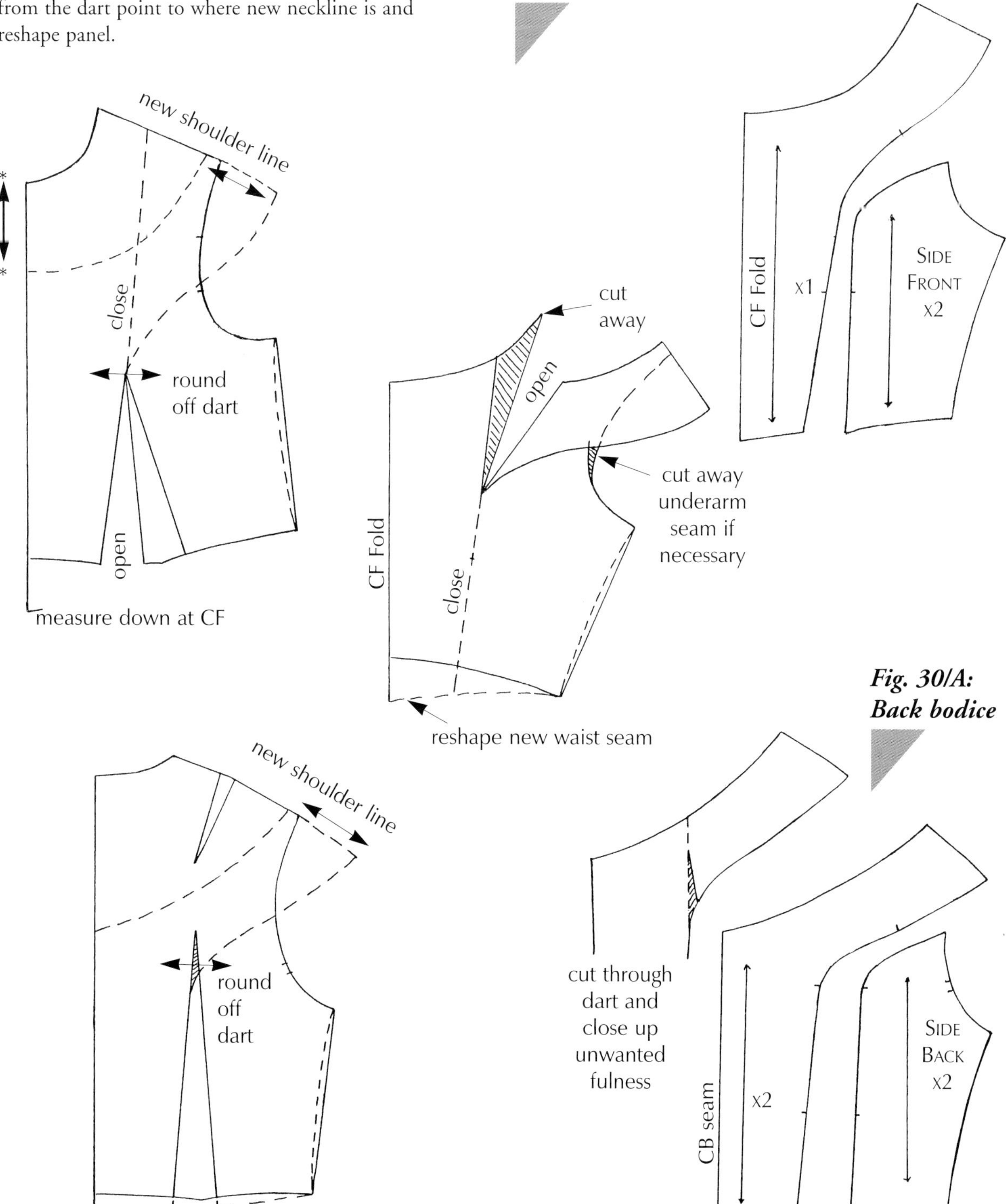

Fig. 30/A: Back bodice

Fig. 31 illustrates a simple use of *gathers* under the bust. *Mark in high waistline (as seen on *Fig. 24*) on front and back bodices. The front neck line is restyled into a *sweetheart neck* shape by closing the shoulder dart and opening it into the new waist seam. Both darts are now opened under the bust to form gathers. Add onto pattern under bust seam for extra fullness if necessary, as seen on diagram of front bodice.

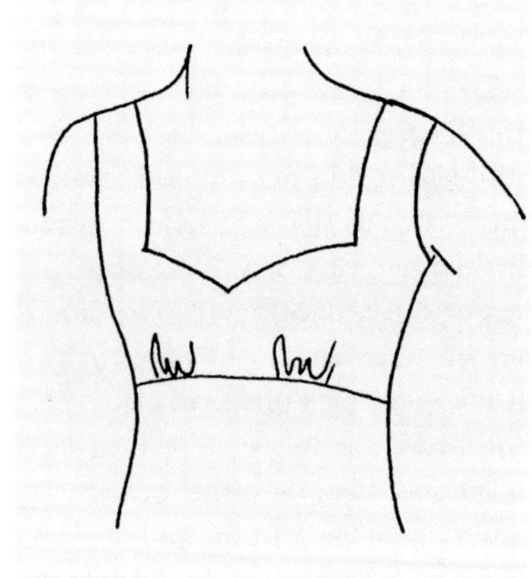

Fig. 31: Gathers

close
*
open
front bodice
CF fold
add extra amount

Fig. 32 has a *gathered cross over bodice* where the neckshape on the *full front bodice* is restyled. Here, extra fulness for the darts are required on both the shoulderline and draping at the side seam. Soft fluid fabrics such as silk satins or a silk jersey are appropriate for this style. **A.***Mark in at centre front, how far down the cross over neckline is to be, and the distance from the neck edge to shoulder line. **B.** Close the waist dart on the *wider* part of the pattern and place into shoulder. If the fulness of these two darts is not enough on the shoulder, slash through to waist seam and open pattern to the amount required. **C.** Close waist dart on the *smaller* part of the pattern and open up into the side seam. **D.** For extra fulness, slash through to centre front, as shown, and level off seam edge. If stretching of the fabric happens along this curved neck shape, it doesn't matter here, because the style lends itself to a floppy and draped look.

Fig. 32

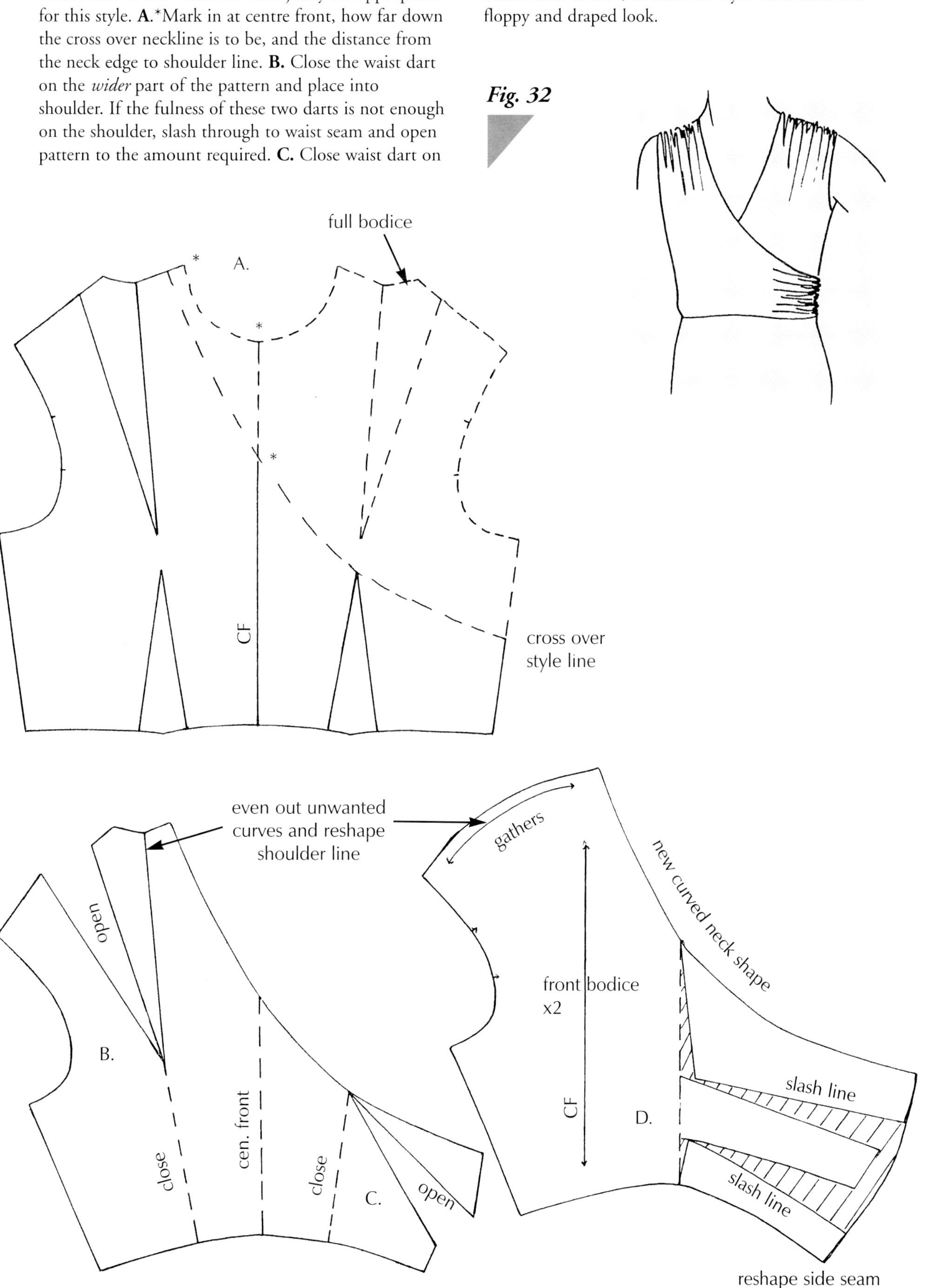

Fig. 33 shows a likeness to a *Victorian bodice shape.* It is an interpretation of period styling, where the style lines are structured to form however many panels required, and they are *boned.* Here the shape becomes more complicated as darts are curved and shaped into panels of exaggerated proportions. **A.** Once the shoulder dart is closed on the CF bodice, *reshape the neckline and mark in style lines. The centre front panel follows through the bust point to a low position below the waist, to a curved point at the centre front. **B.** The waist line drops to the high hip measurement. To achieve this, close the darts at the waist and mark in new style line. Make sure you have *some ease* in this area, so that the bodice doesn't distort its shape.
C. Trace out these panels *keeping the draft* as it is and add seam. **D.** Ignore the back shoulder dart and put in style lines on ***Fig. 33/A.*** *Slash through the waist dart and take the dart point into the new neck shape.
E. Close the dart and reshape waist line. **F.** Trace out the panels and add seam. *Label pattern pieces by numbers* and put in grainlines and notches.
Note: See under boned bodices for more detail on construction and trimmings.

Fig. 33: Front bodice (period influence)

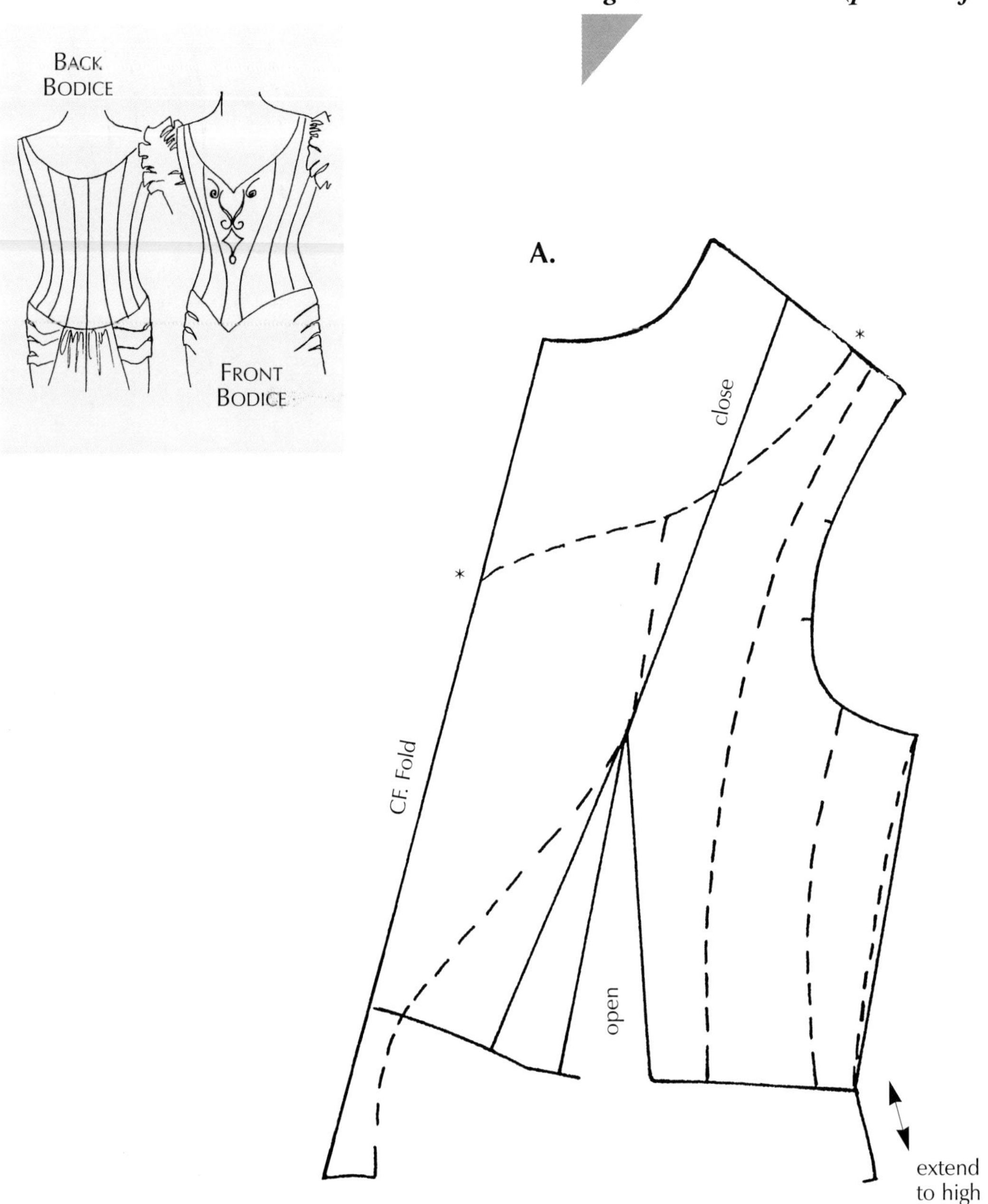

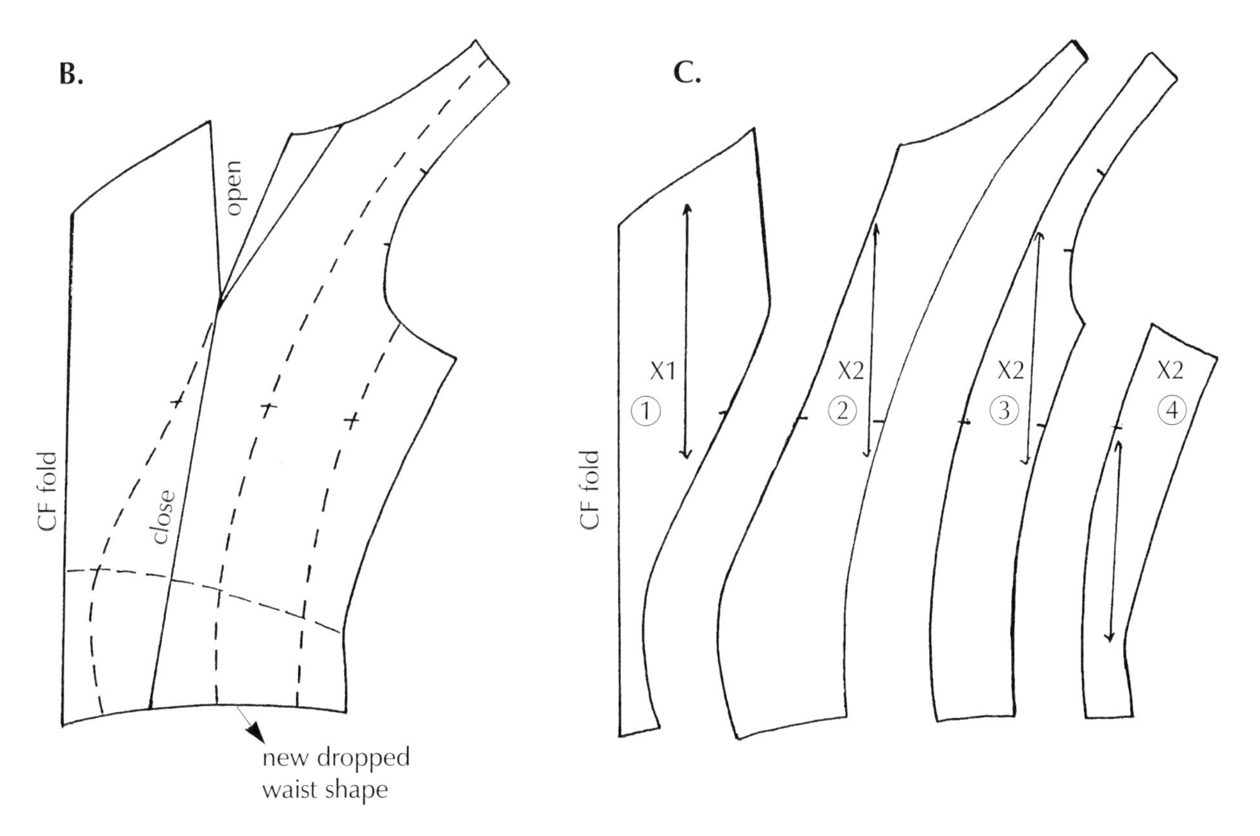

Fig. 33/A: Back bodice (period influence)

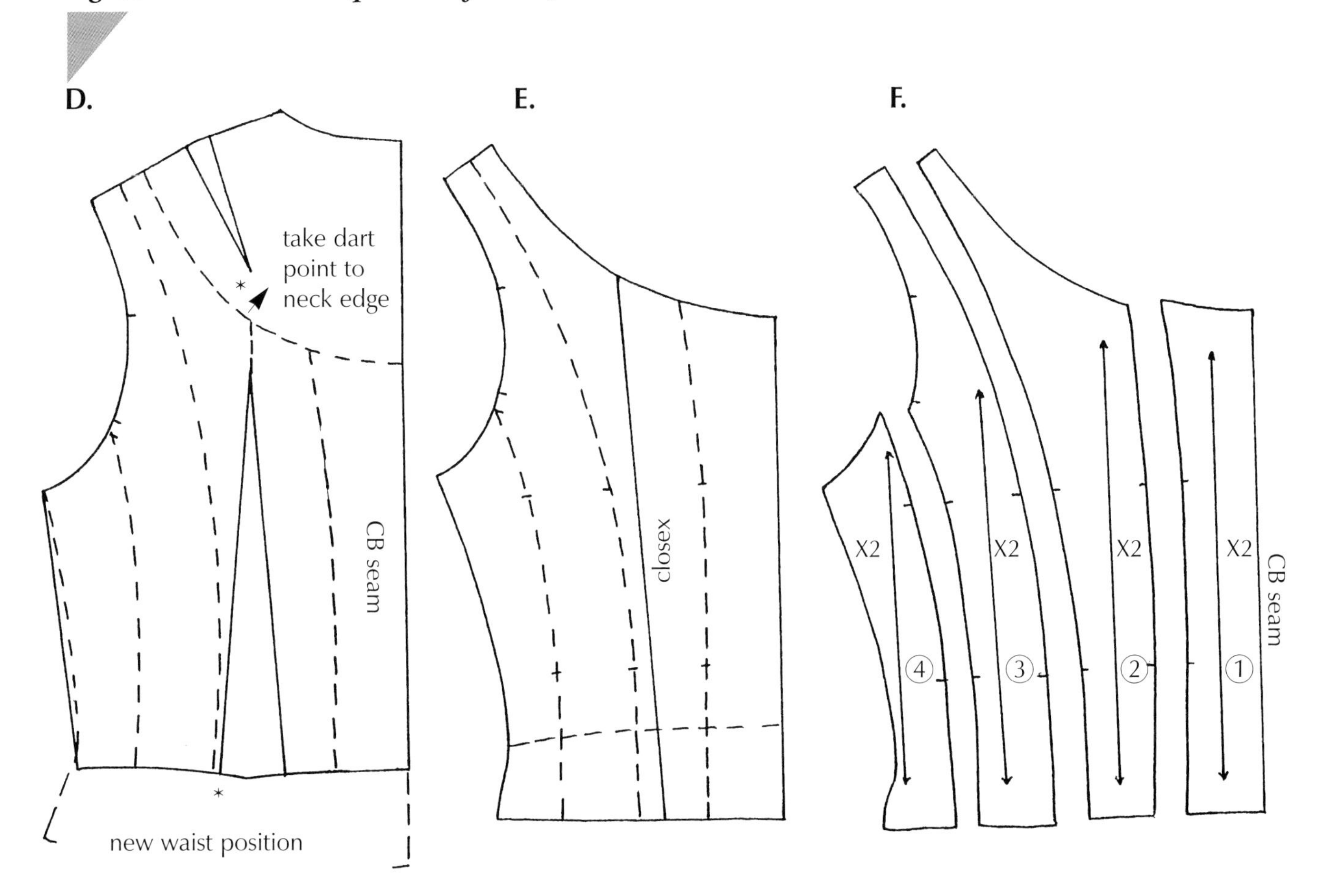

Necklines

We've seen some very elementary and some complicated neck shapes in the examples above. The importance of this feature on the styled silhouette is that the eye is drawn to this area and there's nothing worse than a badly fitted neck line. It's easy to eradicate unwanted fulness, as demonstrated under 'Gaping'.

Other neckshapes important in bridalwear

Fig. 34 shows an *off the shoulder* neckline and how to achieve the fit without it slipping down beyond a point where it becomes uncomfortable. Almost all wedding styles today are designed with bared shoulders. It is also fair to say that because it is very flattering to the wearer, it's easy to get it wrong. Sleeves are often incorporated to enhance this neck shape and to improve its fit. Elastic strips are often used to support the sleeve at the upper arm position. Made to the upperarm measurement, the elastic is enclosed with bias cut fabric and stitched discreetly between the seams of the underlining. The construction of this style is illustrated in ***Fig. 30*** (under panelled seams).

Off the shoulder necklines

Concentrate on the proportions from base of neck at centre front ***a-b*** and to depth of neckline at CF. Measure from base of neck along shoulder line at ***c*** to 2.5cm (1") below where the shoulder blade meets the upper arm socket, then downwards towards the desired sleeve width at ***d***. From the bone at nape of centre back neck ***e-f*** measure down to neck shape at CB. Then join up to measurements on shoulder. * Close up any gaping at the neckline and put into bust dart. *Fig. 34/B:* Do the same for the gaping along the sleeve edge over the upperarm. Make sure that some ease is retained for the movement of the upperarm.

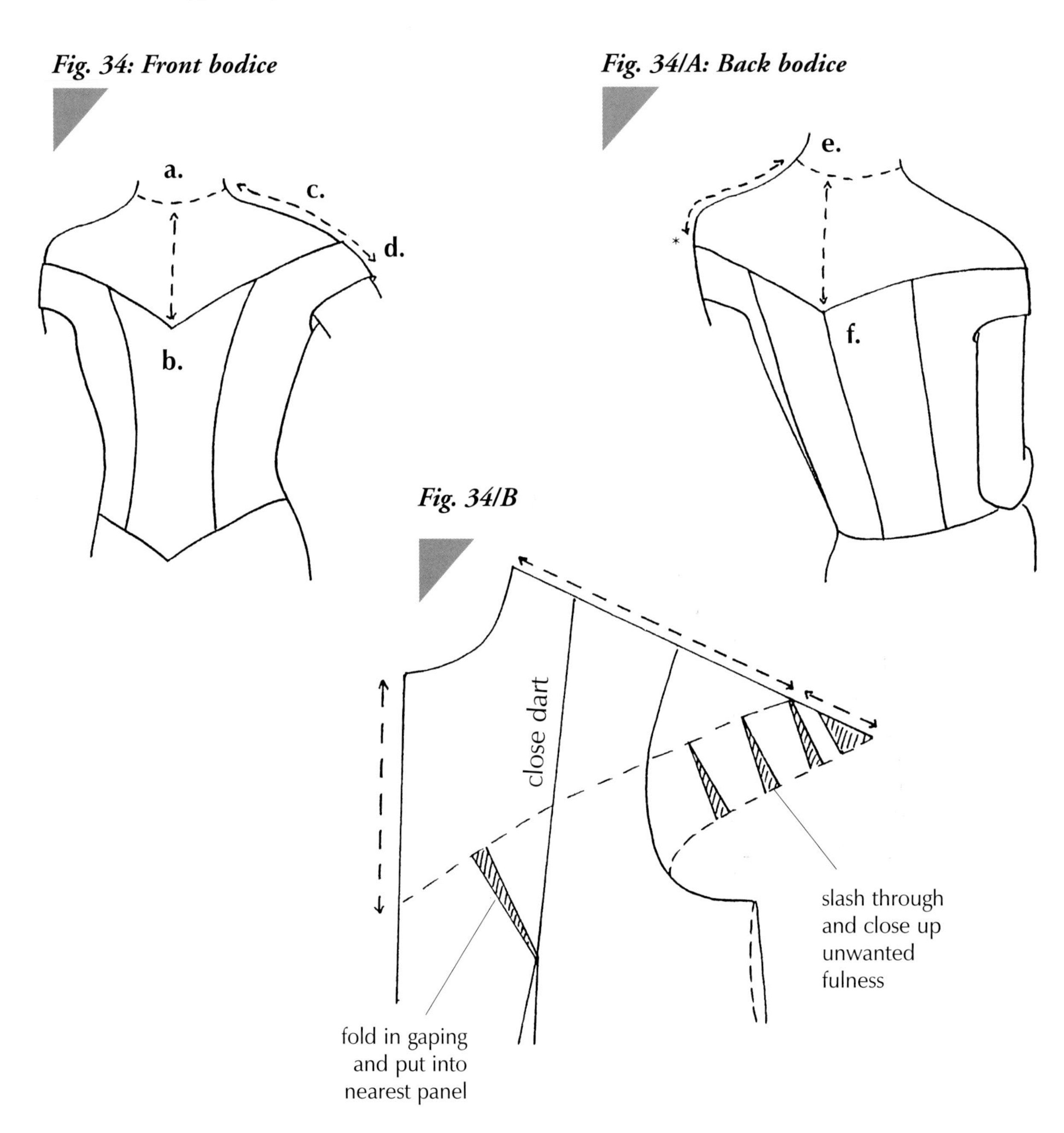

Fig. 34: Front bodice

Fig. 34/A: Back bodice

Fig. 34/B

Fig. 35: The *cowl* neck is used for both front and back bodices. In this design the fulness is draped across the centre front and stops near the bust point. Soft fabrics such as chiffons, silk satins and crêpe de chines are ideal for this type of styling. Where possible, cut the fabric on the bias for a better effect. One would also have the facing made as part of the bodice so that there are no seams at the neck edge. The lower (or wider) the neck shape, the fuller the cowl becomes since there is more volume of fabric incorporated in the design.

Fig. 35/A: *Mark in new neck shape once shoulder dart is closed. The lower the neckline the fuller the *cowl* becomes. Open up a new dart position at CF neck edge and close dart at waist. ***Fig. 35/B:*** Draw a line at right angles from the CF neck upwards, and outwards towards the shoulder at neck edge. Draping across the front can be achieved by putting all the dart fulness into the centre front area and increasing the volume or fabric.

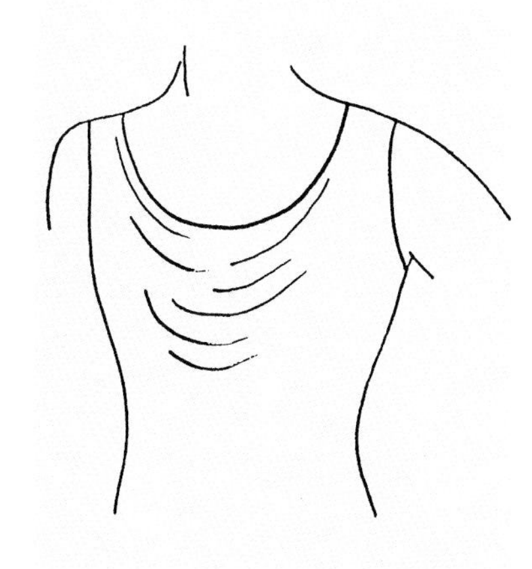

Fig. 35: Cowl neck for front bodice

Fig. 35/A

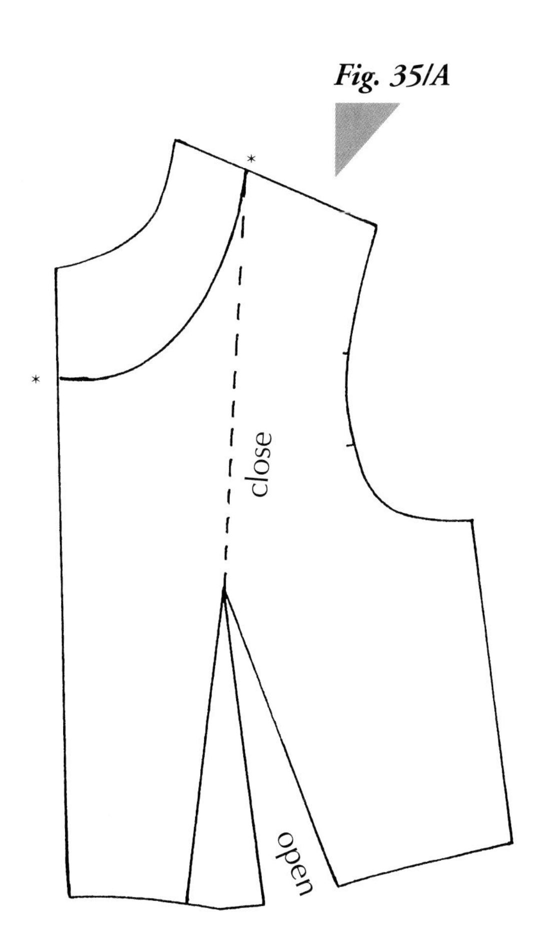

Fig. 35/B

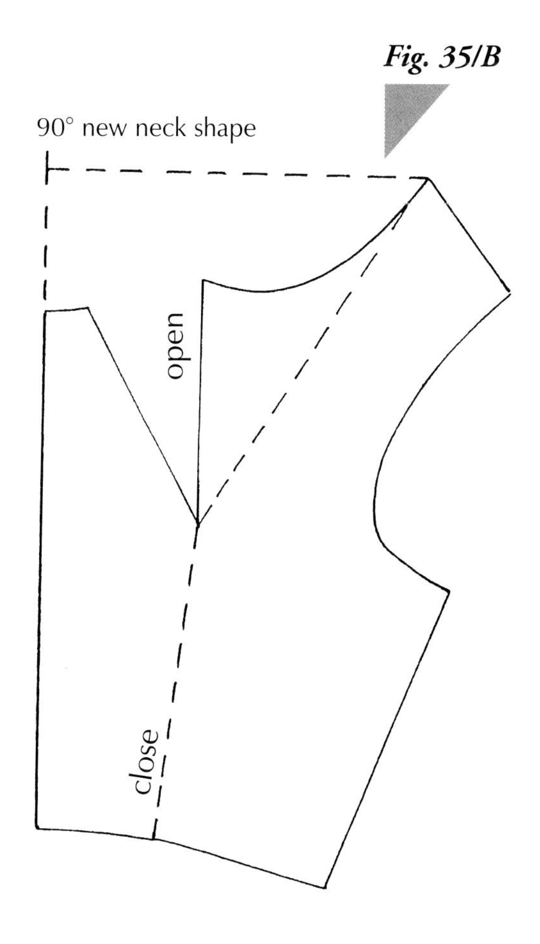

Fig. 36 shows off a *cross-over halter neck*, which is draped to form pleats at the base of the front neck and fastens at the nape of the back neck. The amount of fulness required is optional and then stitched onto the lining pattern (which is made to the foundation pattern). This silhouette looks good in both eveningwear and bridalwear. This *cross-over halter neck* incorporates ruching at the shoulder and side-seams and folding and pleating the fabric onto a flat yoke, for lining. To benefit from a nice flat shoulder line, cut the front and back yoke pattern pieces separately. However, eliminate this seam if you want a closer neck finish.

Fig. 36/A: Once the shoulder dart is closed, shape front neck band *through the bust dart* thus enabling you to close the waist dart, making the bodice or skirt a flat pattern piece as seen on ***Fig. 36/B.*** *Trace out front yoke for lining* and then cut through pattern and spread out evenly on the straight grain for gathers (*Fig. 36/C*).

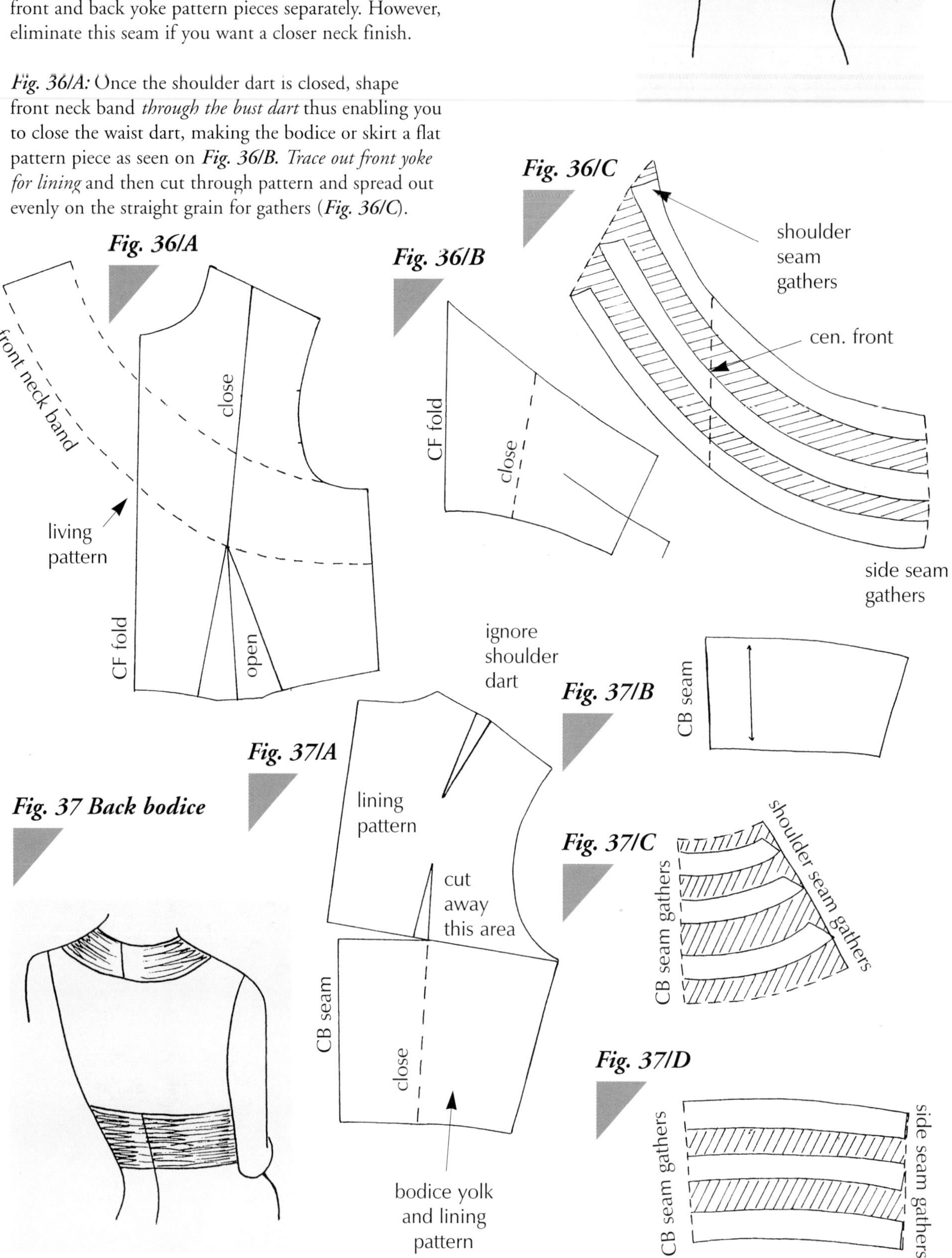

Fig. 37/A: Prepare the back bodice by ignoring the shoulder dart. Cut away the area not required and close the unwanted waist dart. Trace out yoke pieces for lining before preparing them for gathers. *Fig. 37/B:* The back skirt or yoke piece is made without darts. *Fig. 37/C* (neck yoke) and *Fig. 37/D* (bodice yoke), are slashed through to the amounts required on each new pattern.

Gaping: Fig. 38

Where there is *gaping* at the **armhole or neck edge**, correct it at the toile stage. The amount of extra fulness that accumulates in these areas, varies according to the style and the chest measurement.

Fig. 38/A: Close the shoulder dart and mark in your style lines. Cut away the unwanted dart at the shoulder seam. *Fig. 38/B:* Where the neck and armhole seams gap, s*uppress* the unwanted fullness; it can be as much as 1cm (3/8") on small busts. *Fig. 38/C:* *In this demonstration the neck edge, CF seam, and armhole are shortened by placing them into the nearest seam or into the bust dart through the bust point. This can reshape your bust area as shown. *Fig.38/D:* You can take some of the fulness out, if necessary, by rounding off the bust point.

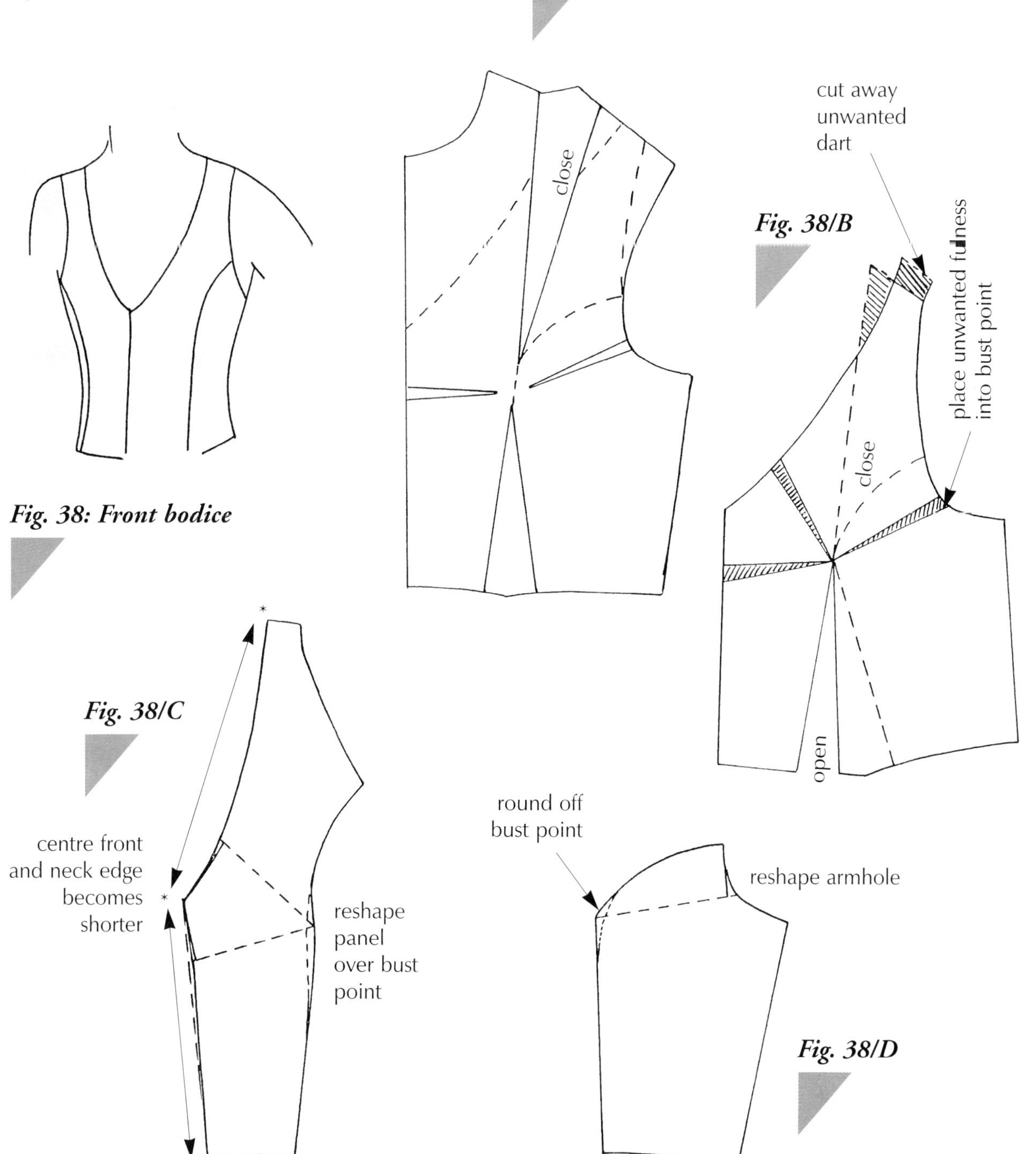

Neck facings: Figs 39-43

Many styles are made without facings and that's because bodices are normally fully lined. However, some styles are made with facings on which linings are attached. Other facings are made for dresses where they are not lined at all, especially those for bridesmaids.

The function of a facing is to neaten and strengthen the neck or armhole edge, or openings where they are required. Facings are lined with interfacing of a quality suitable for the fabric used. Some facings are cut to the foundation patterns with no amendments, others need slight adjustments, made to the CF for button wraps, for example. Ensure that the neck shape doesn't gape before cutting out the facing. Interfacings are cut to the facing patterns but when a very firm quality is used, it is trimmed to the seam lines.

The finished width of a facing is approximately 5-6cm (2"-2$\frac{3}{8}$") on some necklines and between 3-4cm (1$\frac{1}{4}$"-1$\frac{1}{2}$") on armholes. Back and sleeve openings are less: between 2.5-3cm (1"-1$\frac{1}{4}$").

Fig. 39: sweetheart neckline
Trace out the bodice of this style (***Fig. 31***) and decide upon the width of the facing. The neckline is quite low and the facing width should not exceed the armhole width.

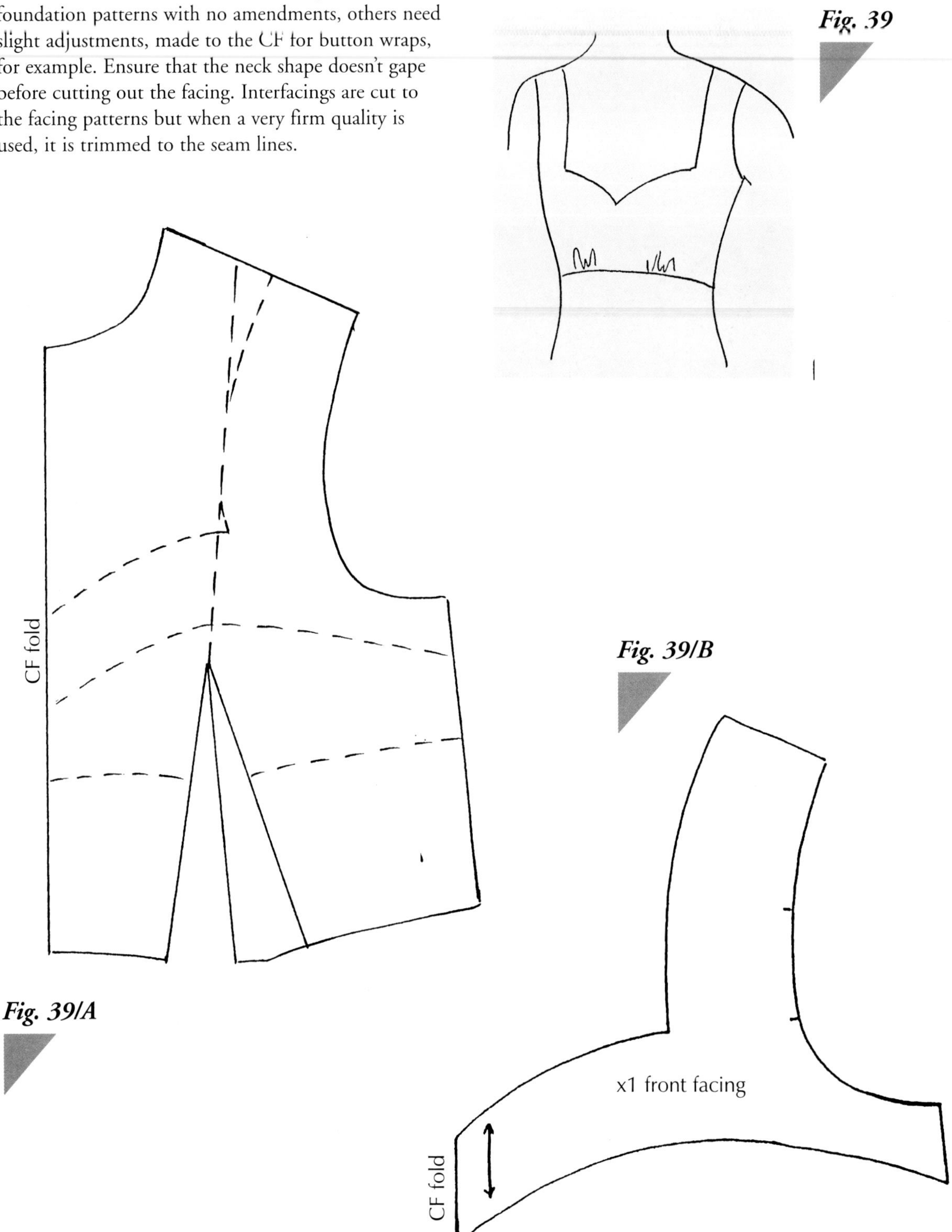

Fig. 39

Fig. 39/A

Fig. 39/B

Fig. 40: Neckband or yoke
Trace off the foundation pattern of the neck band or yoke and include the armhole notches for the front and back. Grain lines are important to mark onto your pattern and it's well to establish whether the facing should be cut on the bias or the straight grain. For example, if the fabric is very rigid then a bias facing can be used. A soft fabric may create stretching on the neck seam and a straight grain facing will help to prevent puckering.

Fig. 41: Boat shape neckline
Here, like the previous style, the facing is cut from the foundation pattern for back and front bodices. The facing is cut on the bias so that when the fabric is stitched onto the curved neck seam and armholes, it can be eased onto the bodice without pulling out of shape.

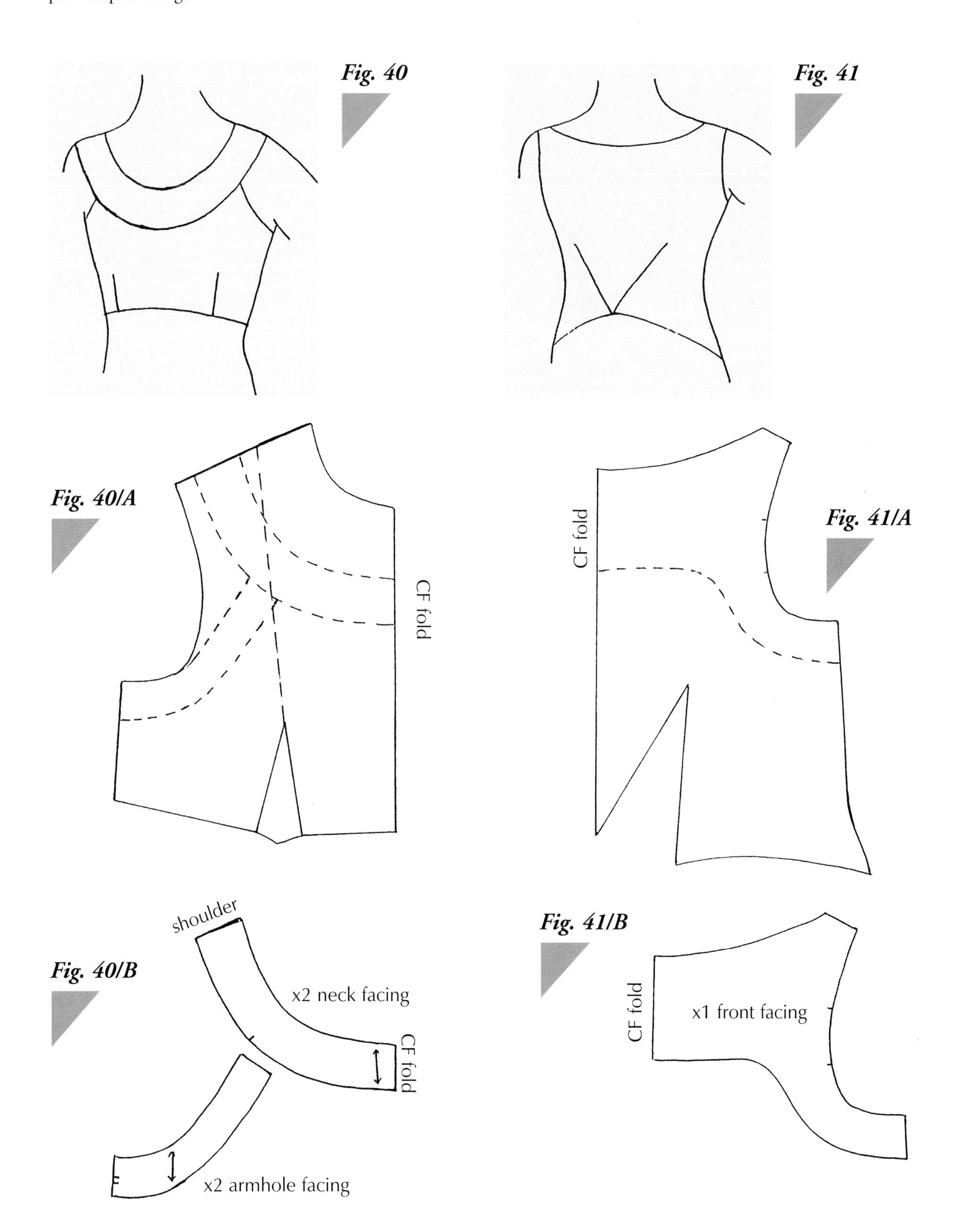

Fig. 42: Scooped neckline and armhole
Once the adjustments to the neck shape and armholes have been made *(Fig. 38)*, trace off the neck line for both front and armholes. The facing pattern for these areas should be cut on the bias.

Fig. 43: The neck facing for a button wrap facing
When a neck line has a grown-on button wrap, the neck facing is taken to the raw edge of the wrap seam and not to the CF fold. Trace out the neck shape and reduce the neck facing pattern by the amount of the wrap, then add your seam allowance.

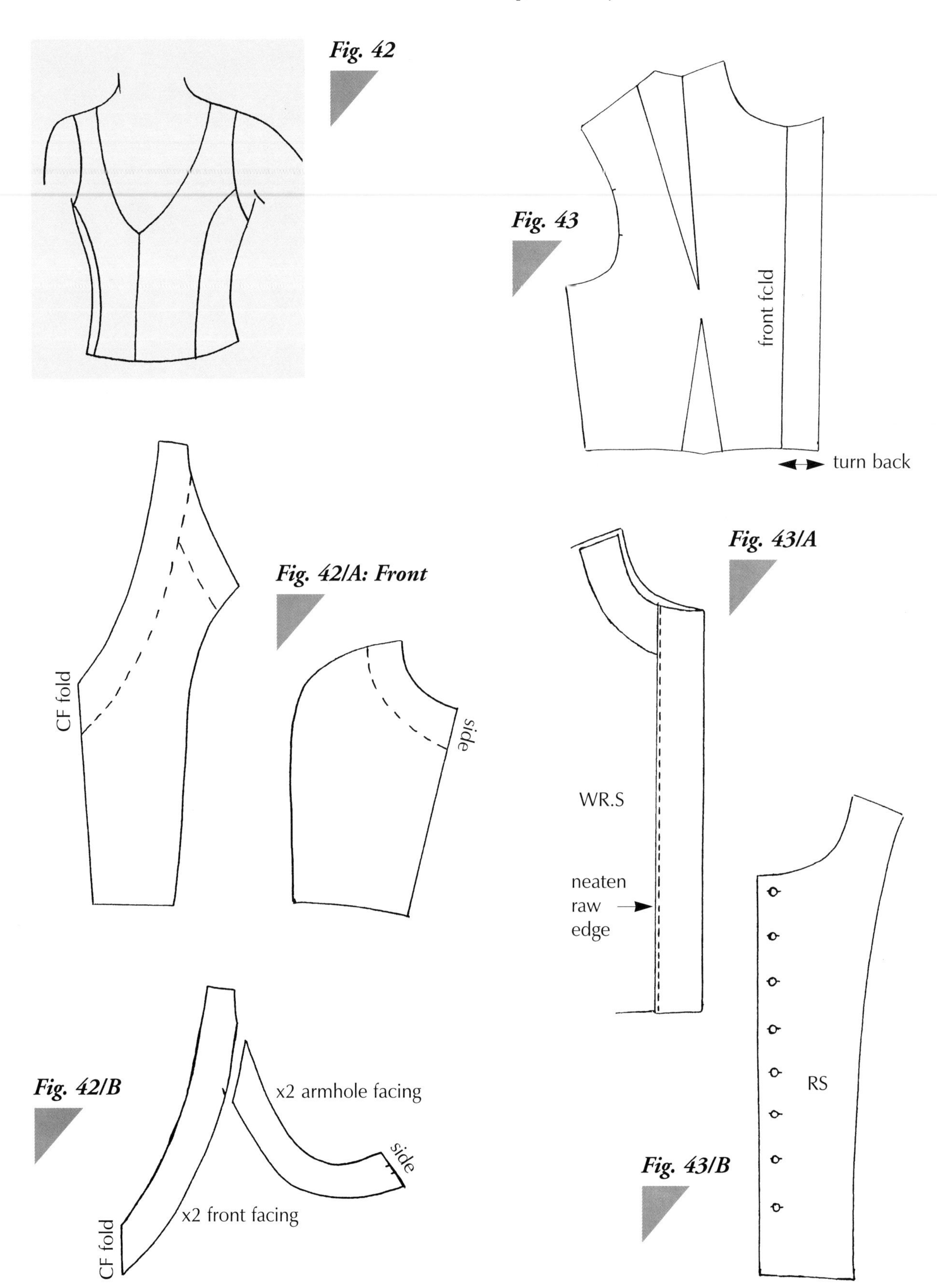

Fig. 44: **Attaching facings**

Stitch the shoulder seams together. Thumb-press them out and iron flat. Place the right side of the facing onto the right side of the garment. Pin and tack and then stitch the facing from the back opening on one side towards the centre-front and over to the other side. At the CF where the neckline dips to a 'V', mitre into the seam. Trim away the excess material of the CF and seams. The facing is turned onto the wrong side of the garment and tacked close to the outer edge. Iron the neck seams flat and the facing away from the actual garment, so that no marks are seen on the right side of the neckline. This method produces a smooth finish to the neck shape.

Fig. 44: Attaching a facing

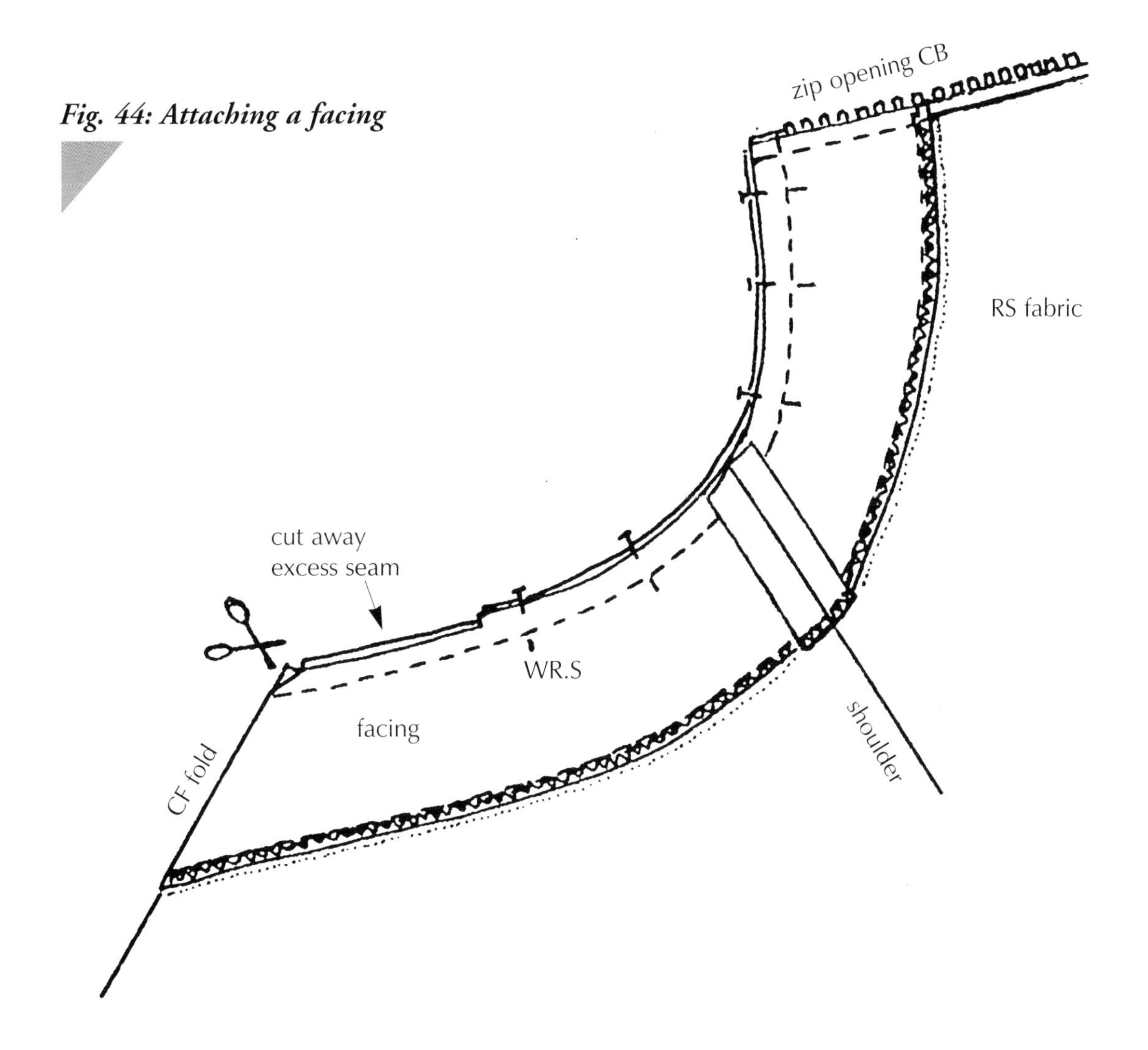

Selecting a style

PART 3

Achieving a silhouette

Designing garments (***Fig. 1***) for the retail market or doing a collection for an exhibition or a one-off for a client, is the most difficult and the most rewarding experience a designer can wish for. Whether you are doing this for yourself or for other people the principle is the same. A few basic points will help to achieve this.

- *Collect as much information* as possible on the sort of style(s) you want to develop. Always carry a notebook around with you to jot down ideas. Museums and libraries, comparative shopping in both garment and textile fashions, film and theatre, newspaper articles, exhibitions, catalogues and dress patterns, they all help to produce creative ideas when you need them.

- You may want to use a theme for a collection. *Fashion forecasting* magazines will help you identify those areas. They predict the trends for future seasons. These magazines are expensive to buy but you can often browse through them at specialist fashion bookshops or libraries.

- Your client may come with a barrage of ideas and come to you for inspiration. Keep an eye on what has been popular in the past: in terms of *colour, fabric, embroideries and trimmings, and style lines.*

- Either way, have a *portfolio with cuttings* out of magazines and rudimentary sketches and fabric swatches to hand. Focusing your ideas on paper enables you to identify your *handwriting:* your originality will develop in this way.

- It might be worth photographing the garments you make for yourself or for other people and placing these in an album.

Fig 1

Design illustrations

Drawing from sketch books (*Fig. 2, 2/A, 2/B*) will give you an indication as to how to improve your drawings and is one way of overcoming your shyness when putting your ideas down on paper. However, it is important to try doing them freehand eventually and this comes with practice. A simple sketch can often be as effective, provided all the fashion details are clearly marked on it.

- There are sketchbooks of *design silhouettes* available from specialist bookshops that would help you produce fine sketches. They are often very stylized and these exaggerated poses may not be suitable for your design idea. Find a template that will enhance your ideas as opposed to making them look ridiculous.
- *Trace off the outline* of a silhouette that would suit your design onto a A4 size marker pad (fine drawing paper), then draw in your style lines putting in all the back and front details like neck and collar shapes, pocket details, buttons and loops, trimmings or anything else you plan to use. Details of faces, hands and feet are not essential.
- *Swatch* your sketches with the fabric you have in mind and write down the necessary details from the labels provided.
- *Make notes* of any changes to the design next to the drawing.
- A *graphic border* around your sketch will give it dimension (like a framed picture).

Fig 2: Back view

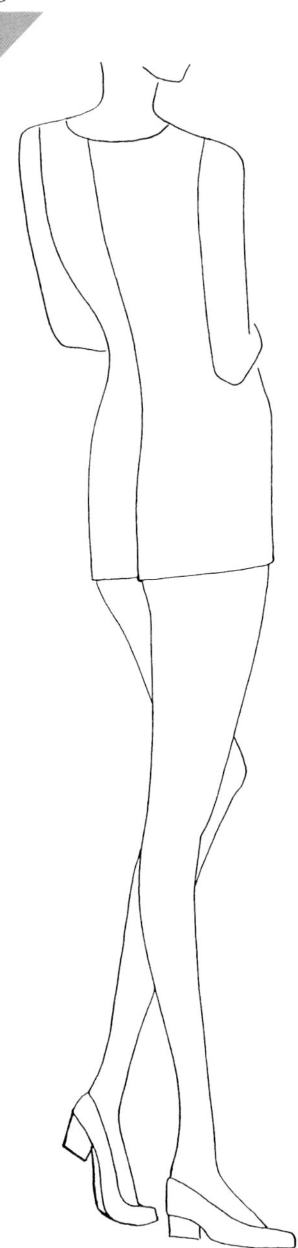

Fig 2/A: Front view

Fig 2/B: Silhouette

Toile

A **toile** (a dress material) is a mock up of the original pattern, styled and reshaped onto a stand or figure to achieve an accurate fit. It's usually made up in *calico.* However muslin, polyester cotton, or even nylon can be used providing it is comparable in weight to the fabric to be used in the style. *Calico* came originally from India. It's a cheap, plain weave cotton which comes in various widths and is very durable. A lightweight calico is normally used for styles with draping like collars and skirt shapes. A medium weight calico is used for tailored jackets (such as riding jackets as worn in Victorian times) and a heavyweight calico is used for structured garments like boned bodices, for instance.

Some shapes are better draped on the stand and often one can incorporate both flat pattern and draped methods on the same design as discussed in Part Four. *Fig. 3* is one example and here I have incorporated the cowl collar to illustrate my point. For a bought pattern, make up a toile to test the fit and establish how much ease is necessary and to see what other changes will need to be made before using it as a basic pattern for other things.

Fig. 3/A: Toile

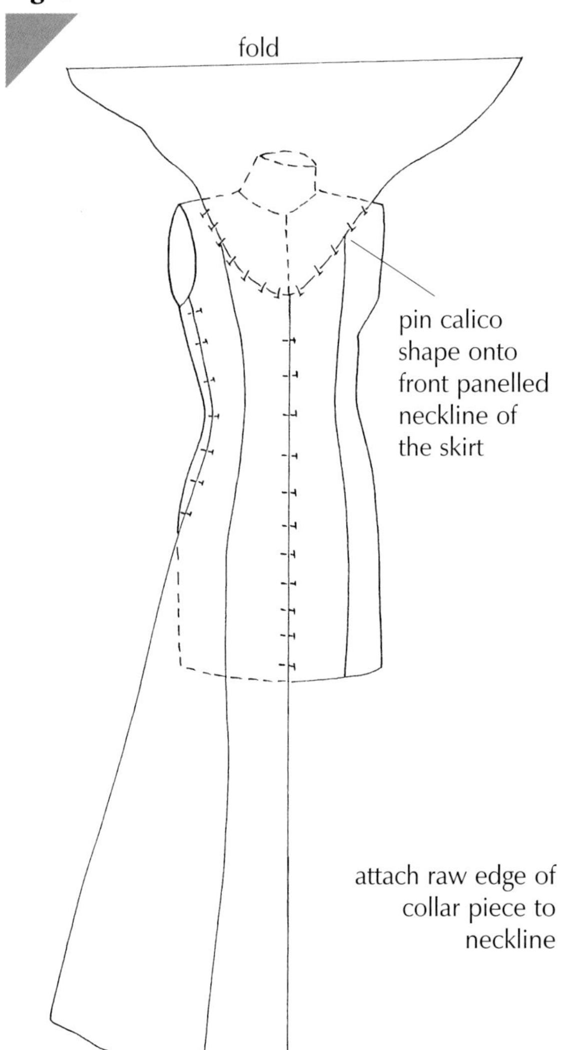

Fig. 3: Silhouette

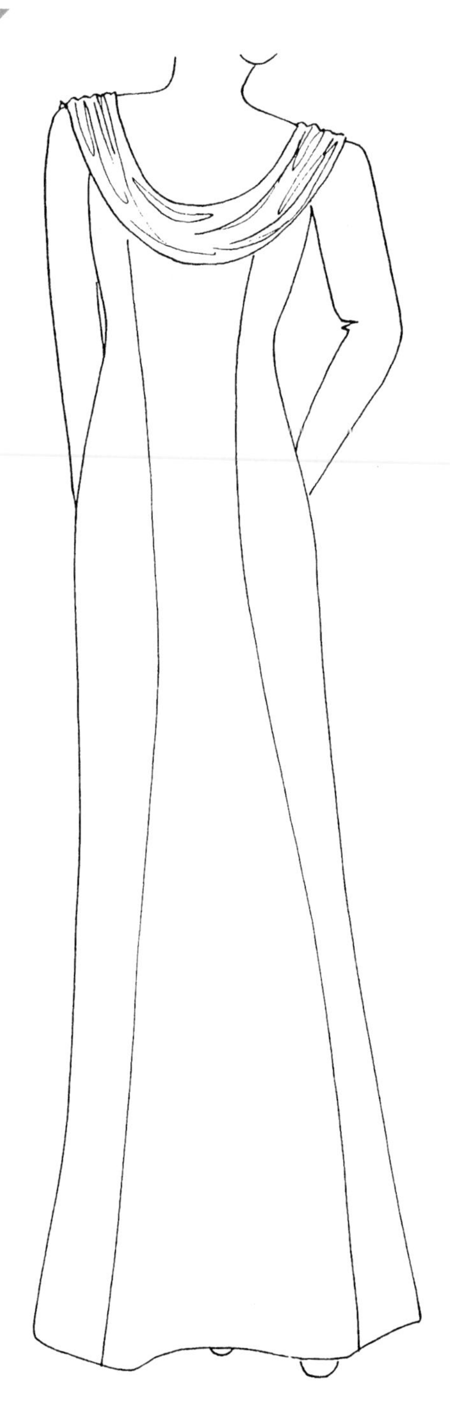

Fig. 3/B

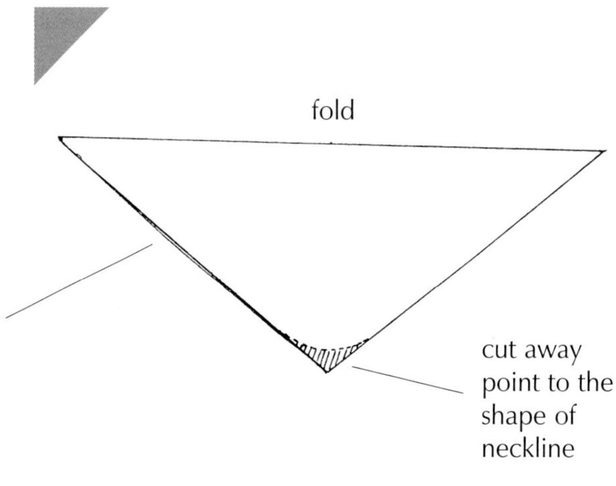

- The fabric for the cowl drape on ***Fig. 3/A*** is the required length of calico needed for the drape. Fold this square in half with the fold placed on the bias. Cut away some of the excess of the triangle at the centre front so that the point is rounded off and corresponds to the front neck when shaping it.

- On *Fig. 3/B*, attach the panelled dress shape from the drafted pattern to the stand. Use a tape measure and some pins and a marker pencil to realign your shape if required, and re-mark on the pattern draft, to ensure that the dimensions are established. Then pin the raw edge of the collar fabric to the neckline. Shape and drape collar to the size and fulness required.

- *Fig. 3/C* is the shape produced from the method used to achieve the cowl neckline. It shows the collar taken from the stand, reshaped into the pattern required and pulled down towards the CF to form a cowl. This shape has shoulder seams which are optional. If the cowl drapes along the back neck you may consider making the drape without these seams.

Fig. 3/C: Cowl neckline

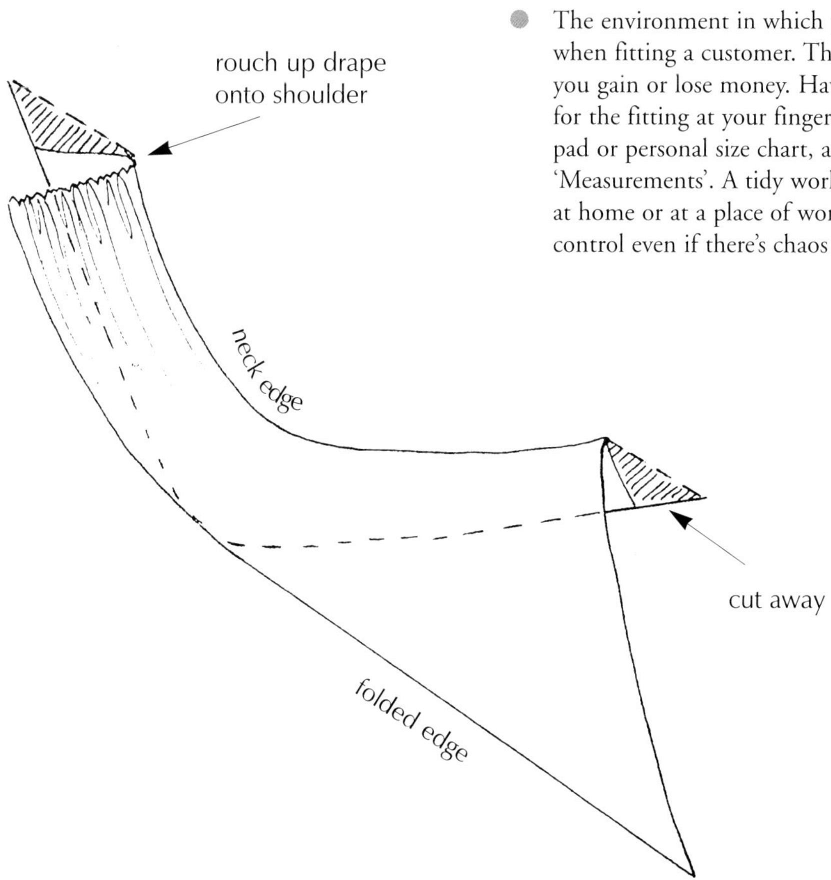

Fittings:

- With the first fitting, puckering around the neckline and armholes often occurs (see the section under 'Gaping'). Any alterations are refitted to the contours of the figure so make sure that with the second fitting, the *correct underwear* is worn. Some brides take a while before focusing on this very important factor. Certain bra shapes do make a difference to the fit of the bodice. For strapless garments, a stretch body or chemise would need to be worn to pin adjustments to the fit (as discussed under 'Taking Measurements').

- A further fitting may be required before cutting into the main fabric allowing for *weight loss,* as some brides, through nervous energy, may lose weight without trying. Taking a fraction out at the centre back can often solve this problem. A final fitting is necessary once the garment is put together, to establish the hem length and ensure that the correct height of shoe is worn.

- Your toile will have *seam allowance* on all the pattern pieces and markings for the position of pockets, buttonholes, darts, and other details like pleats or gathers, if required. Once the style and fitting is correct, first cost out the pattern on the width of fabric you plan to use. It can save you money before buying and cutting into the main fabric.

- The environment in which you work is important when fitting a customer. The *ambiance* could make you gain or lose money. Have everything you need for the fitting at your finger tips, including a note pad or personal size chart, as discussed under 'Measurements'. A tidy work surface, whether it be at home or at a place of work, means you look in control even if there's chaos beneath it!

Fabric and lace selection

The range of fabrics in bridalwear has increased significantly over the years. Silks from the Far East and India have quadrupled in the nineties thus keeping prices in Europe very competitive. The standard width for most silks is between 112/4cm(45") but other widths such as satin qualities, exceed that at 140cm(57"). Silk Organzas are between 105/120cm(41"/47"). The types listed below are among the most popular. Some designers work from fabric lengths or swatches to get their inspiration for their designs; others use a selection of design silhouettes to decide which fabric to use. The latter is based on production lines, whereas the former is based on individual styling.

Note

Many silks can be hand-washed but it is recommended that bridalwear should be dry cleaned, especially since it is usually so elaborate. Dresses have sometimes been ruined through dry cleaning, so make sure you have a good recommendation.

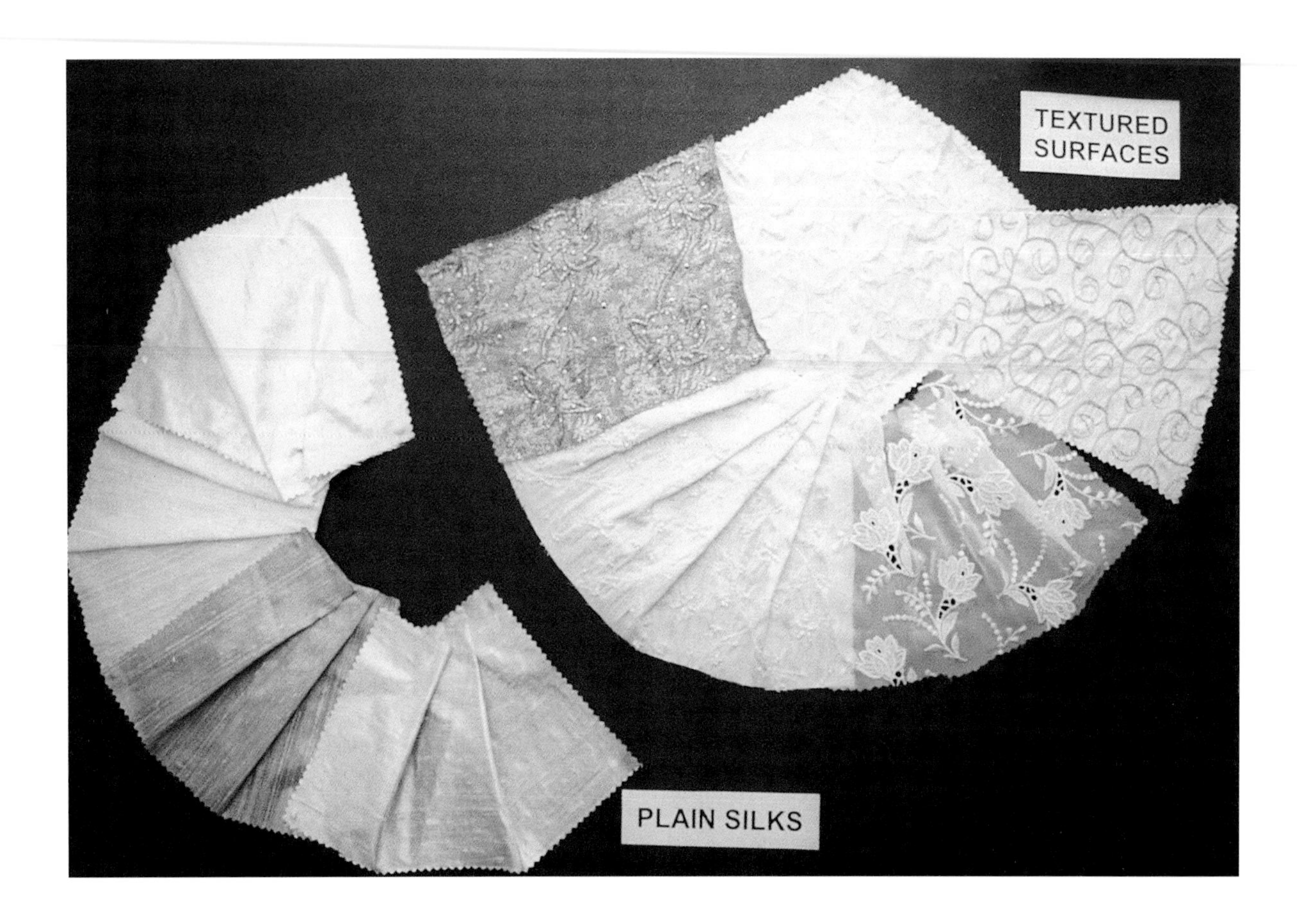

- Dupion silk is one of the most popular natural fibres used in bridalwear, especially for bridesmaids' dresses. Its slightly wrinkled and knobbly appearance and variety of colours, are the reasons for its appeal. It's also crisp and drapes well. Machine embroidery dupion comes as a beaded-all-over or satin-thread embroidery, and these are supplied mainly in pale colours. For darker shades, fabric lengths of no less than a 100 metres (approximately 360 yards) will be dyed up on order, unless the supplier has a quantity in stock.

- China silks are of a better quality and come in 1and 2 ply and are slightly more expensive. The colour range is not as extensive but it does compare favourably with dupion. The surface of the fabric has a slight sheen to it and frays very easily.

- **Jacquard** silks and cottons can be identified by the design seen in relief on the underside. The patterns vary from the smallest to the largest of designs. It is also more expensive than plain silks and comes in a variety of colours.

- Brocaded fabrics come in silk and synthetic qualities. The surface is richly textured and is often threaded with metallic silver or gold. These come in a variety of colours as well and fray very badly. Seams should be bound if possible, and make sure the bound areas don't show on the right side when ironing those seams. Used mainly to decorate parts of the dress, like the bodice, or jacket. This is the type of fabric that is tidal, that is to say it comes and goes with fashion predictions.

- **Velvet** comes in more than one quality. One can now find it in cotton, silk, polyester, and viscose. It is expensive but very durable and comes in several colours. The surface is either *raised* or *crushed* and its width is much wider than is normal for silks. Stretch crush velvets are also used for bridal and evening wear. A combination of nylon and cotton fibres are used to develop this fabric. Devore is a velvet where parts of the pattern have been burnt out, leaving a clear transparent image in some areas of the fabric. Velvet is difficult to handle and to press. A special machine foot can be obtained through specialist shops. This enables you to stitch seams without the underside puckering. It helps to tack all seams before sewing them. Do not press directly on seams but steam iron them through a cloth and have a velvet pad underneath.

- **Dutches satin** is recognised by its sheen on the right side and matt finish on the underside. The quality is heavier than ordinary silks and therefore produces a fuller fold and drape to the garment. Both silk and polyester satins can be found and they come in wider widths than other silks. It's expensive but money well spent.

- **Taffeta** is light and crisp and can crease easily. The texture lends itself to voluminous and extravagant styling. Moire taffeta is another variety and is distinctive by its water mark effect on the surface. Comes in both silk and polyester.

Laces

- They vary from width to price, in quality and design. Most bridal laces are expensive. They are often woven with a multi-faceted amount of thread to give its rich texture. Scalloped edgings or flounces, galloon laces and motifs, which are plain or beaded, are used to trim garments. Whereas beaded allovers are used mainly on the bodice or sleeves of the dress.

- A *guipure* (Venice) lace is made with heavy yarns in matte and mainly viscose (80%) and cotton (20%) and comes in various widths and designs: scolloped edgings from between 1cm(½″) to12cm(4¾″). Allovers comes in widths of 62cm(24½″), 90-92cm(36″) or 95cm(37½″).

- *Embroidery allover* laces are made on nylon and silk tulle and come in widths of between 85cm (33½″) through to110cm(43″),140cm(55″) and as much as 165cm(65″).

- *Alençon lace* is an allover made with fine satin cord stitched through and outlines the design like an applique. *Ribbon allover* laces are made with either shiny cord or ribbon and are stitched onto the design using loops like a spiral effect, giving the lace a three dimensional quality and feel to it. You can buy ribbon threaded lace ready made or have it specially made to order. Laces can also be supplied frilled, gathered, pleated, and layered. A special price is worked out on order for the service.

- **Habotai** silk is very fine and used mainly as a lining to the main fabric. Comes in a variety of colours and in two widths: 112/4cm(45″) and 140cm(55″). It lends itself to screen printing on bridal accessories and underlayers. Sandwashed habotai silks are heavier qualities used for items such as shirts and soft jackets.

- **Sheer** fabrics like chiffon, organza, georgette(polyester and silk), are used for soft flowing styles and come in a range of colours. Chiffon especially, can be difficult to handle when cut on the bias. Pin and tack wherever possible. Using tracing paper between layers before stitching can stop the layers from working against each other. Use french seams to neaten frayed edges.

- **Dyeing** laces can be done but not all suppliers have this facility, especially for small quantities. It's worth contacting the supplier to discuss terms such as: quality and quantity before going ahead. Not all laces are suitable for dyeing, especially those with polyester fibre content, and there is often a minimum charge for dyeing.

Interfacings

- These are essential for the standard of finish on bridalwear. They are used as underlinings and are sandwiched between the outer fabric and the lining. The primary function is to reinforce areas that are exposed to wear and tear in examples such as *neck facings, collars, cuffs, plackets for buttonholes and pockets, hemlines, seams and belts.* For boned bodices, the entire garment is reinforced since the structure of the bodice is to support the bridal gown, and the trim used thereon. The fusible qualities should be ironed onto the wrong side of the fabric with a dry iron. The quality of interfacings mentioned washes and dry cleans. Check the labelling before purchasing a length since some interfacings are not suitable to wash.

- There are many types, and the preference in quality used would depend on the quality of fabric and design of garment. An *iron-on cotton staflex* is suitable for most of the examples of fabrics mentioned, providing the fabric quality is thick enough to withstand shine and puckering. *Muslin fusible*, a light weight quality, is another example which can be used on fine transparent fabrics such an organza. These widths come in 90cm(35½″) through to 145cm(57″).

- *Woven interfacings* such as *cotton lawn,* and *tailoring canvas* are two extreme qualities. One is suitable for fine fabrics and the other for heavy weight fabrics. These interfacings should be cut along the straight grain and are stitched inside the seam width along the seamlines. Widths in these interfacings vary from 61cm(24″)through to 130cm(51″).

- *Bonded interfacings* such as *vilene* are synthetic qualities of thick and thin dimensions. These are used on stretched fabrics or natural yarns and can be cut in any direction. Mostly found in a 90cm(35½″)width.

Collar shapes and lapels

PART 4

During the mid 1600s, collars were as important in design for men as they were for women. These elaborate decorations were known as ruffs and later the fallen collar was introduced. The ruff was fitted round the neck separately from the main garment. As fashion evolved through the noblity, every denomination of the political and social establishment had a particular dress code and style of collar. This accessory, as well as the use of cuffs, plackets, and pockets, enhanced the design and hence the status of the wearer. For the contemporary bridal gown, collars, with some of their more decorative features, are not always functional but are often used instead to enhance the silhouette.

Collar assessment

- There are several stages to the draft of the collar, notably the *fold* line, which divides the stand and fall of the collar i.e. the area that rolls over from the neck seam onto the bodice. The *stand* is the depth of the collar that rests against the CB neck, and where it curves over the shoulder seam. The *breakpoint* is the position at which the collar meets on the CF neck edge, and where the first button or fastener is attached (***Fig. 1***).

- Most collars require a *top and under collar* so that the fit of the top collar rolls slightly underneath at the front and back edges. Allow approximately 0.3cm difference between the two (***Figs 2 - 2/B***). Under collars are traced from the top collar returning to the basic shape at the neckline and corners of the collar.

Fig. 1

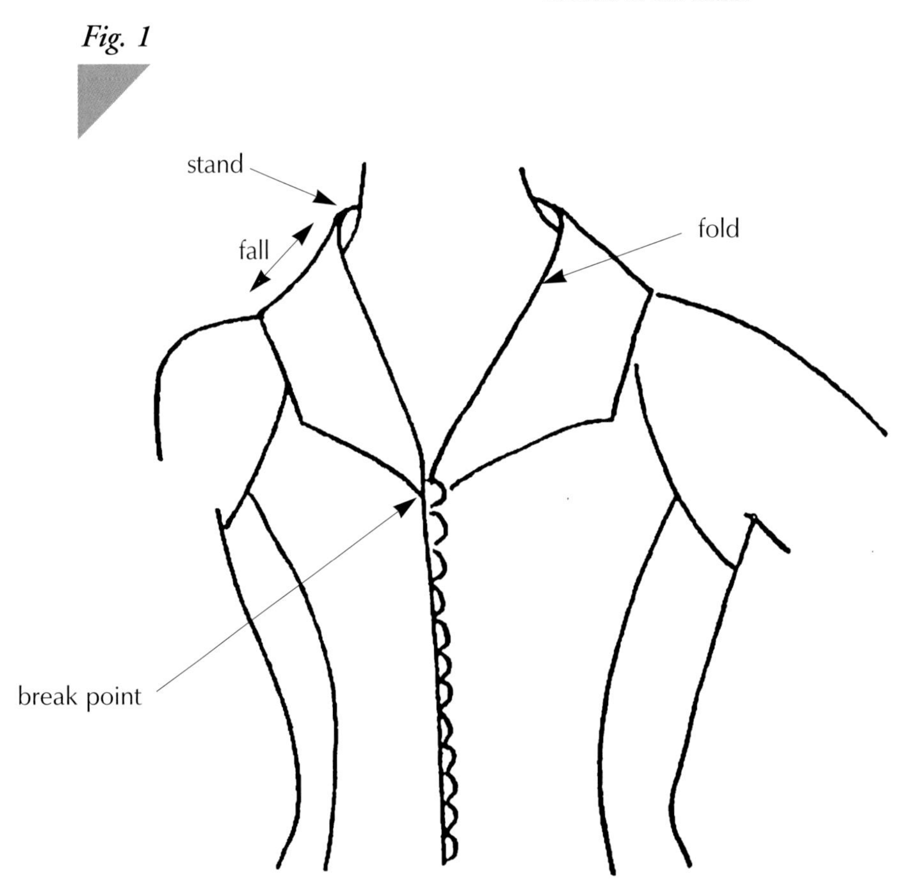

- The *shape and size* of the collar is determined by the style of the garment and to some extent by the bust size and fabric used. A very large velvet collar, for example, would look heavy and out of proportion on a very large chest size. The catagories of collar shapes are enormous and range from the stand collar or mandarin (which stands up against the neck) to the shawl and revers, used mainly for tailored styles. There is also the all-in-one collar, which has no seam along the front neck edge. Some of these shapes are illustrated in this text.

- The *buttonstand or placket* is not regularly used on the bridal gown but when applied on the tailored jacket or similar openings, it is made to fit the size of the button used. The details can be seen under 'Collar Shapes'.

- *Linings* are determined by the thickness and quality of the fabric. The top layer is stitched onto an under layer of a stiff netting or interfacing, and these layers are lined with a soft silk or polyester satin. Fusible linings should be used with caution when ironing on delicate fabrics and raised surfaces.

Collar shapes

The flat collar (***Fig. 3)*** takes the shape of the foundation pattern.

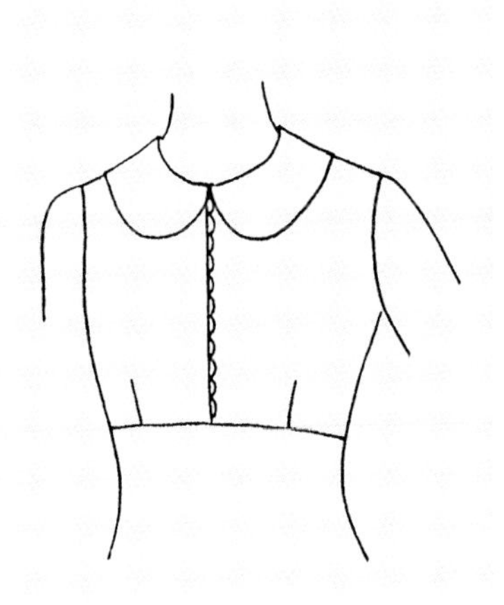

Fig. 3:
The flat collar

Fig. 2

under collar
CB
top collar
neck edge
corners

Fig. 2/B

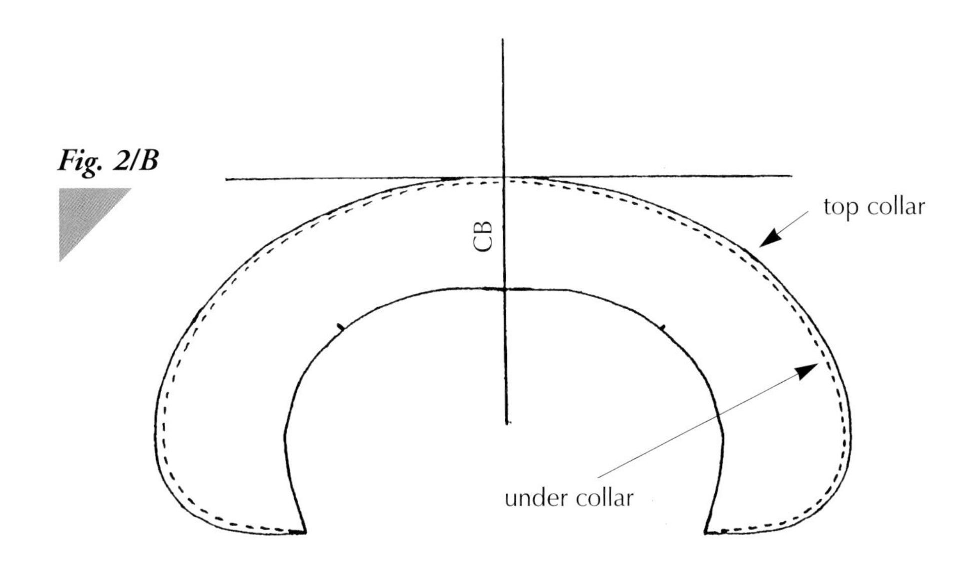

Fig. 3/A shows a flat collar with rounded corners at the front, often seen on bridesmaids' dresses. The back and front shoulder seams are placed together at the neck edge and the armhole seams overlap by approximately 2cm (3/4"). Trace off your shape, marking in a depth of about 6cm (2 3/8") for the CB to 7cm (2 3/4") at the CF.

The shawl collar: worn off the shoulder

The classic shape in bridal wear is the shawl collar (*Fig 4*). Since so many styles in bridalwear have low cut neck shapes, the collar is often worn off the shoulder. For some collars, draping on the stand can work in conjunction with the flat pattern method used on the main silhouette. For this shape, it works well. The toile is pinned onto a tailor's dummy by cutting a square piece of calico, large enough to cover the depth of your collar. Fold it in half so that the two points meet. Cut along the fold line on the bias grain and pin this part to the neck edge of the bodice.

Fig. 3/A

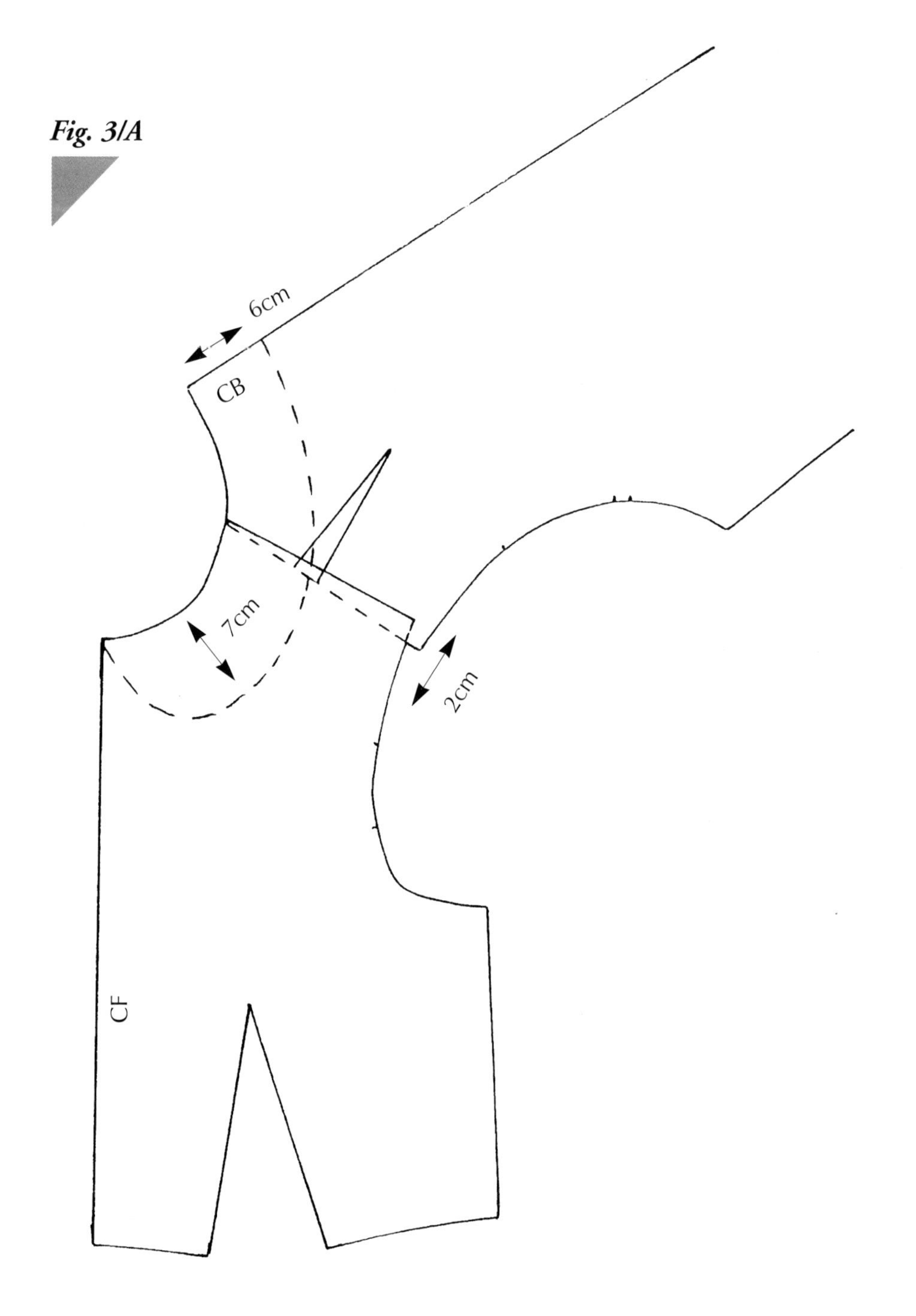

Pattern preparation

a. It is important to suppress the unwanted fulness of the neckline and locate it into the bust point when you are doing the collar.
b. Fit the bodice shape onto the stand or figure. Then drape and pin a large piece of bias-cut calico onto the neckline. Seam allowance is 1.5cm (½") wide.
c. Work your way from the CF neck seam towards the CB. The fabric is pushed up against the neck. It becomes easier to mark in the depth of the collar to the required measurement.
d. For a flat shape, the collar takes the shape of the bodice neckline. You may want to reshape the CB of the collar.

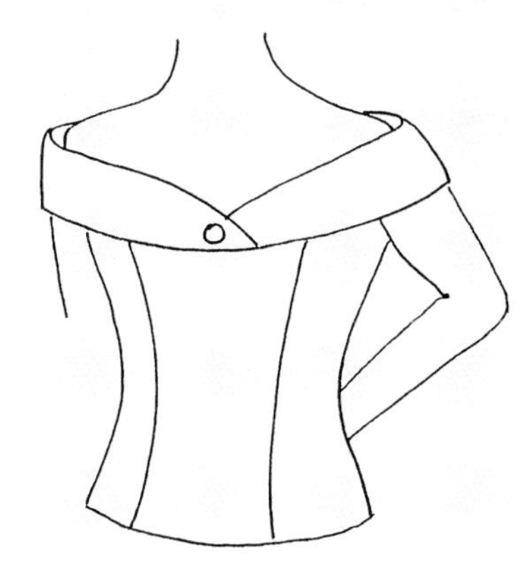

Fig. 4:* *Shawl collar off the shoulder

Fig. 4/A

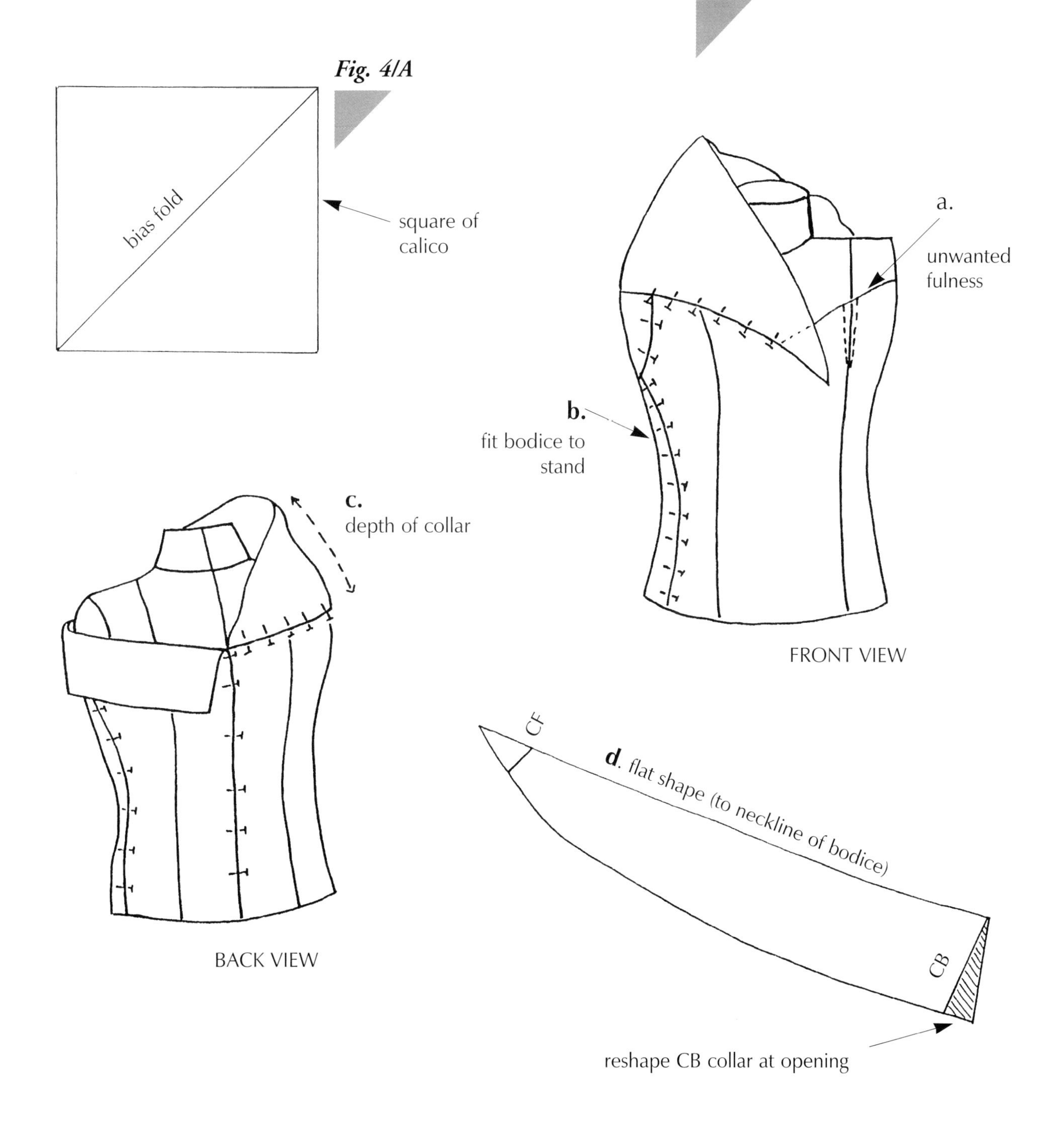

e. To increase the stand of the collar over the shoulder and CB position, reduce the width by folding in 0.5cm (1/8") along the outer edge of the collar to nothing at the neck edge, at regular intervals.

f. The collar overlaps by 4cm (1½") at the CF. The button wrap is shaped to a point, bagged out and neatened. The main part of the collar seam is stitched onto the neck edge from the CF to the CB.

g. A decorative button is tacked onto the wrap where it overlaps and stitched through onto the bodice.

Draped collar: off the shoulder

Use the shawl collar pattern for this silhouette. All that is required from this pattern is to extend the depth, by slashing through from the CF to the CB to the amount of drape required. Reshape the CF and put the CB on the fold of the fabric. The zip opening to this style is along the side seam of the bodice. The lining and interfacing is cut to the foundation pattern and the top collar is ruched and pulled into position onto this under collar. To keep the ruching or pleating in place, tack the fabric down onto the lining at various points. Onc can buy ready-made pleated silk or other quality pleating in preference to making a draped pattern yourself. Use the lining pattern for this.

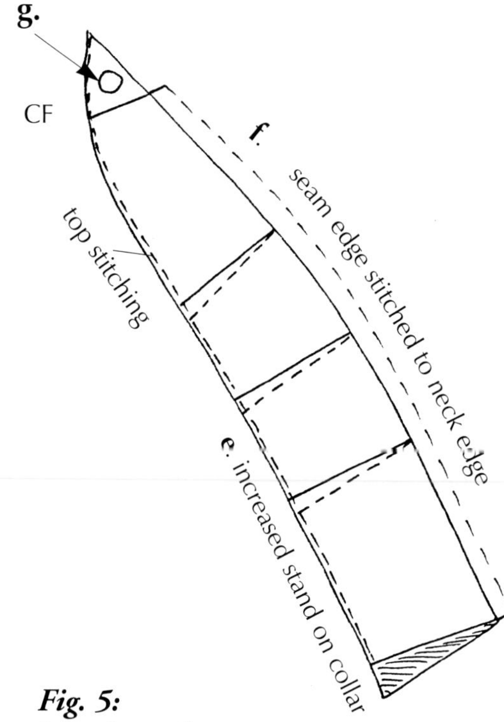

Fig. 5:
The draped collar

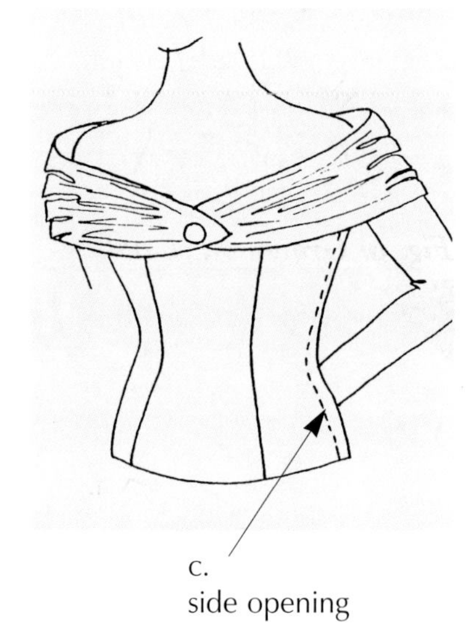

trace out
off the shoulder shawl collar

CF

a.

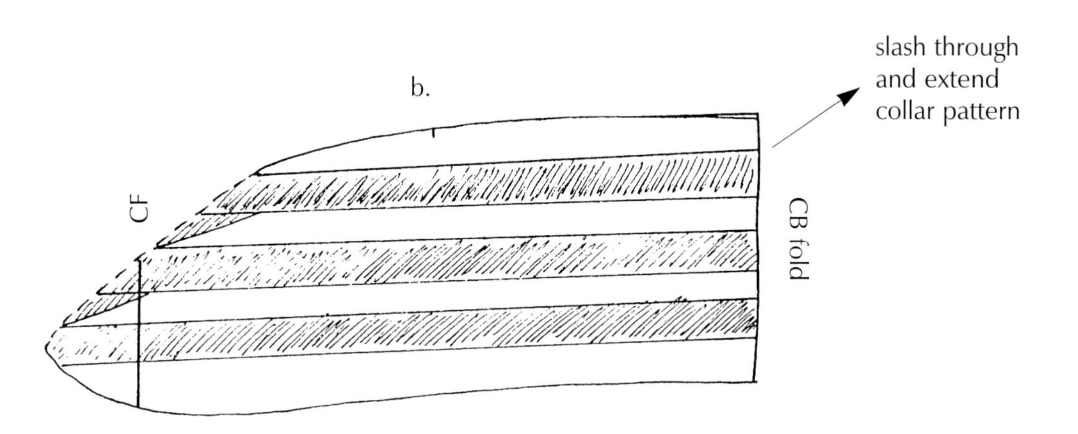

The one-piece collar: the shawl or grown-on collar

This shape is usually made quite close to the neck edge (*Fig. 6*). It is suitable for fur-type fabrics for the winter season, or heavyweights like brocade, velvets and duchess satins. For lightweight fabrics such as jaquards and crêpe back satins, the principle of the draft remains the same. The collar is derived from the basic shape of the front neckline. Trace off the foundation pattern and put the shoulder dart into the waist seam. Add the buttonstand width required and then mark in the neckline.

Fig. 6: Grown on shawl

Prepare pattern

a. Draw a dotted line from a-b at shoulder neck edge, allowing 2.5cm (1")for stand on collar.

b. From a-c measure the neck opening and mark a line down to breakpoint at CF buttonstand.

c. Measure half the back bodice neckline and join up from a-d.

d. Draw a dotted line 2.5cm (1") from d-e which corresponds to a-b.

e. Now measure the required depth of collar from e-f and curve down towards c, allowing it to correspond to the dotted roll line.

f. Complete the dotted line from e-b and c. This roll line for the collar varies according to the depth required.

Note

g. The back neck part is increased to enhance the shape of the collar and lies further over the base of the neck. Slash through from the outer edge to nothing at CB neck line to the required amount.

h. The facing or top collar is made approximately 0.5cm ($\frac{1}{8}$") bigger around the outer edge to break point at buttonwrap. *Allow sufficient width to your facing at both shoulder and hemline, so that it doesn't protrude when the collar is turned onto the RS of your garment.

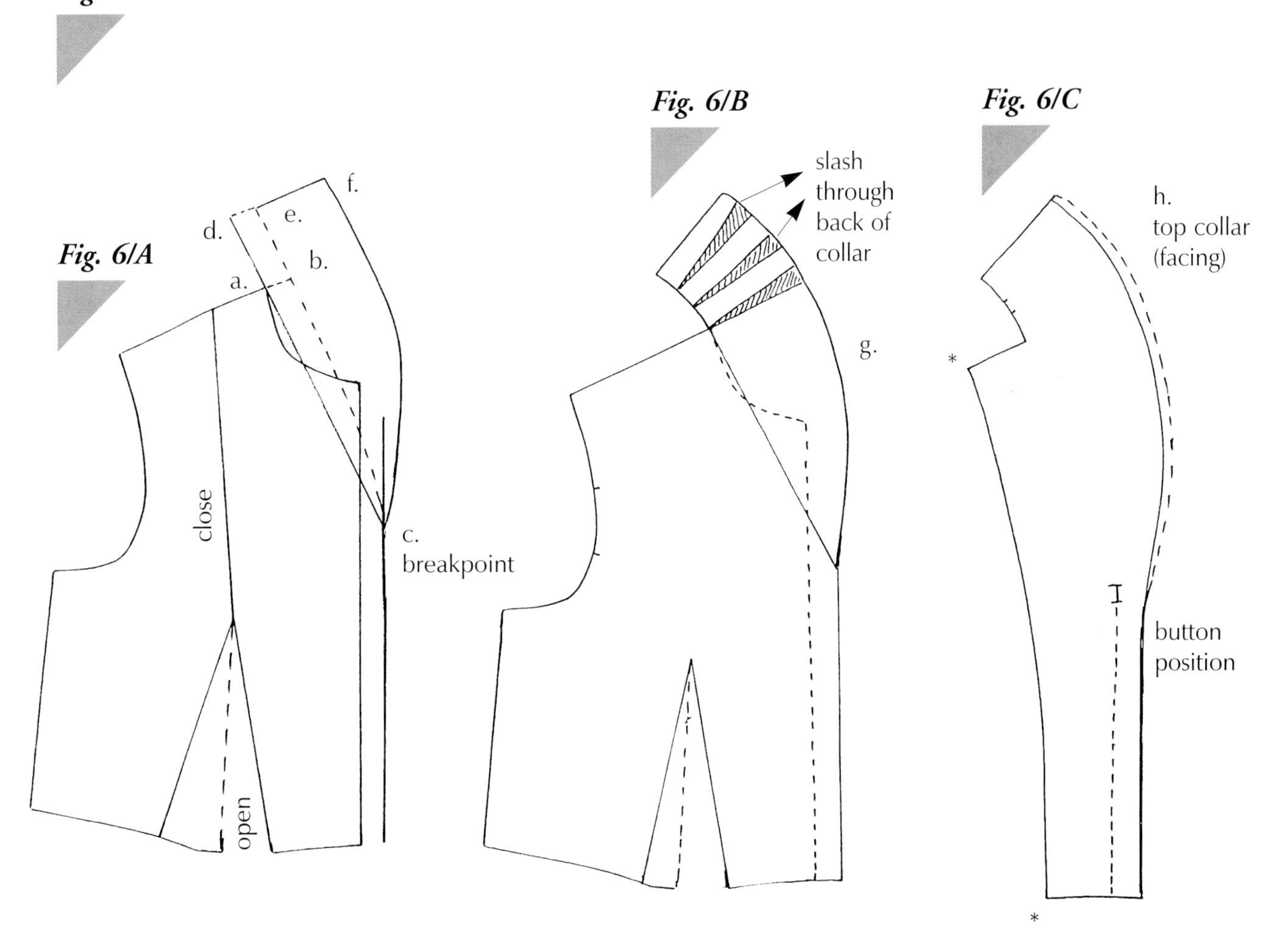

Fig. 6/A

Fig. 6/B

Fig. 6/C

The basic grown-on rever collar

Fig. 7 is drafted in the same way as that of the shawl in *Fig. 6*. The difference in design is the rever shaped along the outer edge of the collar. The position from **f to c** is reshaped by folding the collar along the roll line onto the front bodice and marking in a measurement at **g** from the shoulder line to a point at which the rever starts. Draw a line to **h** and then to a second point at **i**. Now reshape the rever from **i-c**. The measurement between the two points is arbitrary (approximately 5cm [2"]). Trace out the lapel with a tracing wheel and make a separate facing pattern **j** for the top collar 0.5cm (1/8") wider to nothing at breakpoint c. *Allow sufficient width to your facing at both shoulder and hemline as on *Fig. 6/C*, so that it doesn't protrude when the collar is turned onto the RS of your garment.

Fig. 7: Grown-on rever collar

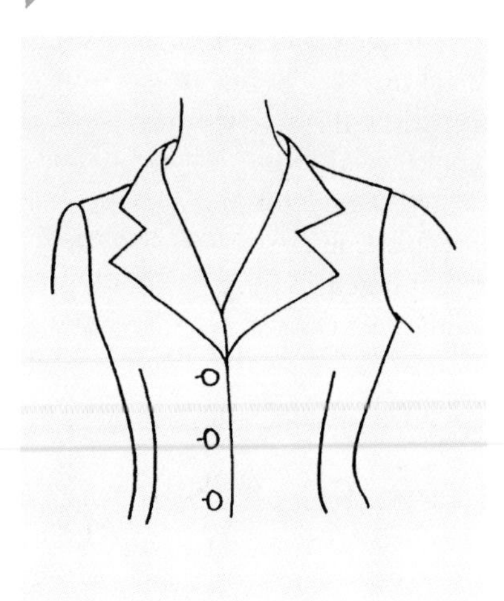

Fig. 7/A ***Fig. 7/B***

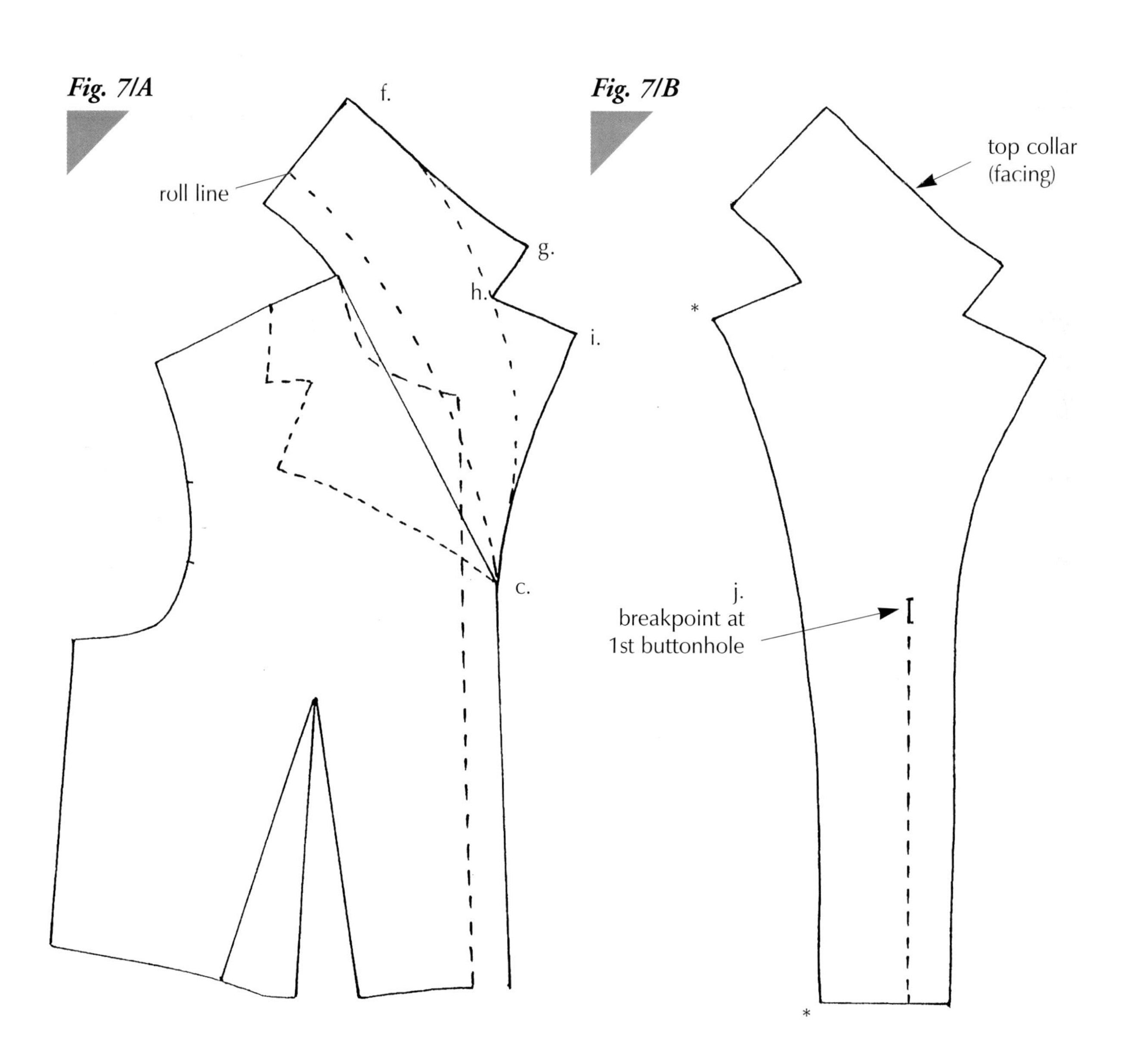

The double-breasted rever: Fig. 8

The photograph illustrates a double breasted rever attached to a scooped neckline. To achieve a military look, use a narrow braid or bias binding in a contrasting colour and stitch this across the centre front panel. Trim each end with large covered buttons that match the colour of the braid or binding. The method used for this collar is much the same as that of *Fig. 4* where the toile is pinned and draped from the neckline of the bodice. Before doing this, fit the bodice onto the stand as before.

Fig. 9 shows how the collar fits onto the CF wrap of the front bodice pattern, where it overlaps and extends to the bust seam of the side front panels. The depth of the collar is cut so that the fall extends low across the centre front and back bodice. The back shoulder dart is closed on ***Fig. 9/A*** and put into the waist seam, and the bodice has a panel cutting through the dart as on the front. Here, the CB panel has a zip opening.
Fig. 9/B: the stand of the collar lies fairly flat onto the shoulder line, with a minimum rise of approximately 2cm (3/4"). Very little suppression is needed on the outer edge as seen in this case in ***Fig. 9/C***.

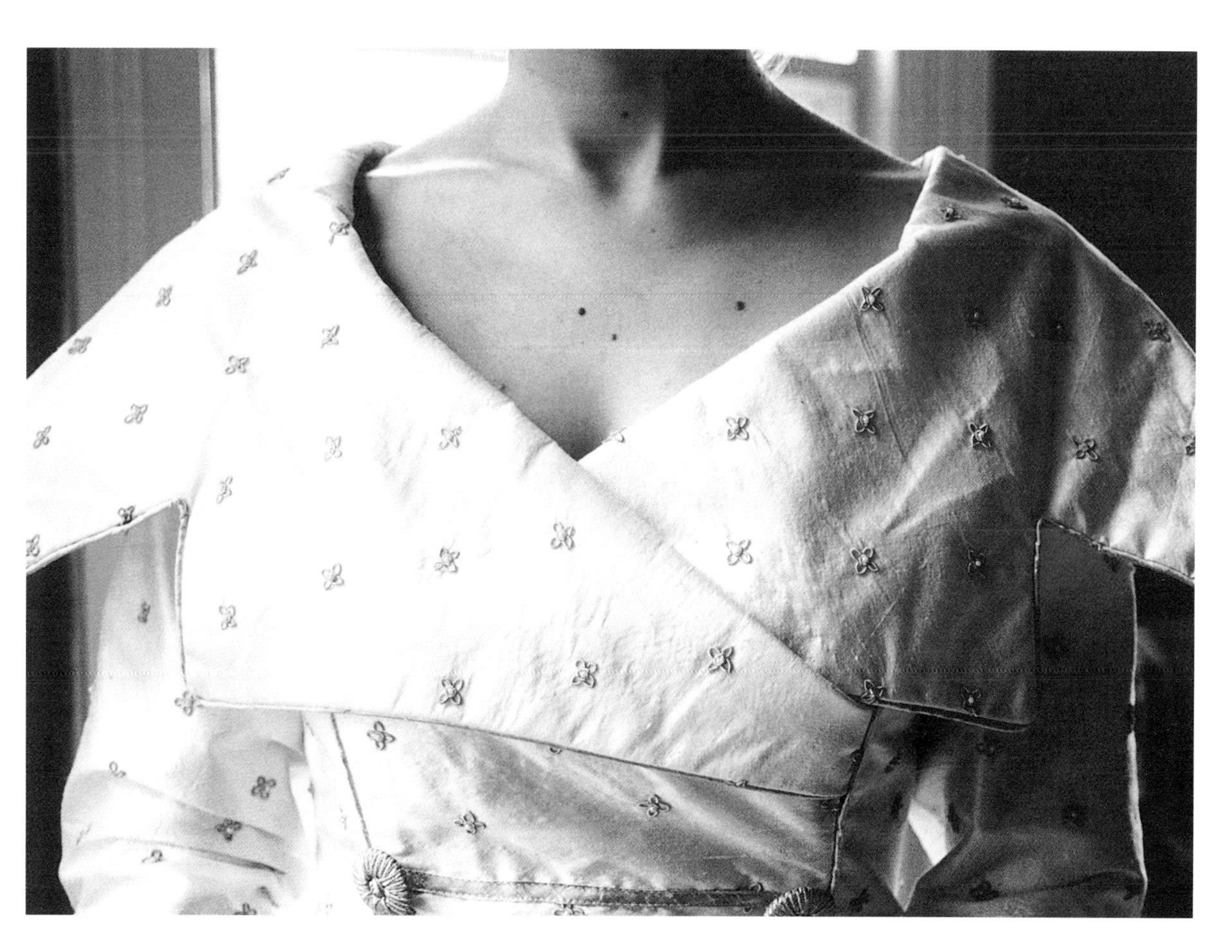

Fig. 8

The double-breasted collar:

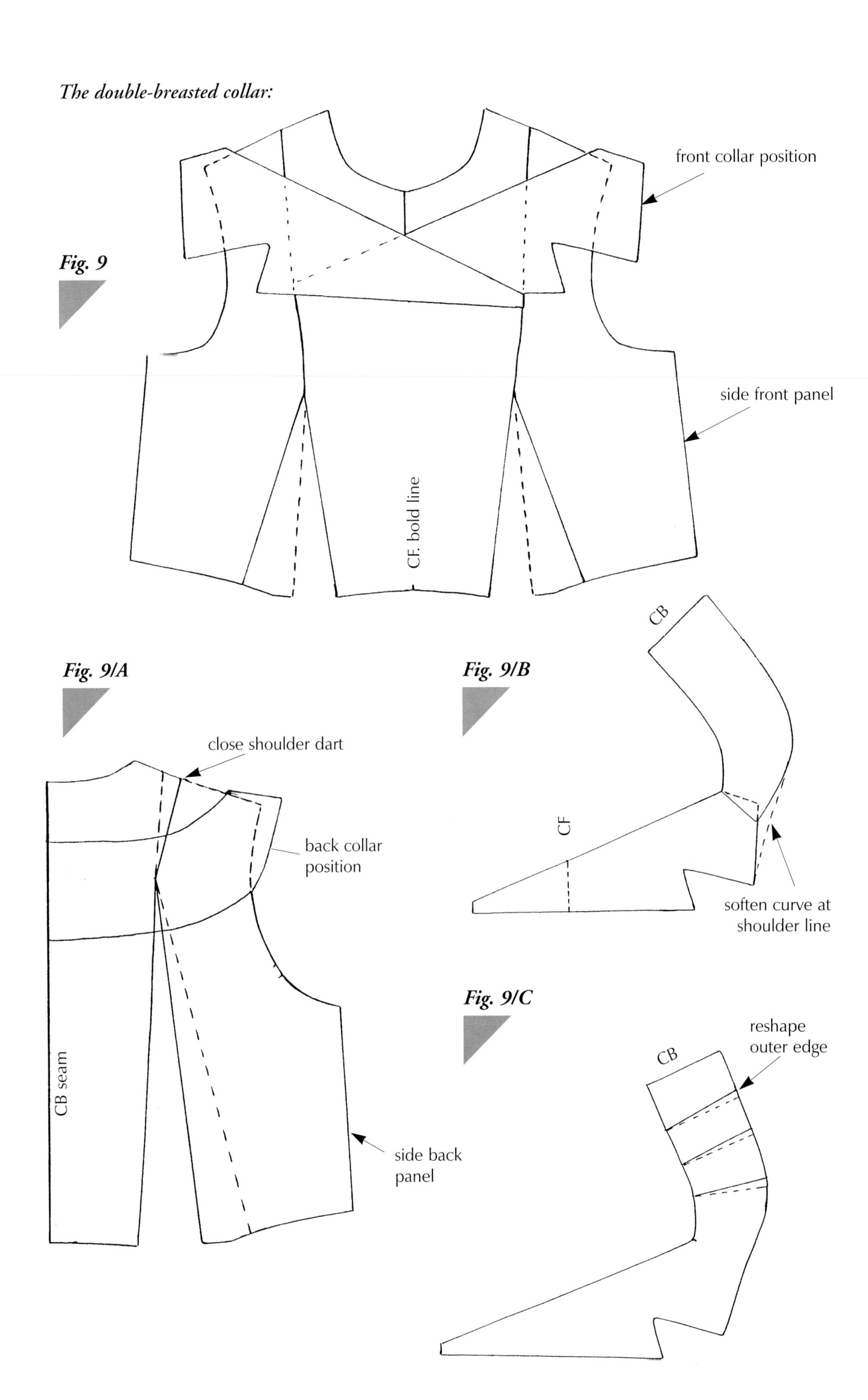

Fig. 9

Fig. 9/A

Fig. 9/B

Fig. 9/C

The straight collar

The straight collar was a feature used in the 60s but not widely used in bridalwear today. *Fig. 10* has a slight variation to the normal straight collar. This styled pattern sits somewhere between a straight and a mandarin collar draft. The straight edge is extended beyond the CF position where it overlaps onto a double-breasted bodice, and reshaped at a side front opening. The collar is suppressed at the top edge of the back neckline and reshaped so that it has a closer fit along the back neck. The kimono silhouette has had a revival in recent times in fabrics such as brocades and jaquards.

a. Take half the back and front neck measurements. Mark in the depth of the collar and draw a line at right angles.

b. Notch in the shoulder and CF positions and measure the extra amount required for the wrap at the front.

c. Reduce the top edge of collar at the shoulder notch and CB by 0.5cm (1/8") or more for a closer fit if need be.

d. The front edge of the collar is placed onto the neckline and reshaped at an angle in line with the straight grain of the bodice.

Note
Covered buttons and loops start from the top edge of the collar.

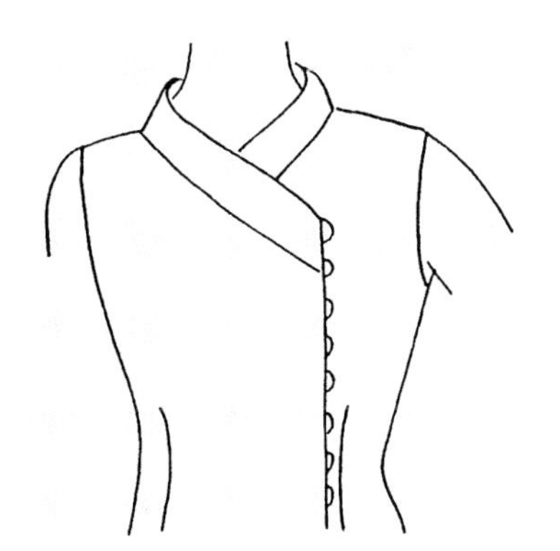

Fig. 10: The straight collar

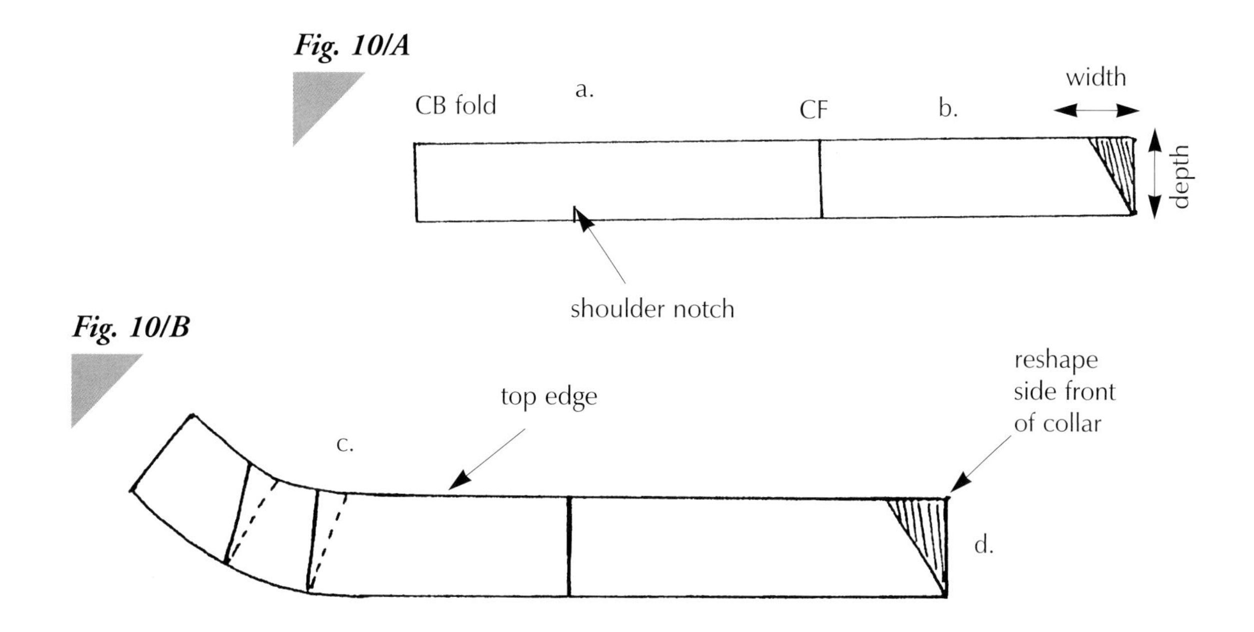

Fig. 10/A

Fig. 10/B

A roll collar

This collar is widely used in bridalwear and opens along the CB seam. It wraps itself around the front and back chest and upper arms of the body, as seen in *Fig. 11*. The neckline is cut low to off the shoulders. This collar is drafted from the front and back bodice neck shape pattern. The bodice has no sleeves so take a measurement for the upper arm instead.

Fig. 11/A

a. Take the full measurement of the neck shape on the bodice and upper arms, and divide the pattern in half and notch in all the positions for the CF, front and back armholes and CB opening.
b. Take the width and depth of the collar and measure down at right angles.
c. To raise the stand of the collar, reduce the measurement at the edge that falls onto the bodice. Slash through to the neck seam and decide how much suppression is required. If the collar is to stand away from the neckline, the measurement for the fall of the collar needs to be quite tight. See ***Fig. 11/B***.
d. However, if the collar needs to lie flat against the bodice not much suppression is required on the fall (***Fig. 11/C***).

Note

The interfacing can be either ironed or stitched onto the top collar depending on the quality of the fabric used.

Fig. 11: Roll collar

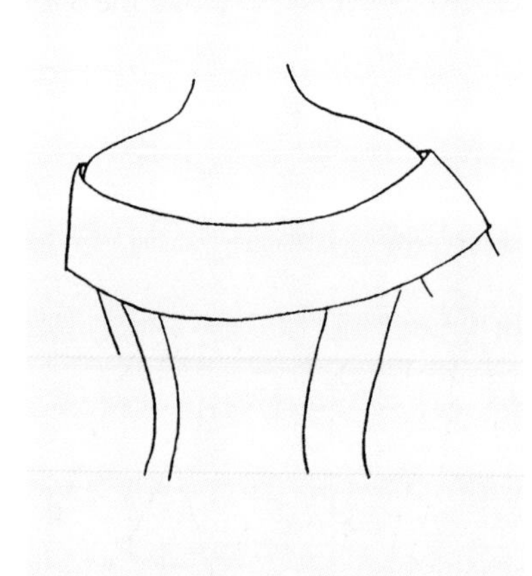

Fig. 11/A

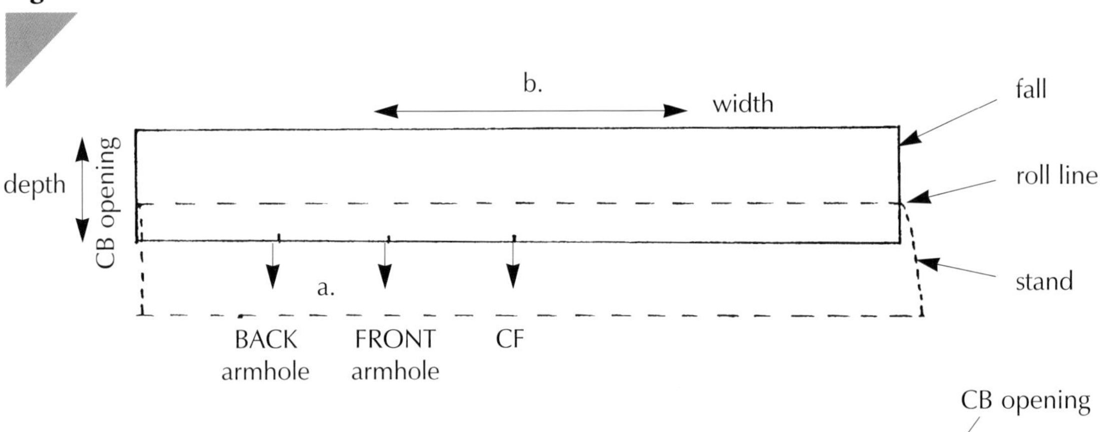

Fig. 11/C

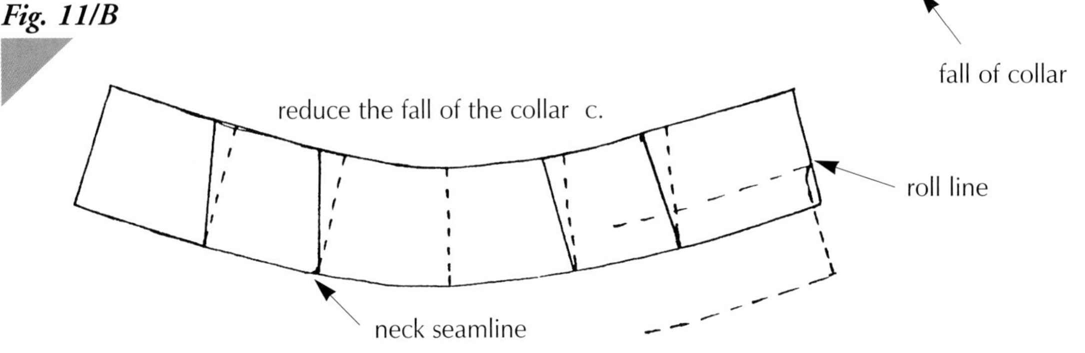

Fig. 11/B

Grown-on buttonstand or wrap: Fig. 12

For front, back and side openings on bridalwear, the popular choices are *loops* and *covered buttons*, *eyelets* and *rouleaux ties* and the *invisible zip*. However, the buttonstand can be seen on styles such as the frock coat, jackets, and some waist fastenings.
For the grown-on buttonstand in ***Fig. 12***, the preparation is as follows:

a. The buttonstand is the wrap that extends from the CF line to the required amount taken from the size of the button (*Fig. 12/A*).
b. The button is centred and then measured either side of the CF.
c. The wrap width is half the button width plus 0.5cm (1/4").
d. From the breakpoint, where the 1st button is attached, measure the 1st buttonhole and subsequent ones down the CF line.
e. Spacing the buttonholes are important: ensure that a button is positioned between the bust points and as near the waist seam as possible, to prevent gaping.
f. The back of the stand is the full width of the buttonwrap plus seam (***Fig. 12/B***).
g. Buttonholes on ***Fig. 13*** are positioned at right angles where the wrap is grown onto the bodice. It is stitched 0.2mm (1/16") from inside the button position to accommodate the shank of the button.
h. A separate stand (***Fig. 13/A***) or placket would require a vertical buttonhole position down the CF because of its seam attachment.

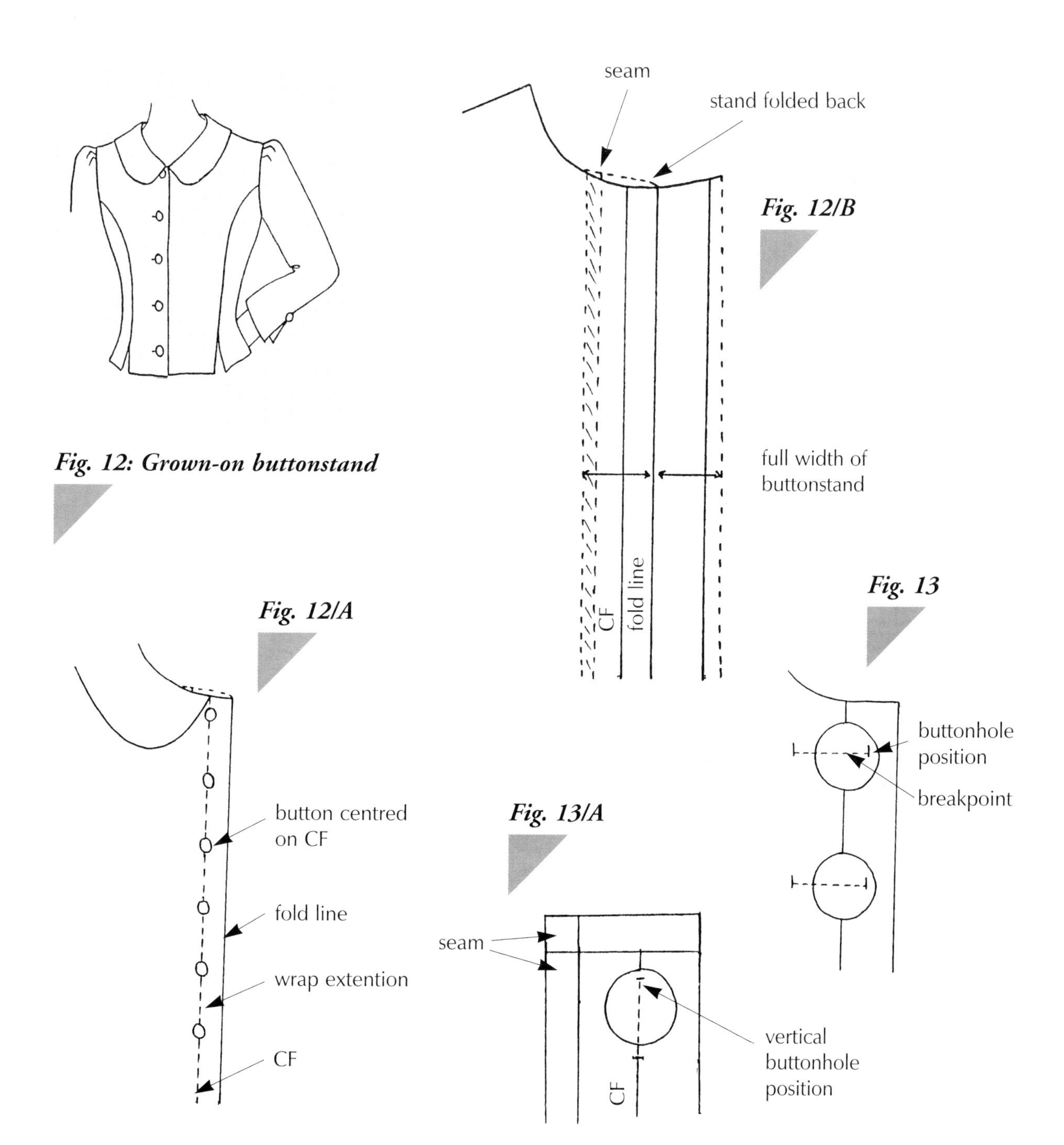

Fig. 12: Grown-on buttonstand

Sleeve styles

PART 5

Sleeve styles for bridalwear have no boundaries and vary according to taste. The length of sleeve, if any, can be influenced by the time of year the wedding is, and the style is often determined by the shape of the bodice. In this chapter we'll be demonstrating the most popular shapes, and to vary the concept of design we'll be dealing with *the basic full-length and short sleeve, the cap sleeve, draping and pleating, the two piece tailored and the leg-o-mutton sleeve.* Cuffs in this section perform a very small function, and are mainly decorative.

For the most part, *a style is derived from the foundation block* even when using a bought pattern. Make sure that with each new design you adapt from the basic sleeve shape, a *toile* is made to ensure a good, if not a perfect, fit. There are several key points to remember when using either of these foundation patterns, as seen below:

Fig. 1

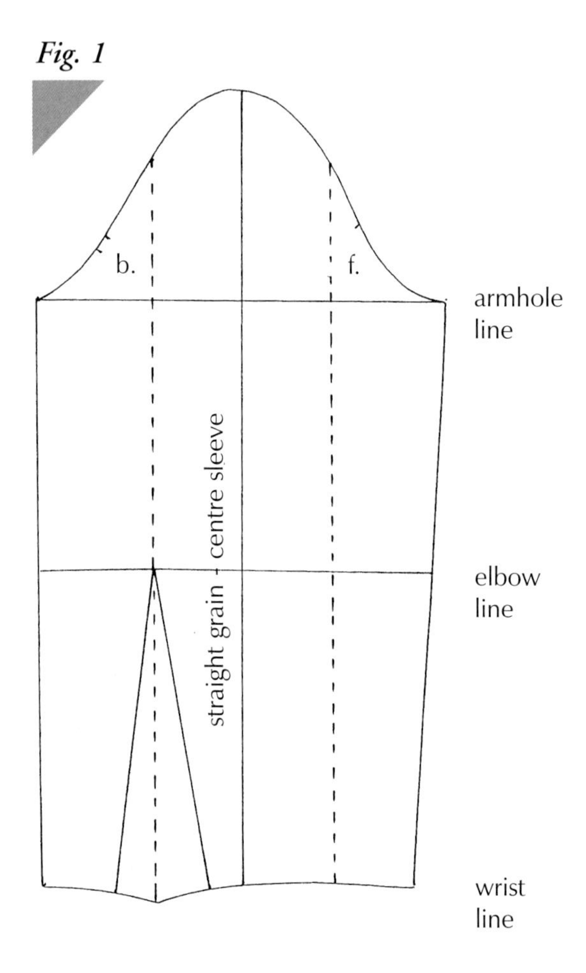

Fitting lines and darts: Figs 1-2

1. The *armhole line* corresponds with the armhole of the front and back bodice.
2. The *elbow line* is midway between the base of the crown depth and the wrist line. Measure the fullest part over the bone at the elbow joint, for ease of movement. Reduce or increase wrist measurement from this position if no dart at wrist is required.
3. A *dart position* extends from the elbow line, midway between the centre sleeve and back seam and down towards the wrist. The width of the dart is normally between 5cm (2") and 6cm (2½") placed either side of the centre line. A small elbow dart could be used instead of the wrist dart (***Fig.2***).
4. The *wrist line* is just below the wrist bone. Styles without wrist openings need to be as wide as the *fist* measures on non stretch fabrics.
5. The *grain line* follows down the centre (when folding the sleeve pattern in half). Bias grain lines are marked at 45% to the straight grain.
6. *Notches* for the sleeve crown vary from pattern to block. But in general, the centre notch meets at the shoulder line. The front position has one notch and the back has two notches. Those for gathers are put in as the style dictates.
7. *Bias binding* is used to cover seams of the armholes for most sleeve finishes. See 'Materials and Decorations'.

Fig. 2

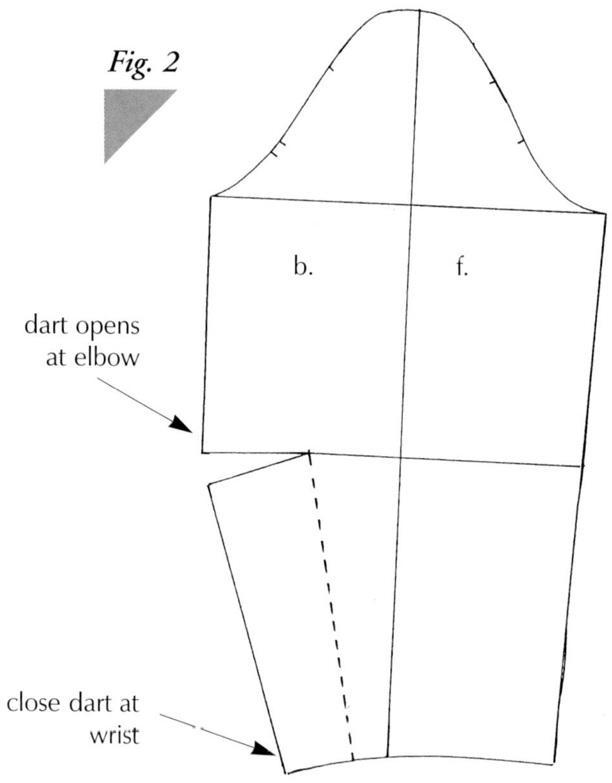

Tolerance on the sleeve crown: Fig. 3

The sleeve head is always eased and never stretched into the armhole, unless the fabric has a degree of stretch in it. When the sleeve crown is shallow and doesn't fit into the armhole, add between 0.5cm (1/4") and 1cm (1/2") at centre notch, starting the increase between back and front notches as seen on *Fig. 3.*

Should you want to reduce unwanted fulness on the crown, slash through the centre sleeve down the crown depth, approximately 5cm (2"), then outwards towards the back and front notches. Fold in the required amount at the centre notch, which shouldn't exceed 1cm (1/2") (***Fig. 3/A***).

Note
Remember to check the upper arm measurement and the armhole depth for each of these alterations to ensure the fit across this area meets with your requirements.

Tolerance on the sleeve head would vary according to *fabric quality and thickness.*

The *scale* below applying to some fabric qualities and a degree of tolerance gives you an idea of what to expect when sewing a sleeve into the armhole.

- For example, a tailored sleeve using damask or brocade, the tolerance would be between 1.5cm (5/8") - 2cm (3/4").

- *Heavyweight* fabrics: (duchess satins, velvets, brocades and some taffetas) - allow between 1.5cm (5/8") - 2.5cm (1").

- *Mediumweight* fabrics*:* (open-weave silks and linens, soft taffeta, sequined and embroidered fabric) - 1cm (1/2") - 2cm (3/4").

- *Lightweight* fabrics: (chiffon, organza, habotai silk, voile, muslins, cotton lawn) - allow 1cm (1/2") - 1.5cm (5/8").

Linings: Without a sleeve lining of some sort, most sleeve shapes would droop except for those with very fine fabrics. It's therefore necessary to apply more than the top layer of fabric. An under lining of firm netting or a soft non-fusible interlining is backed onto the top layer and the silk or satin lining is applied after that.

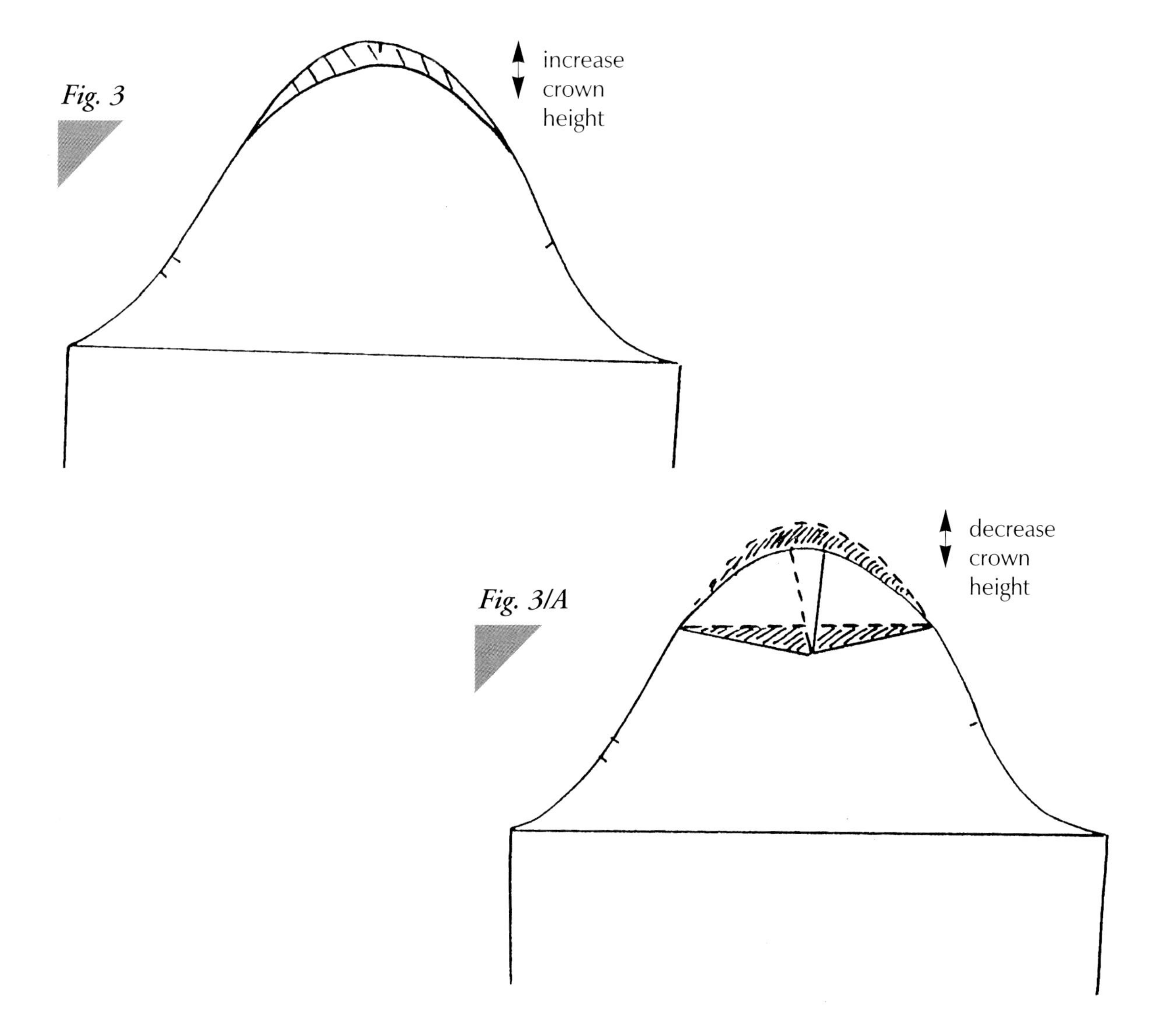

Fig. 3

Fig. 3/A

Sleeve styles

The cap sleeve

Chosen by many brides, this sleeve is made either by stitching it in the armhole or as an extension of the bodice. An example of the latter is demonstrated in Part Two under 'Bodice Shapes'. For this section the *set-in cap sleeve* is concentrated in two areas (*Fig. 4a-b*).

Fig. 4 illustrates the sleeve length which is short and fits snugly across the upper arm. Measure down from the armhole at underarm seam, to about 3cm (1⅛"), and across at right angles. The required measurement can also be taken from the wrist upwards if you prefer.

Cut away the unwanted sleeve piece.

Fig. 4a: Slash through the required sleeve pattern (evenly across the sleeve head) to nothing at the crown. Spread out the pieces to almost straight at hemline.

Fig. 4b: for a tight fit, the sleeve shouldn't be too wide at the hem edge and yet the arm shouldn't be too restricted in its movements. Straighten the hem edge and reduce the hem width from the underarm seams if necessary, and sleeve depth at crown by 0.5cm (¼"), if required.

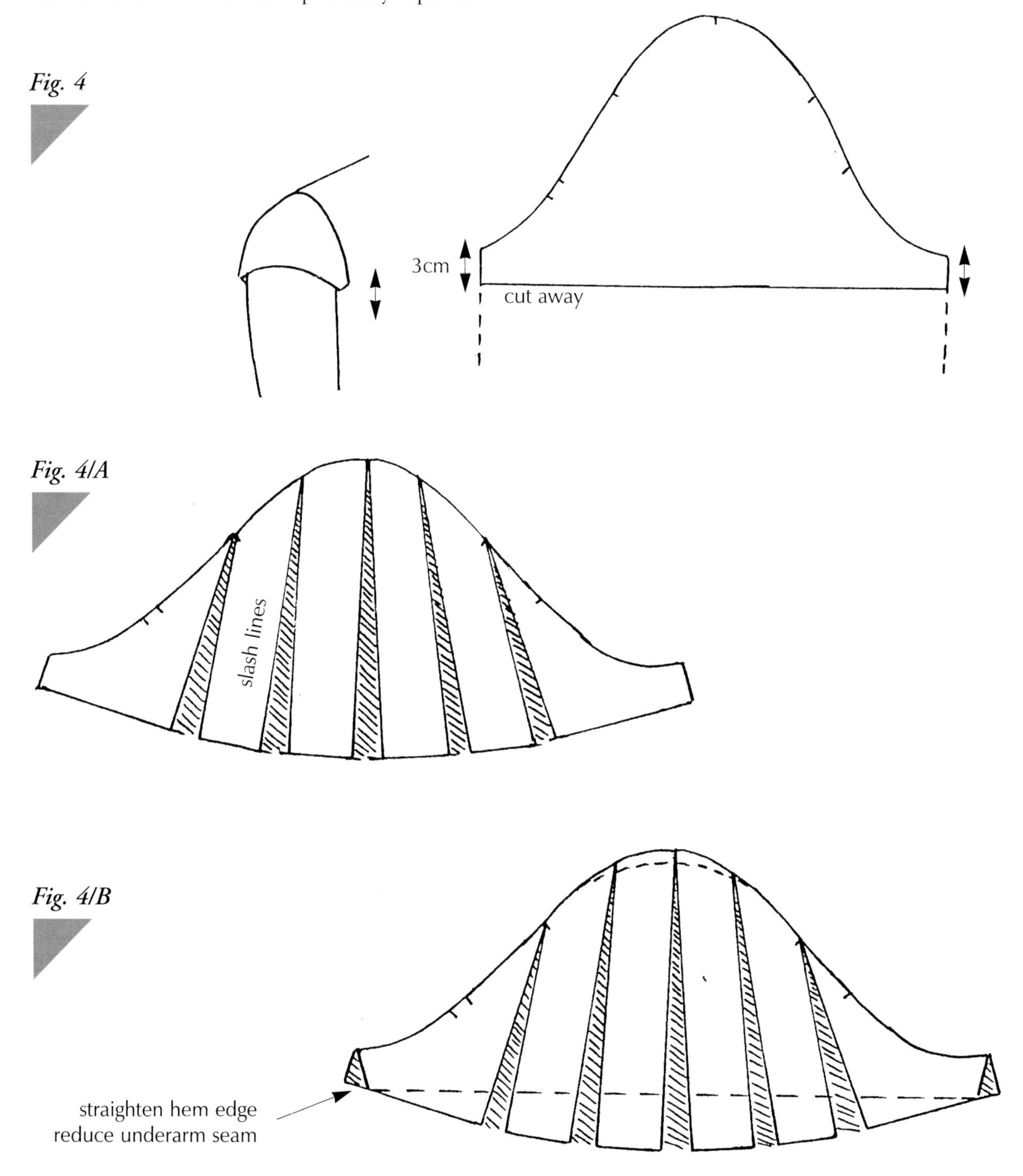

The cap sleeve is fully lined and therefore has a fabric hem width of approximately 3cm (1⅛") as shown in *Fig. 5.* Trace off the existing pattern and mark in length of actual hem for lining. Then add seam allowance of 1.5cm (⅝") to finished edge.

Fig. 5a: shows an alternative method which is to cut the sleeve in double fabric with the pattern piece placed on the fold of the fabric.

The short sleeve (petal shape):

The short sleeve depends on the sleeve shape and to some extent the design of the bodice. Some brides like having the widest part of their arms covered. The petal shaped sleeve length is measured midway between the elbow line and armhole line. ***Fig. 6*** demonstrates this sleeve which crosses over at the centre front and is pleated at the top. It is worn off-the-shoulder and covers the upper arm. The foundation pattern can be used as a reference to other styles of the same proportions.

Fig. 6

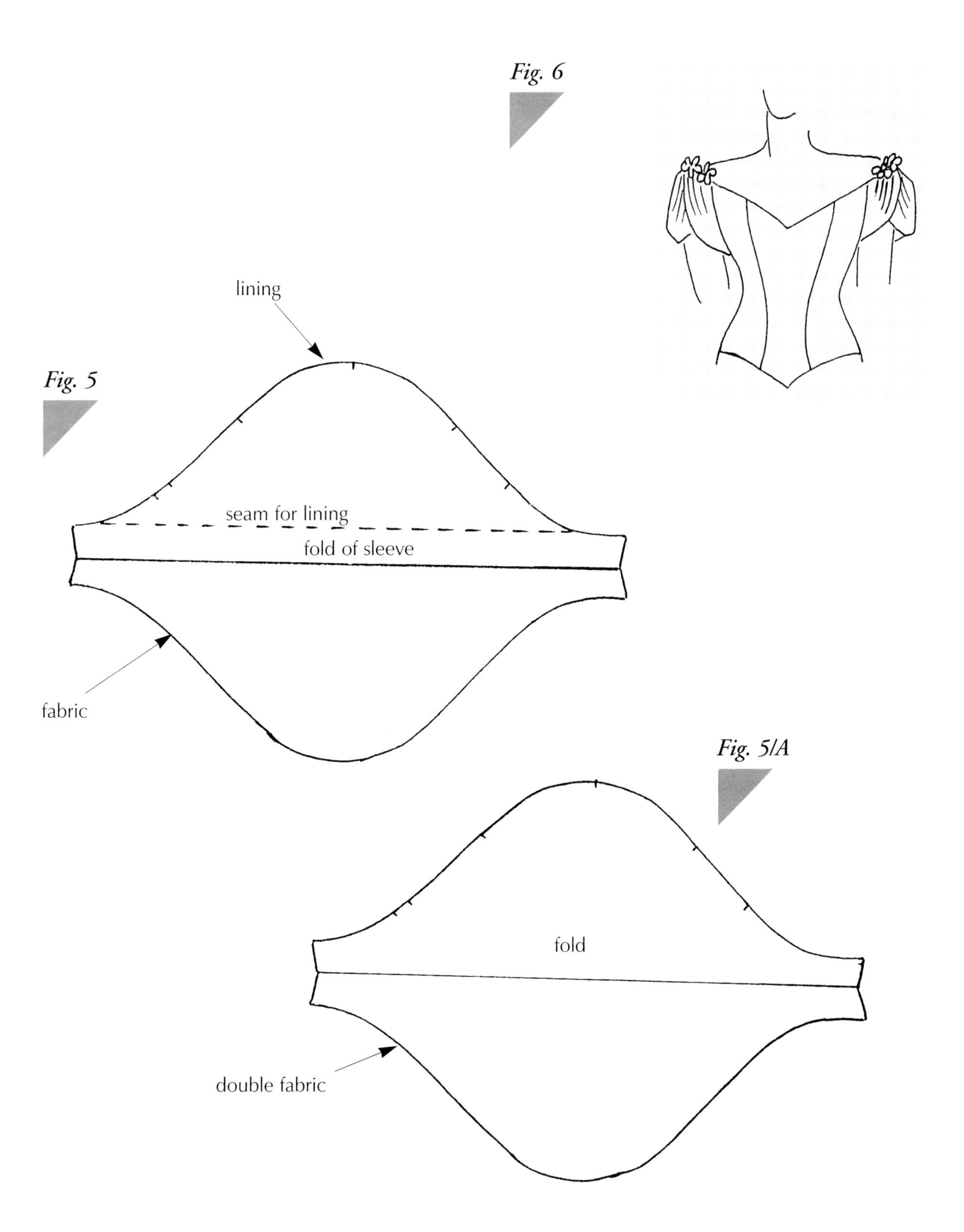

Fig. 5

Fig. 5/A

Preparation for pattern on short sleeve

a. Trace off the basic block and mark in style lines. *Measure the required length of the under arm seams and draw a line across the upperarm at right angles.

b. Centre the curve lines of the cross-over, making it equal for both front and back panels.

c. Measure the depth of the armholes on the *back and front bodice.* This will determine the measurements of the armholes on the sleeves. *Draw a line across the top of the crown between the corresponding measurements.

d. Mark in grain lines, notches and label panels, before seperating the two pattern pieces. Now trace off each piece and cut out.

e. The *sleeve lining* is made to the foundation pattern and then retraced for the preparation of the top layer.

f. For the *pleating,* slash through each panel between notches to nothing at hem edge. Spread out evenly. This method makes the hem edge curve outwards.

Make-up

g. Base the top layer with an underlining (netting) on each of your panels to give it body. Once this has been prepared, stitch the top layer and lining along the seam line at the curved hem edges, encasing the seams.

h. Then pin and pleat your top layer onto each panel of the under layer at crown, and stitch down.

i. The lining and top panels are then stitched together along the underarm seams, boxing in the raw edges and made to lie flat between the two layers.

j. Cross over the two panel pieces at notches on crown of sleeve before inserting the completed shape into the armhole of the bodice.

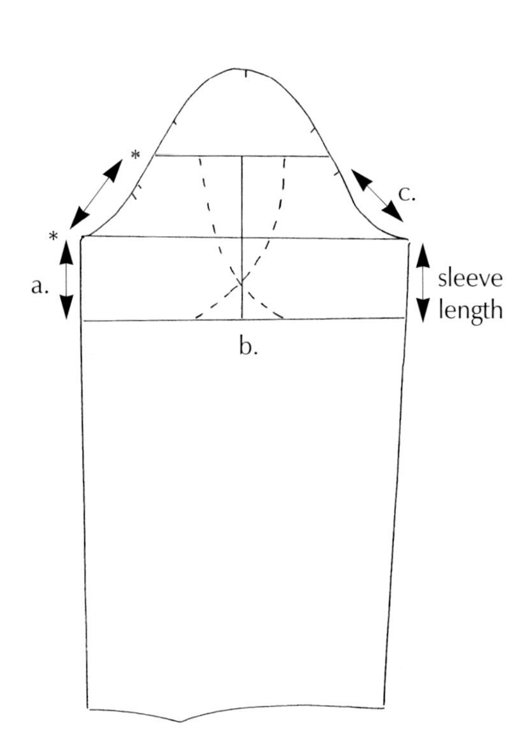

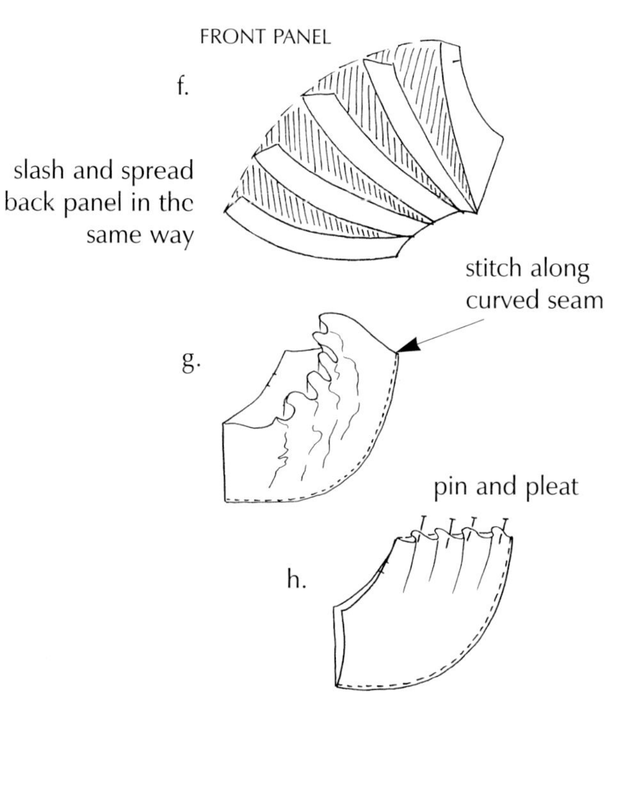

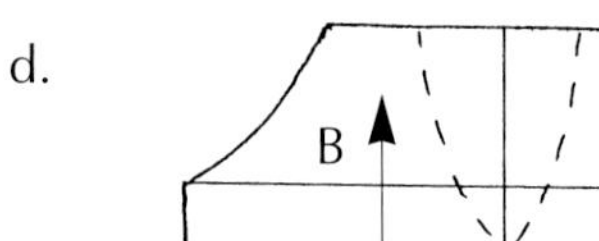

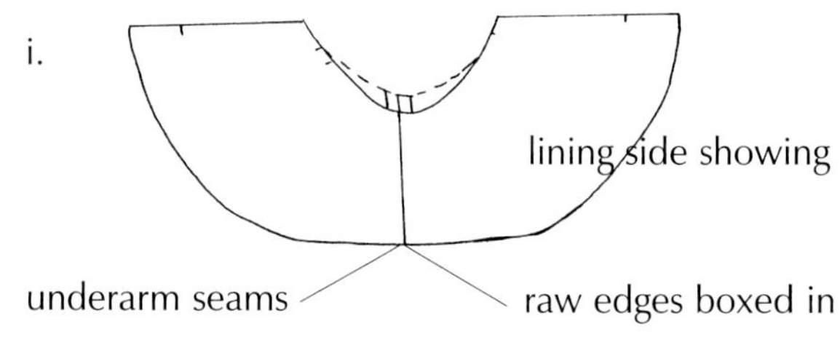

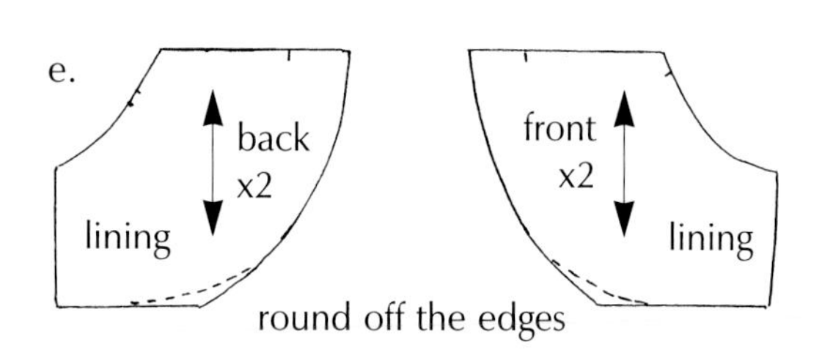

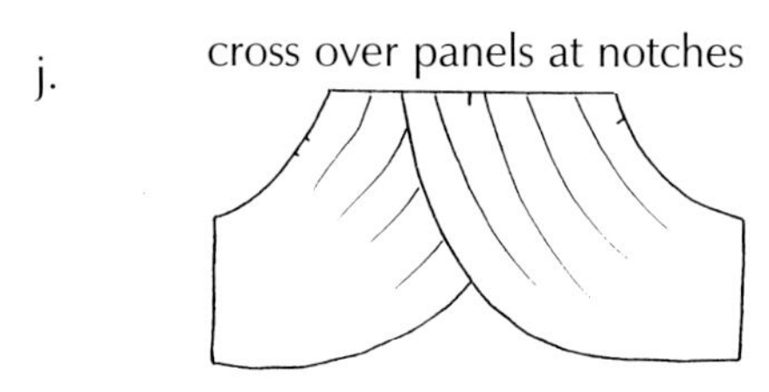

The cowl and drape on sleeves

The cowl shape (*Fig. 7*) lends itself very comfortably to soft flowing fabrics such as crêpe back satins, chiffons, soft velvets, some jaquards and other fluid fabrics. It's a shape that was often used in the 1920s and early 30s where the emphasis on drape and intricate bias-cut seamlines was paramount.

Pattern preparation

a. For the short length in *Fig. 7* trace off the block and measure down from the underarm seam to the length required.
b. Discard the unwanted area and reduce the hem edge of the required pattern, to fit tightly over the upper arm.
c. Mark downwards from the centre notch at the crown to the hem edge and cut through to nothing at the hem.
d. Open the pattern so that the side seams meet at the centre to a 90% angle. Cut out in double fabric, with the cowl line on the fold.
e. Measure the upperarm girth and cut through the slit opening, where the sleeve edge is to be and where the arm slides through.

Note

Stitching along this edge requires careful planning, as the split needs to be mitred in the corners and the raw edges boxed in before doing up the side seams. It would be advisable to make a mock-up of the sleeve at this stage before cutting into the main fabric. The side seams are also bagged out before bringing the two ends of the cowl opening together at the crown. At this point they overlap slightly and are secured before stitching it in the armhole of the bodice. The cowl, (which is on the fold of the fabric) falls open, allowing the upperarm and part of the shoulder to show through.

Fig. 7

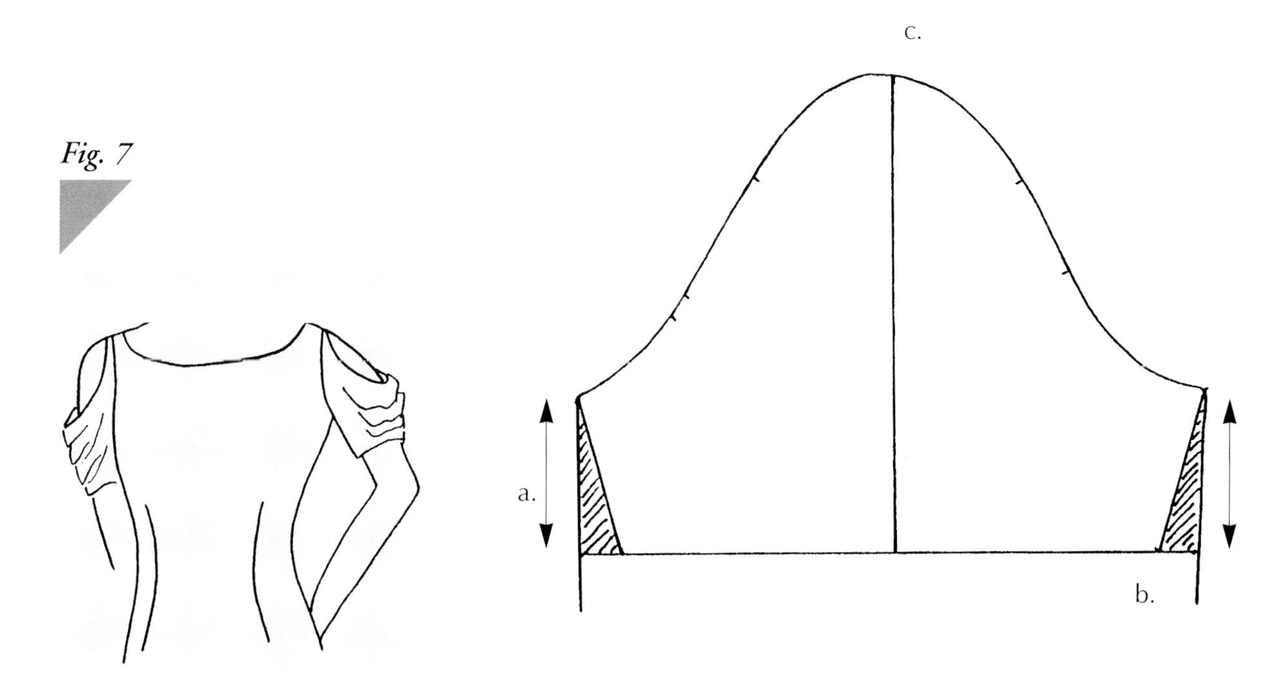

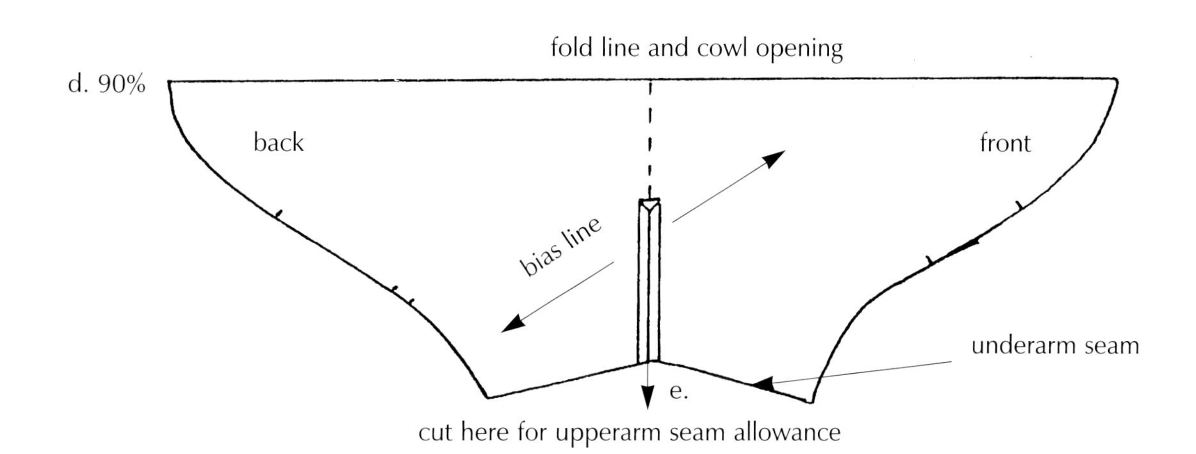

The full-length sleeve with draping: Fig. 8

This full-length sleeve fits tightly at the wrist. It has gathers on the crown and draping starts from back and front notches to armhole depth. Fabric qualities which are recommended for use are firm and yet have drape: dupions, crêpe de chines, satins and taffettas. The foundation block is used to create this shape but one could toile it on a person if preferred. The outcome will be different and not as accurate as a sleeve block.

Preparation for sleeve pattern

a. Trace off the sleeve block and mark in notches for the position of the gathers, drawing in lines across the crown of the foundation pattern for the draping. Put wrist dart into elbow.

b. Allow approximately 2.5cm (1") between each line and 5cm (2") for each drape. Fold in these pleats on your paper pattern to work out its accuracy and mark in your seam allowance. Cut along the crown seam with the pleats still folded up, so that the edges take on the shaping of the pleats. At this stage the sleeve takes on the shape of an ice-cream cone.

c. Slash down the centre through draping towards the armhole line and outwards to underarm seams. Spread the pattern evenly to the amount of gathers and fulness required on the crown and across the upper arm.

Note
The lining is made to the foundation pattern so that your draping and gathers have a flat pattern to attach it to.

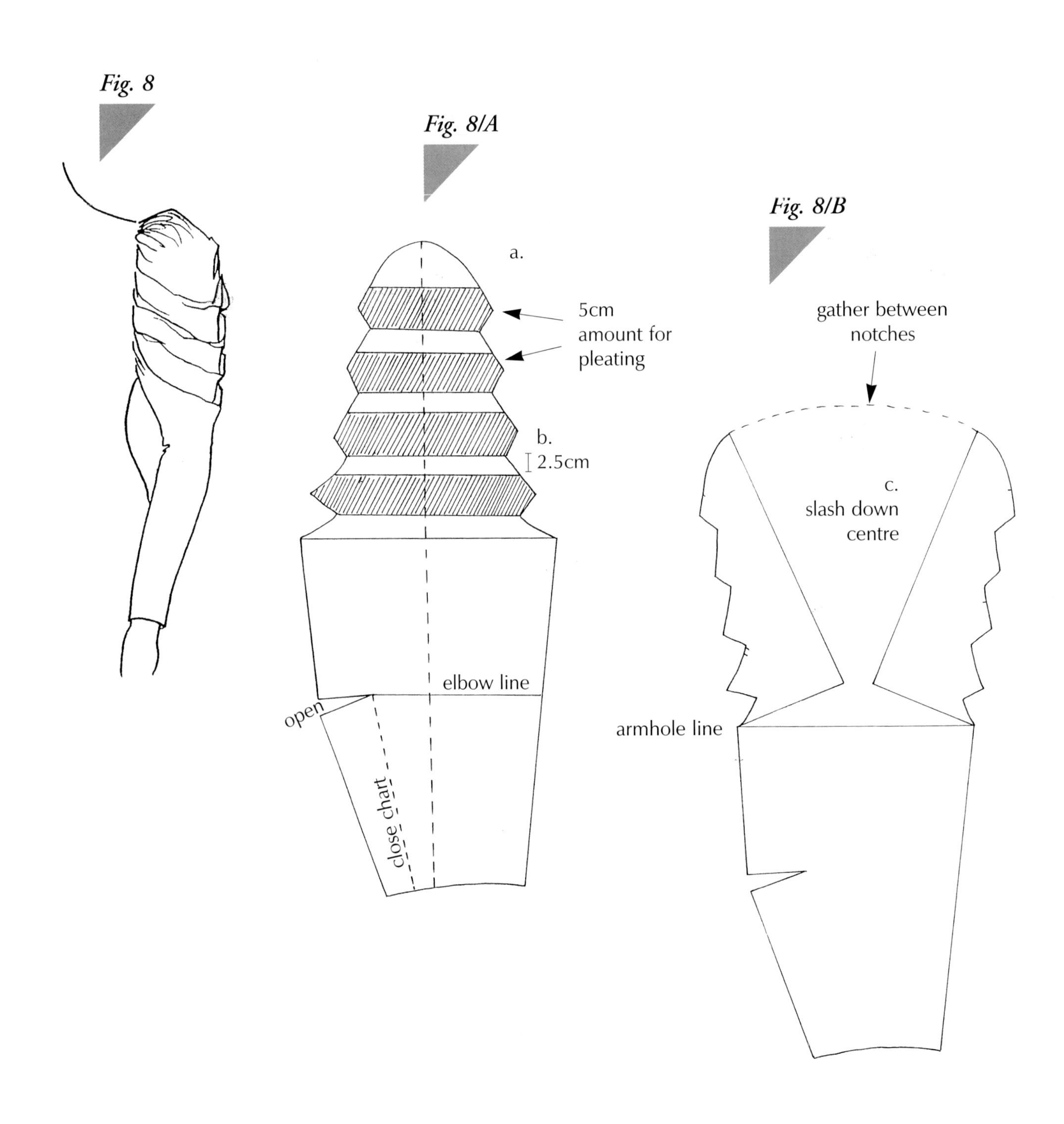

The tailored sleeve (fitted, and with a pointed shaping at the wrist)

The tailored sleeve is used more than any shape in fashion clothing and this particular shape, which points at the wrist, is constantly used in bridalwear. In *Fig. 9* it has a back opening and replaces the dart at the wrist. It is not essential to take the opening as far up as the dart point i.e.to the elbow line, and the wrist measurement is made to the actual size. In order to reduce any unwanted fulness, reshape the side seams from the elbow to approximately 1.5cm (⅝") at the wrist.

a. The opening is trimmed with covered buttons and loops, a method most brides prefer. If an opening is not required, make sure the wrist measurement is wide enough to ease the hand through.
b. The sleeve point comes down to about where the thumb joins the fingers. On very exaggerated sleeve shapes it sometimes extends to beyond the forefinger.
c. A sleeve heading or small shoulder pad enhances the shape of the garment and fit, so ensure you have enough tolerance on the crown.

The use of an *elbow dart* is optional but better suited to this style, as it gives the shape a nicer fit. (*Fig. 9/A*).

a. Close the dart on the foundation pattern at the wrist and open it at the elbow line.
b. Make sure the dart folds in along the side seam of the back before stitching the dart seams together.
c. The point at the wrist may have to be realigned and adjustments made to the centre line of the sleeve.

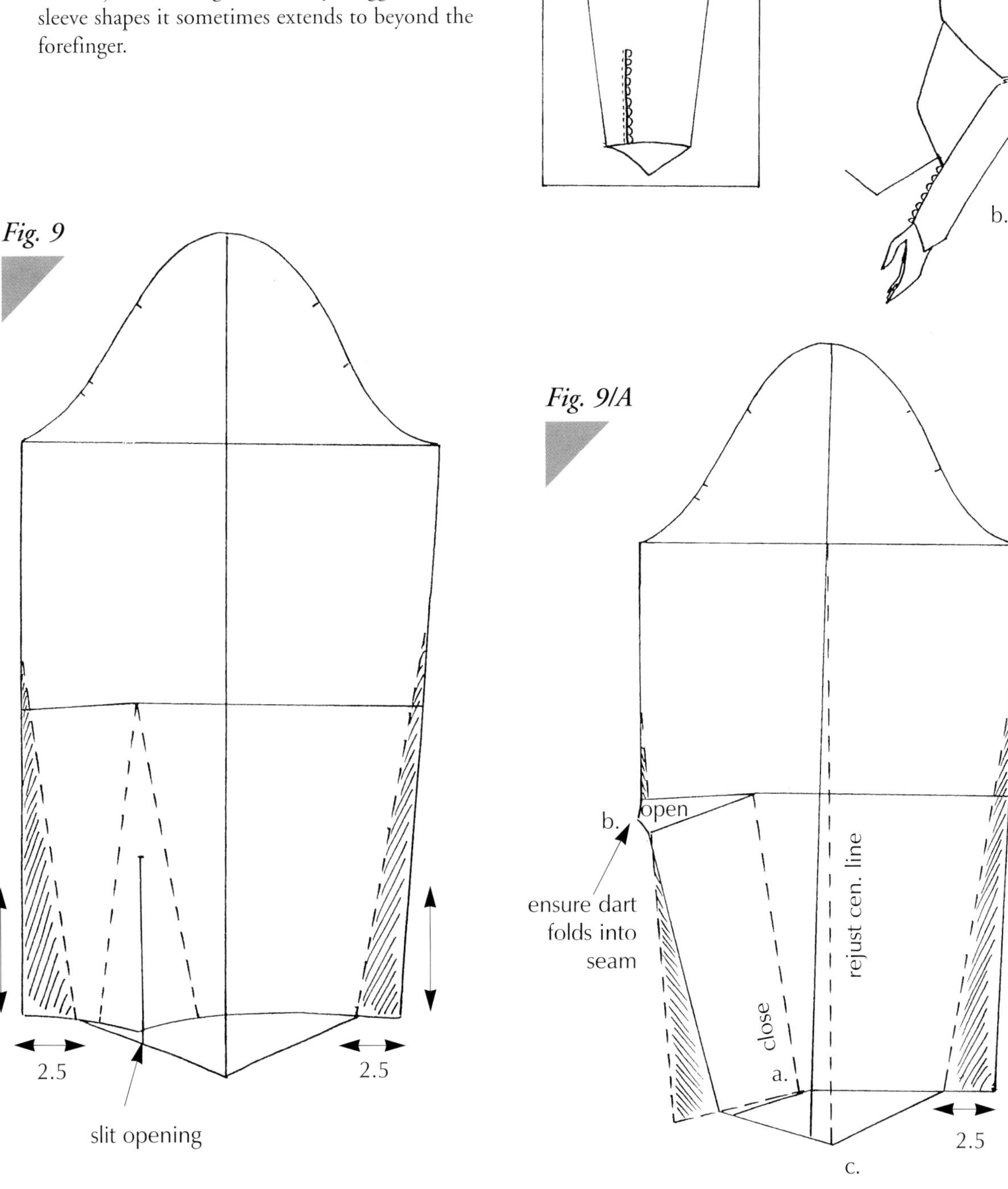

The two piece sleeve

The riding habit, worn from the late 1800s onwards, has caught the imagination of many brides. The jacket for the two-piece outfit was quite structured and the shape of the sleeve changed according to the fashion of the day. Today, brides are increasingly wearing period-styled outfits and so I've included this sleeve shape in the text.

Fig. 10: The proportions of this two-piece sleeve fit rather well. However, for some brides, the choice is to stick to the conventional two-piece suit, and not the riding habit. For this, one can buy a suitable pattern. Adaptation for the sleeve can be achieved if it's a one-piece pattern.

Preparation for the pattern

a. Trace off the foundation pattern. Close the dart at the wrist and open up at the elbow.
b. Fold the sleeve in half and allow the underarm seams to meet at the centre and tape them together.
c. Make sure the underarm seams are positioned on the centre line of the sleeve, so that there is equal distance on either side from fold to seam line.
d. Mark in new seam lines for the underside of your two piece sleeve, by measuring down from the back and front notches at the armhole to 1cm (3/8") from fold at wrist.
e. Cut throught the new lines and straighten out the folds of the larger piece. Make dart equal on either side of seamline. The dart is also now smaller, about 1cm (3/8"). This amount of ease is fine.
f. Match up the seam lengths on the corresponding patterns. Cut along the elbow line from CB on the *smaller piece,* to the CF seam and overlap the line by 1cm (3/8").
g. To increase the amount of ease on these patterns, if required, open the area at the elbow on the larger pattern and add a further 0.5cm (1/4").
h. Then match the seams on the smaller pattern.

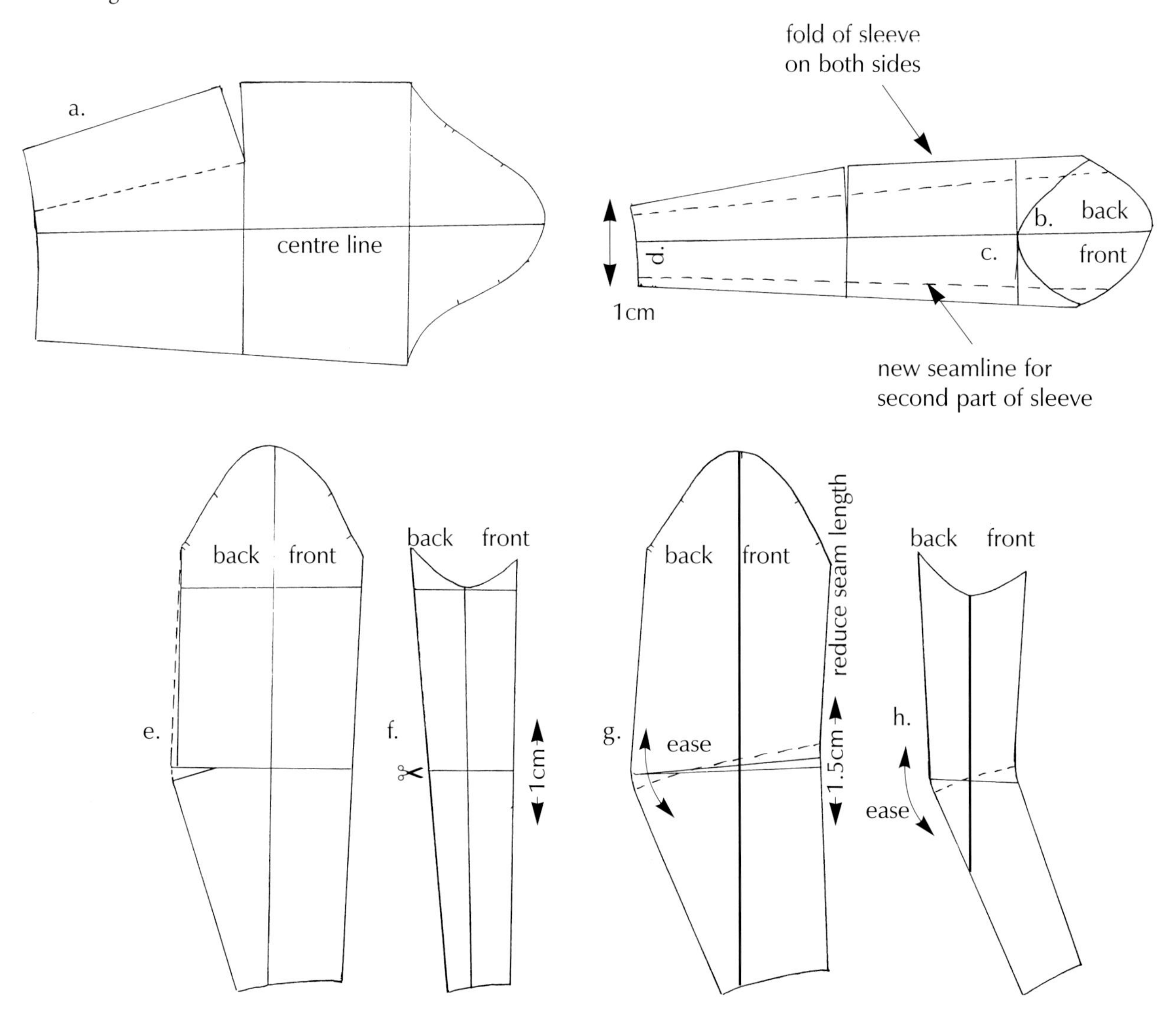

The leg o'mutton sleeve

The riding habit as mentioned before, included the leg o'mutton sleeve, particularly in the late nineteenth century. Its fulness at the crown can be very flattering on a bridal gown when the bodice is worn long and quite fitted over the torso. The sleeve pattern is slashed from just above the elbow. However, there are no hard and fast rules about the shape and the amount of fulness you want to use. ***Fig. 11*** illustrates a full crown and which fits tightly from the elbow down to wrist. Here, the opening becomes a feature at the centre front of the sleeve.

a. Mark round the foundation block and draw in slash lines from top of crown to elbow line.
b. Reduce the wrist measurement to actual size and ignore the dart. The slit opening becomes a feature at the centre front and is fastened with loops and covered buttons.
c. Slash down centre of sleeve crown and outwards on elbow line towards the underarm seams.
d. Then slash down remaining back and front crown sections and spread out evenly. The fuller the gathers, the deeper the crown becomes.
e. Soften the sharp curve at the elbow line on the underarm seam.

Note

The lining is made to the foundation pattern with new wrist measurements. The top layers are attached to the lining after it has been prepared. Cut the new sleeve pattern for a top layer and an under layer (of netting) and stitch them together. *Use two rows of tacking stitches to draw up your gathers on the crown. The button loops are sandwiched between the fabric and the lining. (See 'Method' under Part 6).

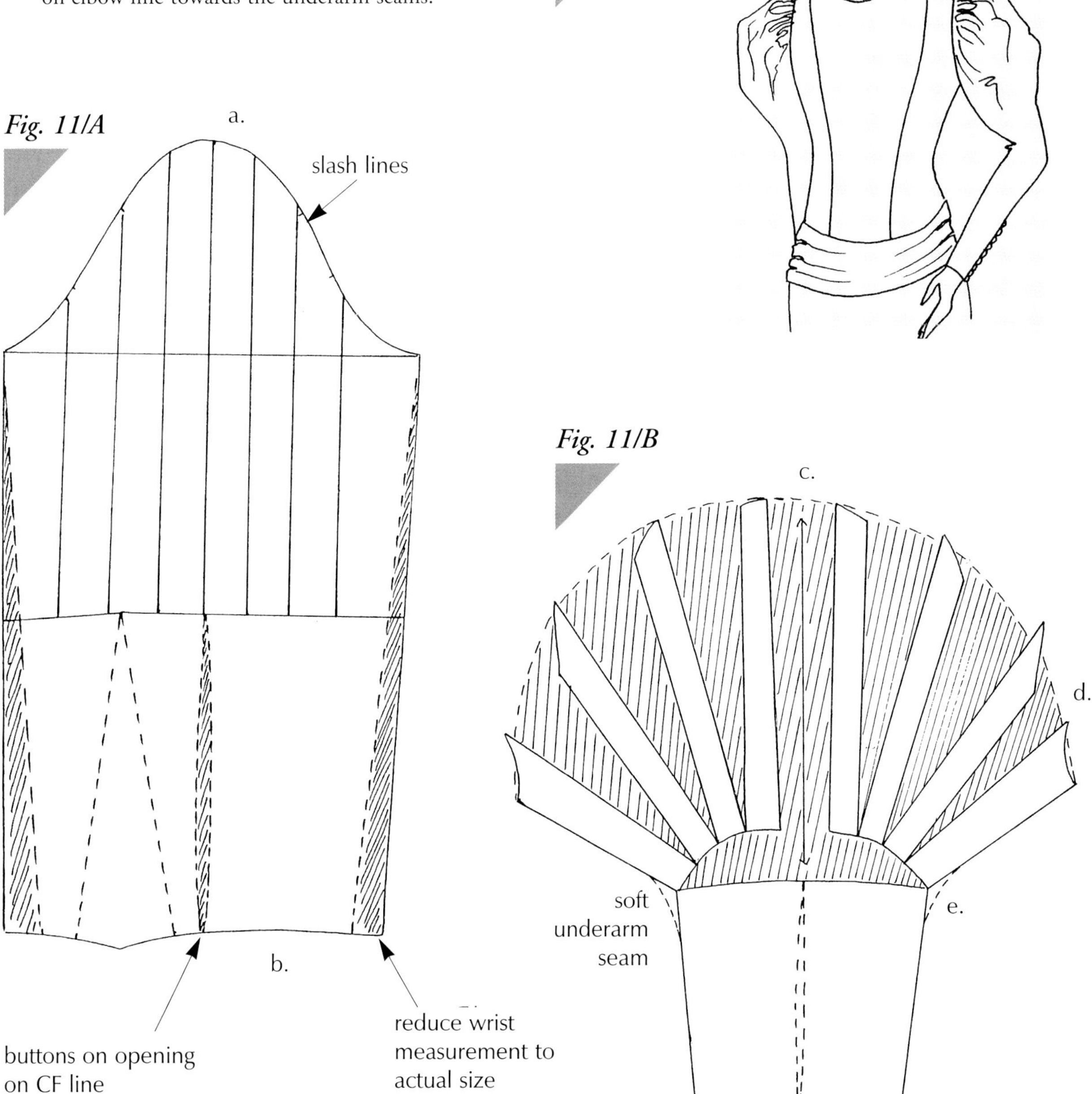

Fig. 11

Fig. 11/A

Fig. 11/B

Sleeve cuffs

Most bridalwear styles in recent times are made without cuffs, unlike in the 70s when sleeve styles bellowed out from fitted cuff widths. In this section an example of a plain and a stylized cuff is demonstrated.

Fig. 12

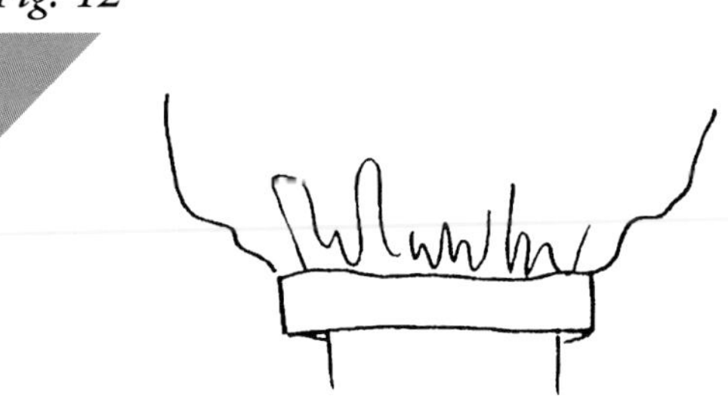

For ***Fig. 12*** the cuff width is determined by the shape of the sleeve. A short puff sleeve as illustrated, and used frequently on bridesmaids' dresses, requires a cuff width of approximately 4cm (1½"). Reduce the actual sleeve length by this measurement and add seam allowance. The length of the cuff is taken from the upper arm measurement with some ease of movement, approximately 2cm (¾").

Fig. 12/A

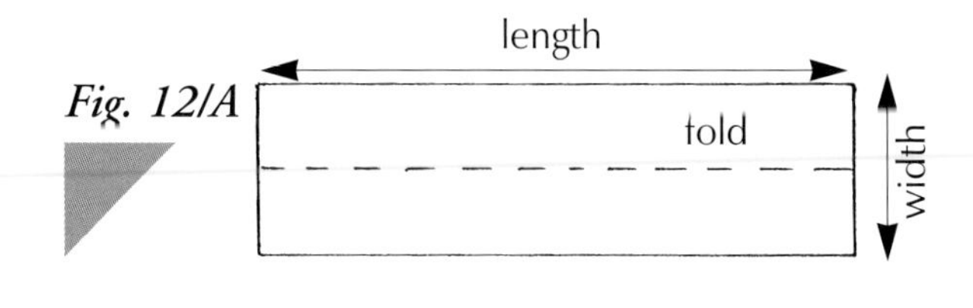

Fig. 13 shows an elaborate design for a full-length sleeve made in either silk organza or taffeta. The opening on the cuff is held together by covered buttons and loops.

a. Trace off the foundation block and reduce the width of sleeve at elbow by 1.5cm (½") and increase the wrist measurement by the same amount. This produces a bell-shaped style using the dart width for gathers. Reduce sleeve length by the cuff width and add seam allowance.
b. The *cuff* has an opening along the centre back seam. Take the width and length of the cuff measurement. This straight piece lies flat onto the wrist.

Fig. 13

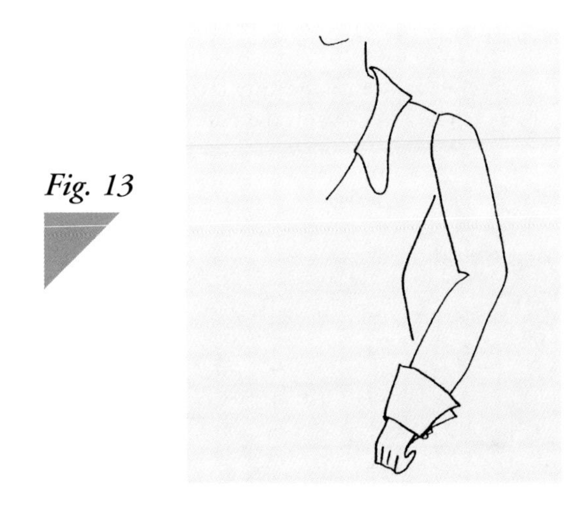

Fig. 13/A Bell shape

a.
reduce width of 1.5cm at elbow
increase width at wrist
reduce sleeve length

sleeve edge
fold line
cuff width
length
b.
c.
the extended length

c. Add to this the extended length which turns up over the sleeve and reshape the hem edge.
d. Notch where the shape starts to increase in width. Slash through lines that would determine the new shape and spread out evenly to the width required. The hem edge is reshaped to an exaggerated point when folded over the sleeve, as illustrated.
e. The finished cuff shape is lined with a fine muslin interfacing. When folded back onto and over the straight part, it hangs loose.
f. The sleeve opening is bound with a narrow bias binding. Use a small size for your covered buttons.

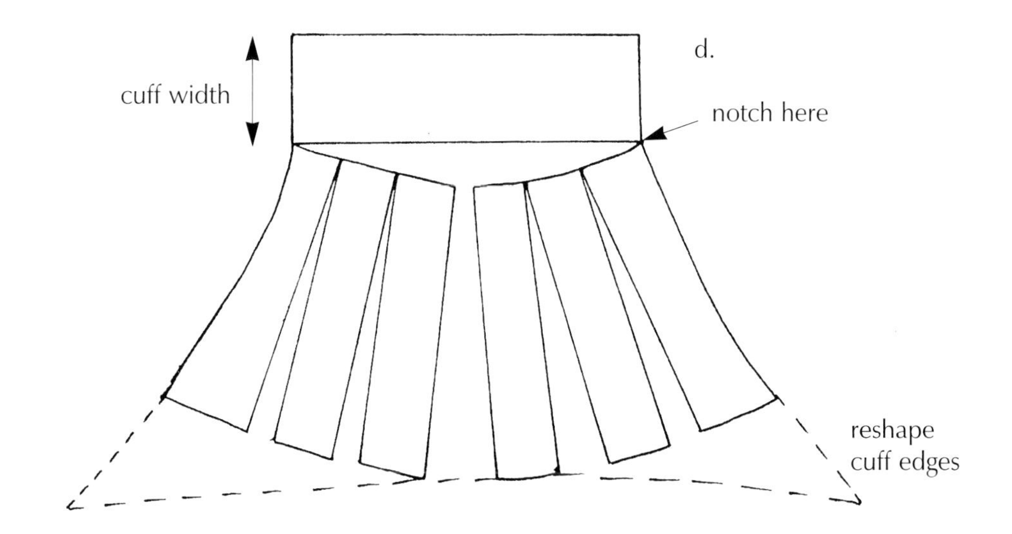

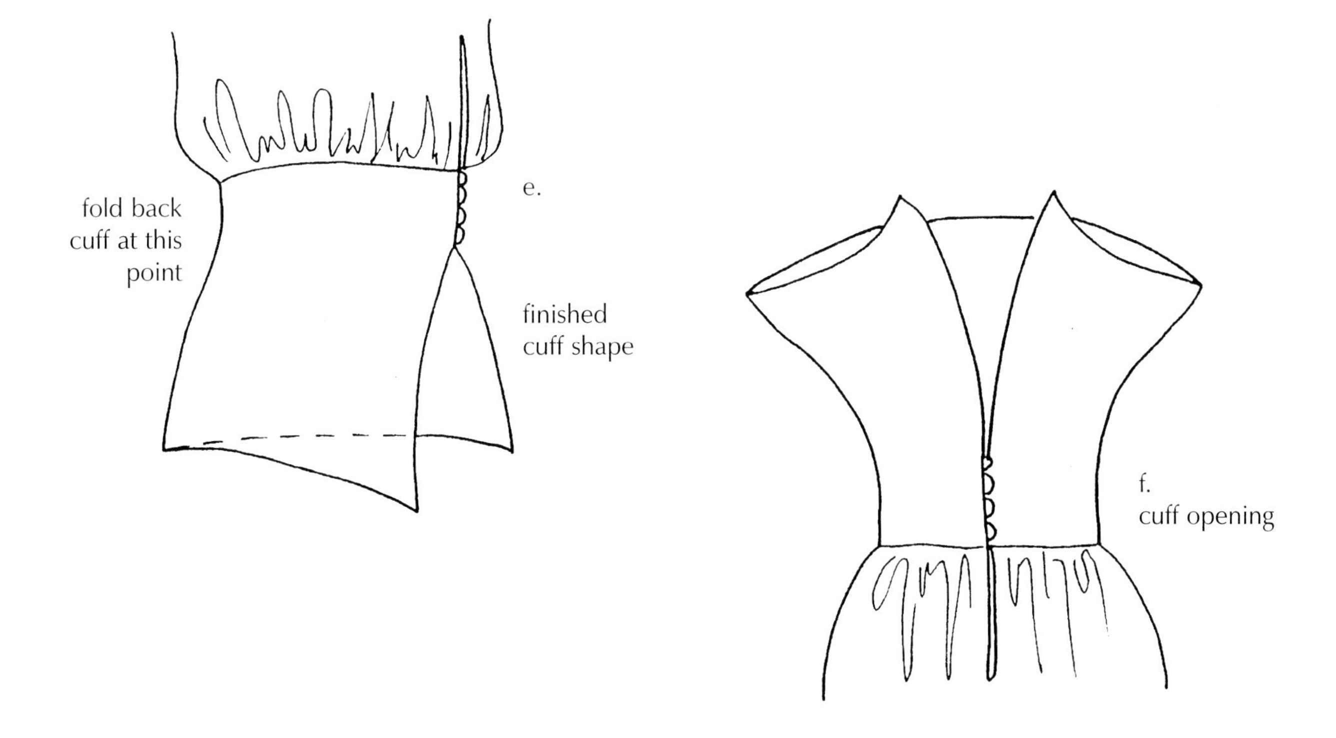

The boned bodice

PART 6

A brief history

It is difficult these days to imagine why anyone would want to imprison their bodies in the way women once did. But fashion and image has, and always will be, an important feature in our lives. The construction of the *boned bodice* developed as early as the 15th century, when women wore an understructure, a stiffened bodice. Later, this bodice became encased in *wood and whalebone* that moulded the body into an unnatural shape and distorted the figure. By the 16th century this bodice was called a *corset,* derived from the French word '*cotte*' (a rib sticking garment).

The corset or *stay,* as it was sometimes called, took on all forms of restructuring over the centuries as new and more flexible materials developed. For example, a lighter whale bone replaced the iron and steel strips used in the 16th century.

The stay was made of two layers of heavy *linen* and *canvas* often stiffened with *glue* or a *paste,* and the whale bones were then inserted between seams and kept in place by long rows of stitching. These seams shaped the contours of the figure. There was no use of dart suppression. That came much later. The opening of these stays were usually fastened at the back with eyelets and ribbon.As the waist seam rose or fell below or above the waistline, according to the fashion of the day, so did necklines, sleeve shapes and hemlines. The *stomacher,* for example, a long central triangular piece of material, made fashionable by Elizabeth I, was worn when the bodice was elongated and dipped at the centre front to form a point. Often heavily embroidered, it became the central feature of the dress and would change to suit different bodices of the wearer. It was fastened either by means of bows or with eyelets.

Materials were very expensive too. Silks, velvets, damasks and lace, some of which were threaded with fine silver and gold, were only used by the aristocracy. Over the years the Sumptuary Laws in England failed in the attempt to ban imported materials from France and they remained in exclusive use for the upper classes for some time still.

The making up of corsets was predominantly a male preserve. In 1675 French Tailors lost their monopoly and were forced to recognise women in a newly formed guild of lady *mantua* or dress makers *(couturières).* However, these women still had a while to go yet before they were able to make stays. Certain tailors called themselves the 'Tailor of the Whale Bone', because they claimed that the skill and strength needed to cut and make these heavy stays were beyond the capabilities of women.

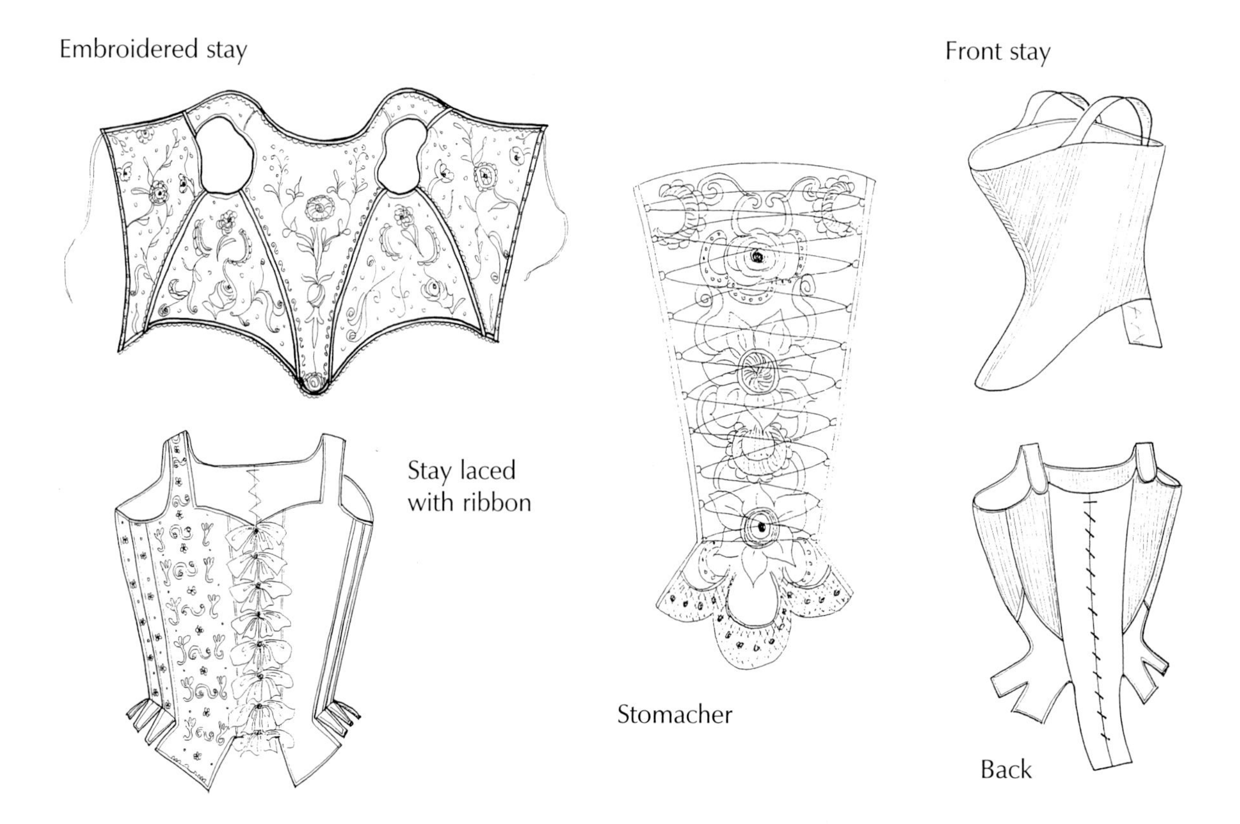

Contemporary bodices

There are parallels drawn from the past from which boned bodices are designed today. With new and innovative fabrics, couturiers have created a wealth of innovative ideas that have enriched the silhouette. Bustiers are now worn over garments as well as for foundation. Designers such as *Jean-Paul Gaultier* and *Versace* created a new look for women in the early eighties and revolutionised the corset. Contemporary fashion has given women the freedom to wear what they want and to feel less restricted than in the way that fashion dictated in the past.

The bodices designed on the following pages, give you a cross-section of styles that can be used on a variety of fabrics and trims for both bridalwear and eveningwear. A fabric width of 112cm (44") for a bodice, shouldn't take more than a metre unless it is bias cut.

In this chapter the application of pattern layout for each style is quite complicated, even though the principle of the dart manipulation is the same. Each of these six examples are here to develop your pattern cutting skills and to encourage the use of your own creative ideas. One can adapt from *bought patterns* providing the shape is that of the complete bodice, with waist darts, side seam or armhole darts. Panelled seams already in place will prove to be more difficult to adapt into other shapes.

A few key points to remember when developing your own designs

- These bodices have very little ease, unlike the normal amount used for flat pattern methods. The areas you would need to concentrate on are across the bust and across the back. Remove unwanted fulness, especially under the bust, and place it into the nearest panelled seam, as seen in Part Two under 'Darts'. Measurements are taken quite tightly, and ensure that the *high hip measurement* is correct before, and when reshaping your pattern.

- For a perfect fit on those styles with bra shapes, model the toile over the *bra* you plan to wear with the garment, *or stretch body.* However, fitting these shapes on yourself can be difficult, so try and find someone who could do it for you. Tailors' dummies are essential for this type of design level.

- All pattern pieces must have *grain lines and notches* marked on them to ensure the correct pieces fit onto one another. Number each one of them as it makes all the difference when cutting the panels out on fabric.

- *Openings* of several types that would complement each design and fabric used are illustrated; the most difficult method is for hooks and eyes, as seen under that section.

- All bodices require *three or more layers:* the top layer, under or middle layer and the lining. *Boning* is essential for the structure and contours of the silhouette.

- The *bodice length* of each style depends on the shape of the figure naturally. Some styles look good finishing at the waist and others look better starting from the high hip position.

Pattern layout

Using embroidery on silk

Figs 1-2: The two embroidery designs are examples of the different methods one can use to create the same effect in embroidery panelling.

Fig. 1: For this style, an *allover machine embroidery* patterned width of about 135cm (53") is used, but these widths do vary. Pattern pieces are *laid out* across the width (matching up the design if necessary) of the fabric, and then cut out. Here, the fabric colours are restricted and manufacturers tend to do them in white, ivory, gold and other pale shades for the bridalwear market.

Fig. 2: For this style, an *embroidery design* is created to fit into the desired panel(s). Here you have the choice of developing your own design and chosen colours. It is a more expensive way of achieving the desired effect, and should be calculated into the cost of making the bodice, dress or jacket.

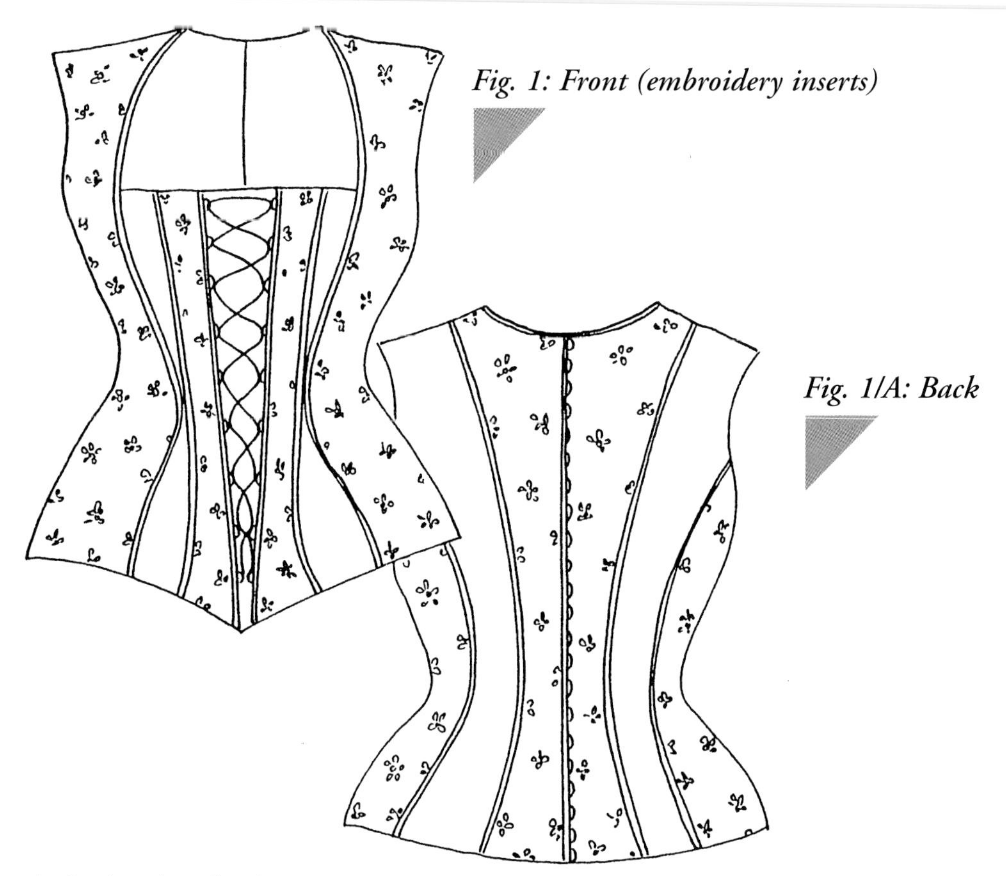

Fig. 1: Front (embroidery inserts)

Fig. 1/A: Back

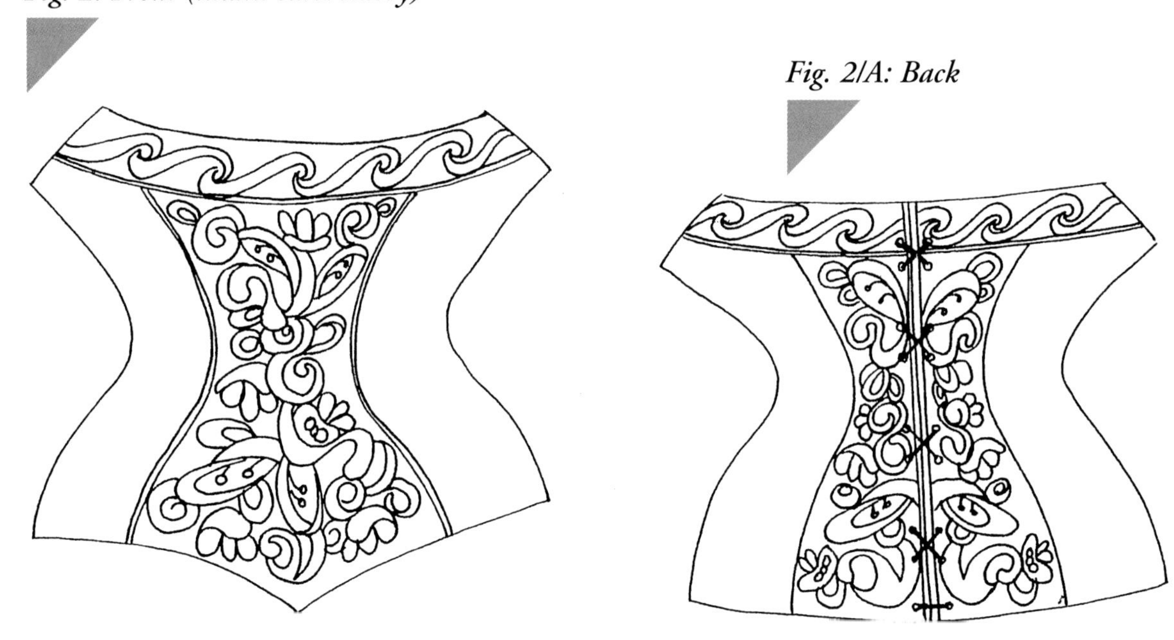

Fig. 2: Front (inlaid embroidery)

Fig. 2/A: Back

Embroidery allover inserts

Fig 3: Pattern layout

a. Trace off the front bodice and close the shoulder dart in the usual way.
b. Open up the dart into the waist seam.
c. Mark in style lines: the neckline, centre front panel and other notches, grain lines and loop positions.
d. Now close waist dart (***Fig. 3/A***) and cut through new neckline. This is made to fit quite closely to the base of the neck.
e. Mark in side panels, which extend to the high hip, and new curved waistline, with the CF point shaped at the navel. Label and put in notches and grainlines (***Fig. 3/B***).
f. Draw in centre back and middle panel style lines through shoulder and waist darts (***Fig. 3/C***).
g. Draw in new waist line for the back and curved side seams on side back shaping.
h. Label panels and put in grainlines and notches. (***Fig. 3/D***).
i. The centre back opening fastens with rouleau loops and covered buttons with 11mm (½") width mouldings.

Note
The centre front panel loops and the draw string threaded through the loops, are prepared and stitched onto the CF panel before it is stitched into the middle panels. To make a feature of the seams, bind it on the outside including the neckline.

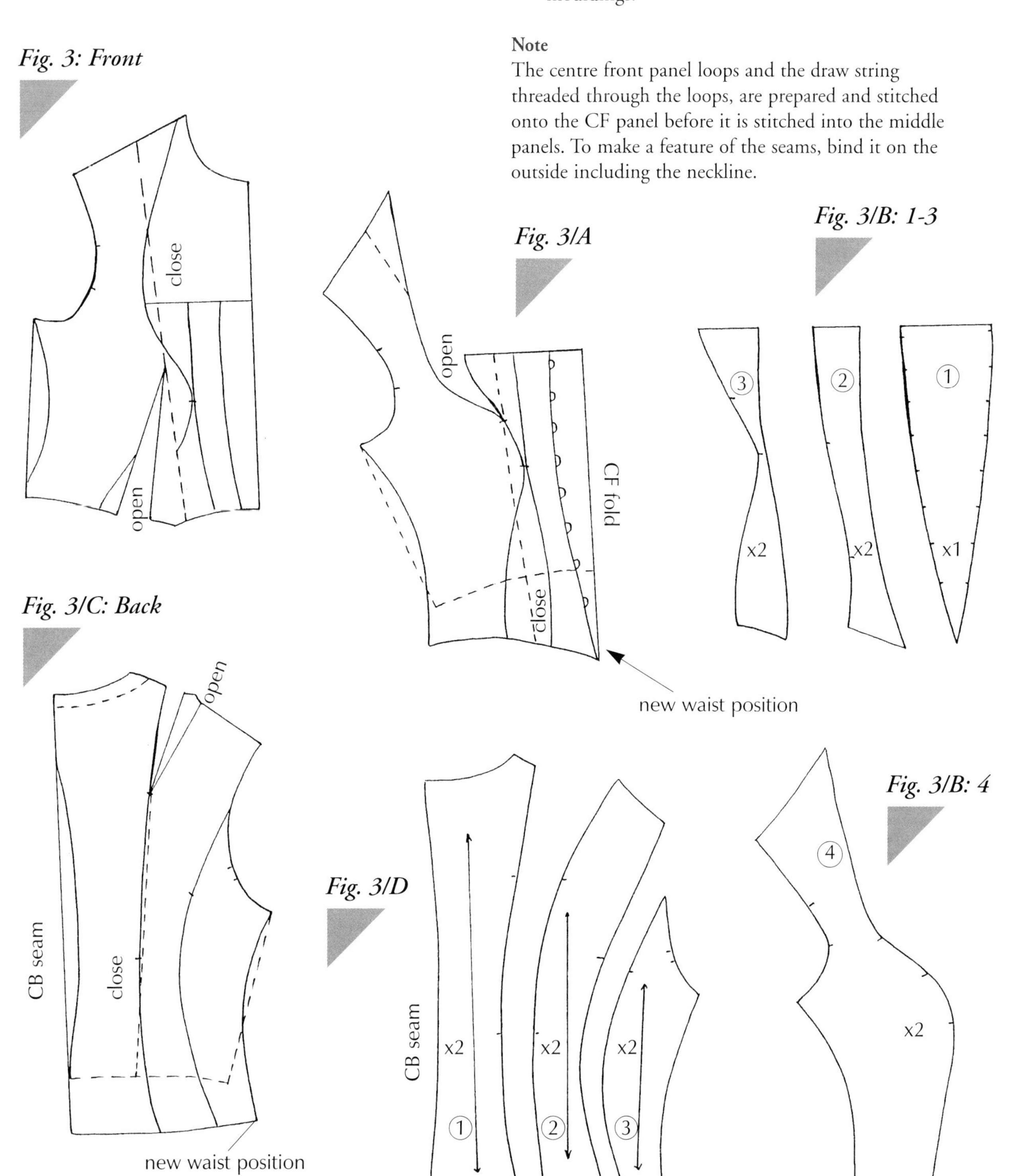

Inlaid embroidery panels

Fig. 4: Pattern layout

a. Close the shoulder dart and open up in the usual way.
b. Draw in style lines (*Fig. 4/A*). Panelled seams are marked through bust points, which leave the centre front panel nice and wide for your chosen embroidery design.
c. Neckline shape is drawn low over shoulder for both front and back (*Fig. 4/B*). Ensure that the width of the neck panel is wide enough to include your embroidery design. Mark in grainlines and notches.
d. Back panelled seams are drawn through the back dart on *Fig.4/C* as you have for front panels. Ignore shoulder darts. *The back opening is threaded with a draw string through metal eyelits. Bind the opening and insert a placket of approximately 2.5cm on the back of the left side facing you. *Fig.4/D*: Mark in the grain lines and notches.
e. Now work out your embroidery design to fit into your panels.

Note: Books of stencil designs are just one of a few sources you can use to feed the imagination. Once this is done, make a template of your design. *See under materials and decoration.*

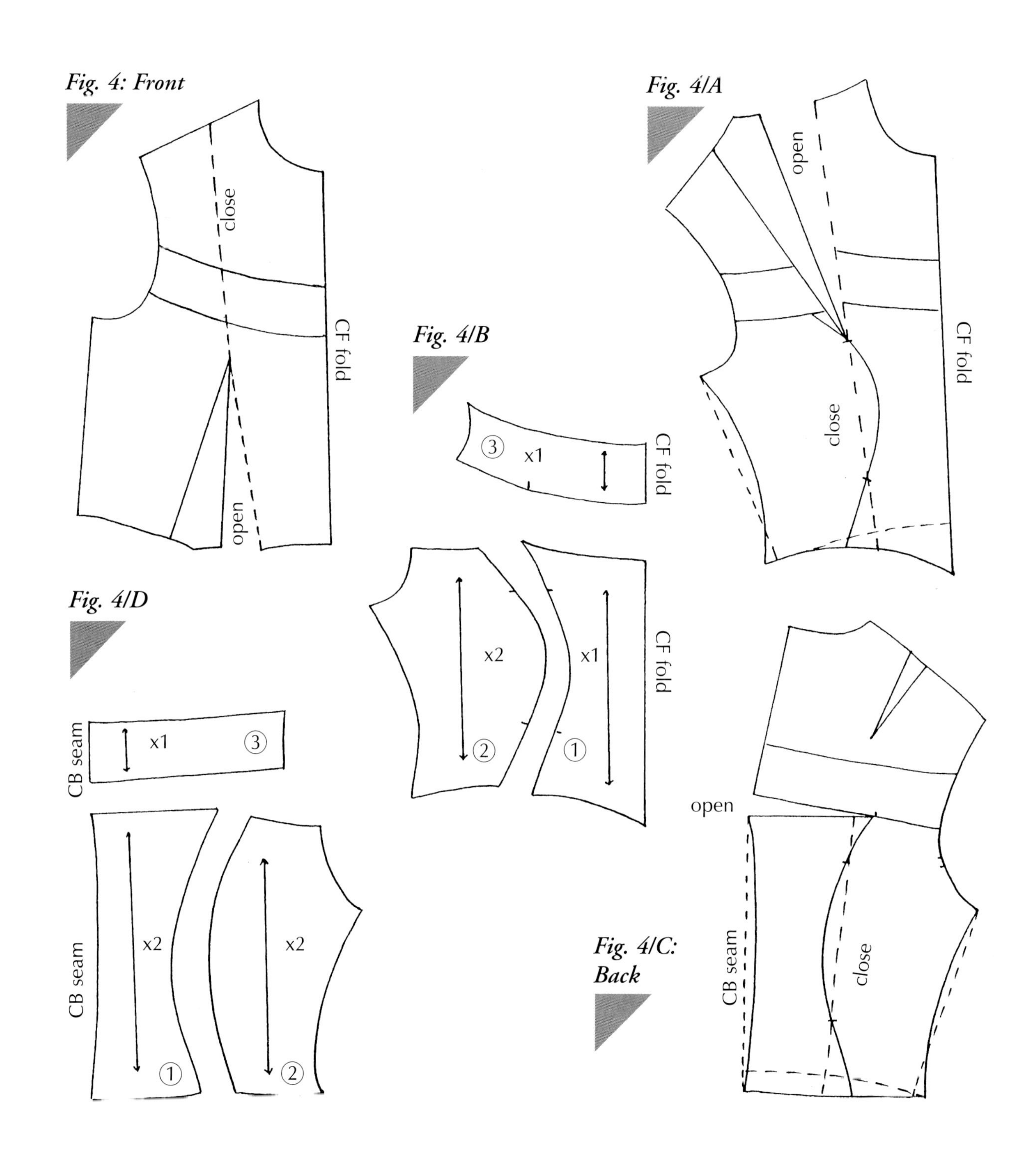

Duchess silk satin bodices

The two styles illustrated in this section are not only bridal but also sporty in appearance and would lend themselves to fabrics such as: leather, tactel, brocade, velvets and pvc-type fabrics.

Fig. 5: The panelled seams are trimmed with bias-cut binding of a contrasting fabric such as a shiny satin, which is then stitched on the right side of the garment. This makes a channel for rigilene boning to be threaded through. The opening at the back is held together with loops and buttons.

Fig. 6: The panels for both styles are cut on the bias. If one is using velvet, however, shading may be a problem for some qualities. A large chunky-toothed nylon zip lends itself to this back opening, or the use of an invisible zip, for a bridal creation.

Fig. 5: Front

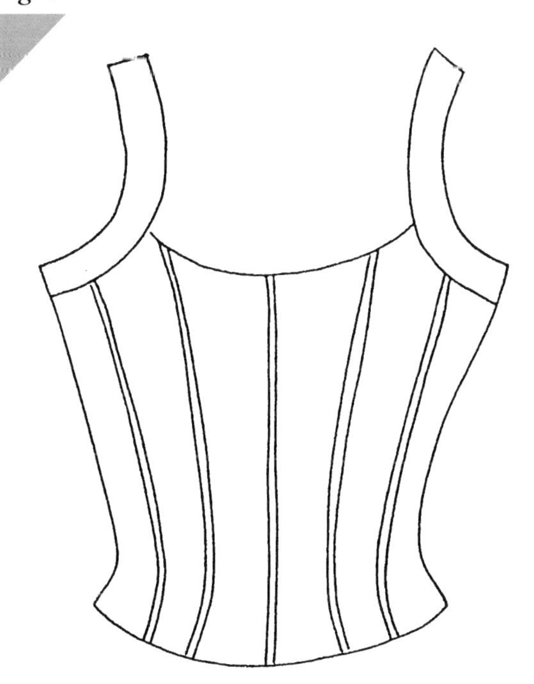

Fig. 5/A: Back

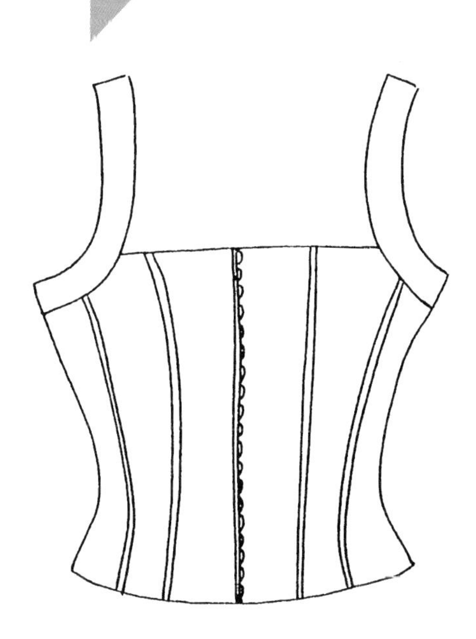

Fig. 6: Front

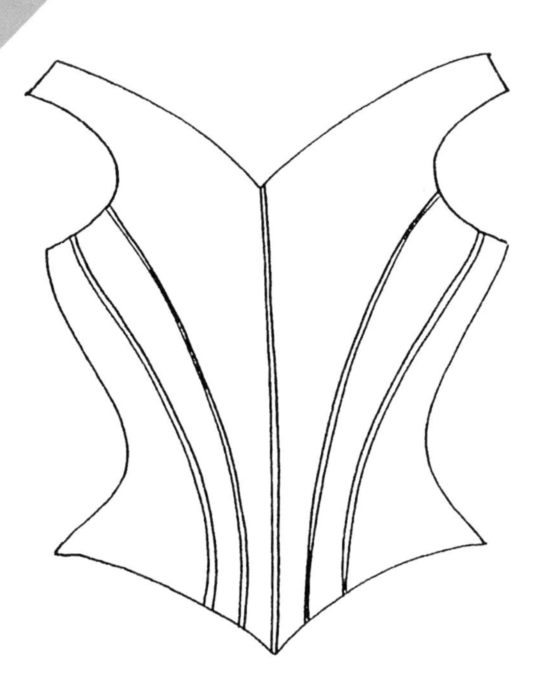

Fig. 6/A Back

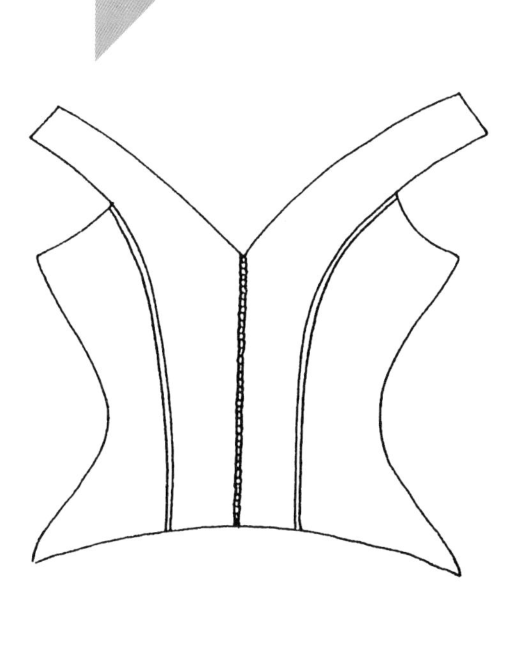

A bias trimmed bodice

Fig. 7: pattern layout (of *Fig.5*)

a. Close the shoulder dart and open up as before.
b. Narrow shoulder strap width of 4cm (1½") approximately, follows the curve of the armhole.
c. Mark in style lines: on ***Fig. 7/A*** the front neckline is lowered to about 12cm (4¾") above bust point (or to your taste). Panels are drafted to create a fairly tight fit across bust, so that the cleavage is on full display.
d. Make sure that the length of your darts at new waist seam are equal. For *Fig. 7/B* mark in the grainlines and notches.
e. Ignore shoulder dart at back on *Fig. 7/C*. Draw in style lines for back panels making sure that your neck shape corresponds to that of the front neck shape, which is *cut low*.
f. Join the shoulder seams and make the shoulder strap as one piece (*Fig. 7/D*) *For a snug fit over the shoulder, overlap shoulder seams by between 0.5cm to 1cm on the *inner* seam. Reshape underarm seams if too wide.
g. The shoulder strap is cut in fabric for top and under pieces with a stiffening sandwiched inbetween.
h. The back opening for this shape is fastened with hooks and eyes and the method for make-up is illustrated under the next section. *Fig.7/E*: Mark in the grainlines and notches.

Note

The length of this bodice is meant to be short. It stops at the waist and dips down at centre-front above the navel.

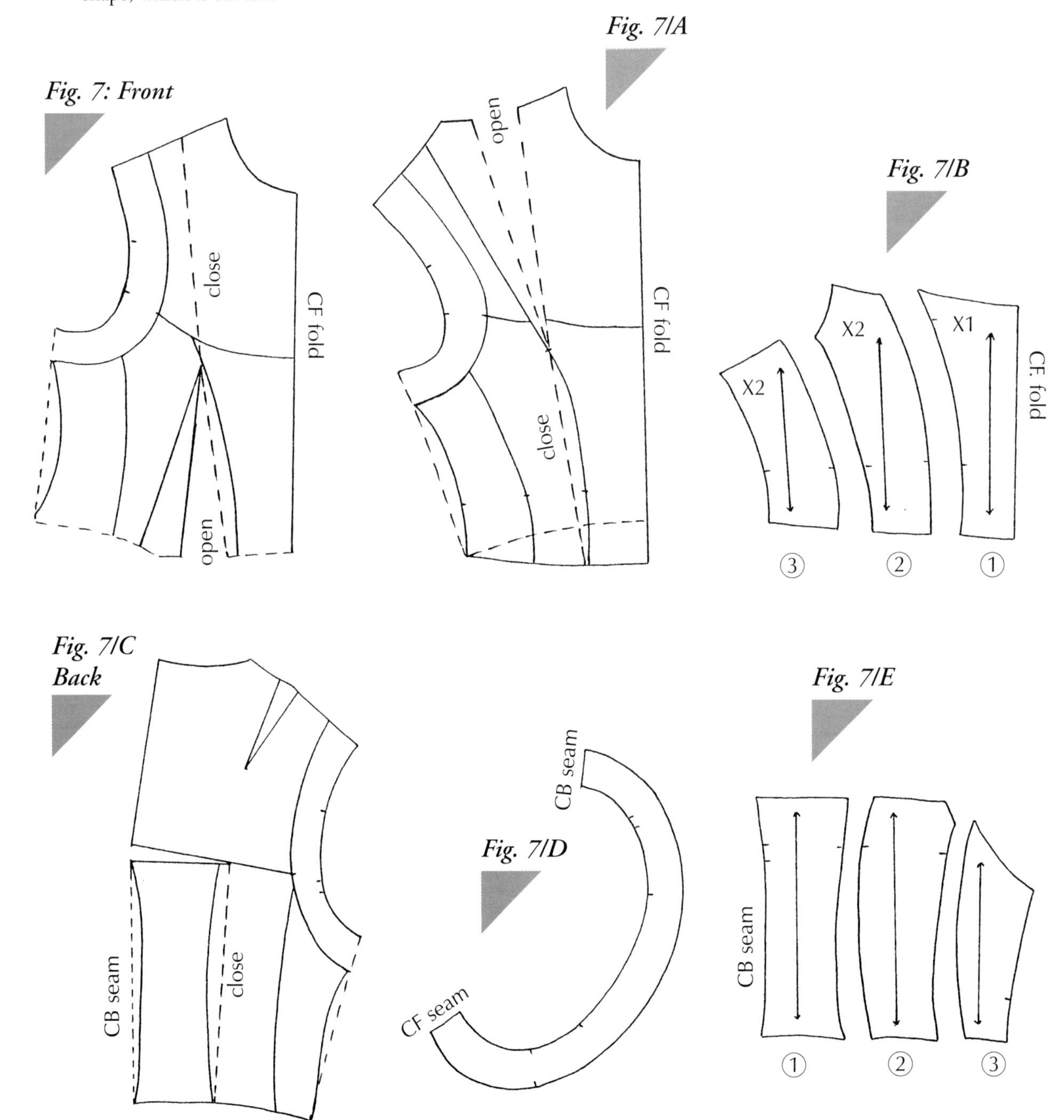

Off the shoulder strap

Fig. 8: Pattern layout (of *Fig.6*)

a. Close shoulder dart and place it at the waist. The CF on this style has a *seam* which is purely decorative.
b. Curve neck shape into armhole which is over the upperarm. *Draw in new shoulderline between 4cm-5cm (1½"-2") in width.
c. Now curve in the new armhole shape and measure the upperarm girth for length and allow for ease of movement.
d. *Fig. 8/B:* Mark in the dart panels from the armhole to bust point, and curve the line down to a point at the centre-front on new waist shape.
e. Extend the centre-front point to below the waist by about 10cm (4").
f. Draw in another panel between panels 1 and 3, following the curve line to the shoulder to create a cap sleeve and panel 2. *Fig. 8/C*: These panels enhance the overall shape adding a slimline look to the bodice. Add notches and grainlines.
g. *Fig. 8/D:* Mark in style lines for back panels*; cut the CB shape approximately 15cm (6") from nape of neck to zip opening. Apply the same method for the shoulder line as that of the front, allowing ease across the upperarm.
h. The waist shape at side seams fit onto the high hip measurement of the front on *Fig. 8/E.*
i. A placket of about 2.5cm (1") finished width is stitched onto the back zip opening.

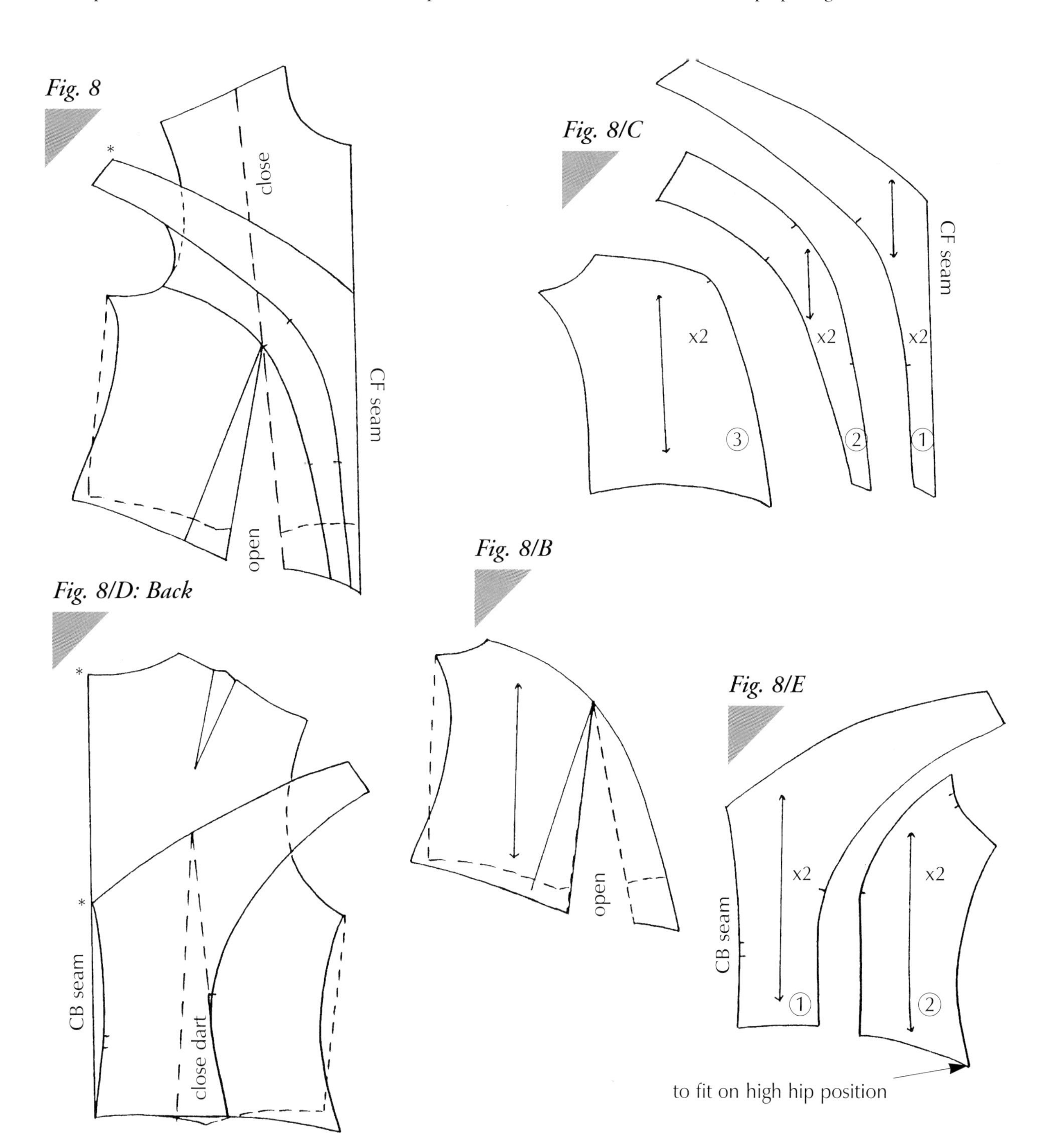

Lace on silk

The two styles below have bra cups and have to be manipulated and moulded onto a body or tailor's dummy to achieve the desired effect. Underwired casings can be bought to the size you require or rigilene boning can be used. A softer finish can be achieved by using just a firm interlining or inserting a wadded padding between fabrics.

The difference between these lace methods are similar to that of the embroidery designs. *Fig. 9* has a scalloped lace edging of a required width, where the scallops are fitted onto the bra and centre-front pattern pieces and matched to pair up, before it is stitched on. However on the allover lace (***Fig. 10***) the pattern pieces are cut out at random on the lace. The width varies according to the design and is an economical way to use lace, because any amount of panels can fit across the width.

Fig. 9: A tight fitted strapless bodice, which could be worn as part of a bridal ensemble or for eveningwear without lace trim. Both designs are made to fit the high hip measurements. ***Fig. 10***: An allover lace and contrasting plain silk fabric is used for this shape and here the front opening has small covered buttons with buttonholes. One could also use stud fastenings or anything of your choice.

Fig. 9: Front

Fig. 9/A: Back

Fig. 10: Front

Fig. 10/B: Back

A laced strapless bra shape

Fig. 11: Pattern layout

a. Close shoulder dart in the usual way and put dart into waist seam.
b. Draw in style lines for bra and fitted panels.
c. Cut through bra shape across bust point, and close waist dart and re-open the shoulder dart so that you can mark around the under bra panel, making dart seams equal, and reshape the waist seam. (*Fig. 11/A*). Mark in bias grainlines for the bra pieces and straight grainlines for the bodice panels. Label and notch these as before (*Fig. 11/B*).
d. Ignore shoulder dart for the back and mark in style lines. The shape across back could be straight as pattern illustration indicates or curved slightly, as shown on *Fig. 11/C.*
e. Close dart at waist and draw in new waist line. The back opening is made for punched eyelets.
f. Mark in grainlines, notches and label the panels.

Fig. 11/B: The deep cup on this shape can also be achieved by using a padded bra on your tailor's dummy. *This is particularly useful for the fully-busted figure.

1. Trace your front block on paper or calico and pin the shape onto the stand or mould it onto a figure.
2. Draw in your style lines. Suppression of the dart around the bra cup will vary according to the bust size. Several fittings are required before the desired shape can be achieved.

Note
See under next section for more comprehensive illustrations of the layout of the scalloped lace.

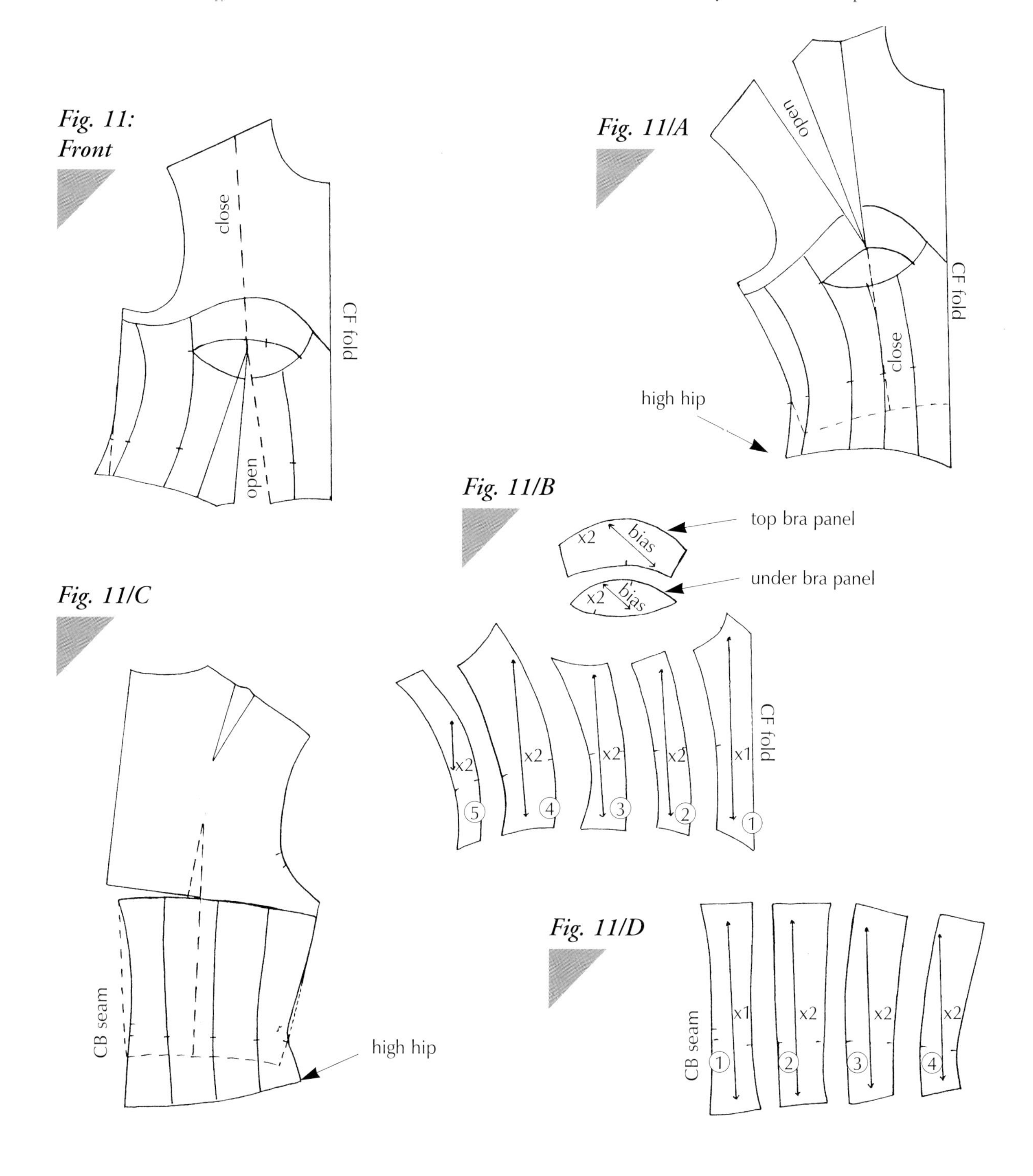

Allover panelled lace bodice

Fig. 12: Pattern layout

a. Close shoulder dart and open up in the usual way. Measure how far down the bra cup is from *shoulder strap to top bra panel.
b. Draw in style lines: the shoulder width is approximately 5cm (2") wide. The armholes on the front remain unchanged.
c. *Fig. 12/A*: Close waist dart and put it into the shoulder seam. Now mark in under bra panel. *Calculate how wide you want the CF placket to be, and deduct the measurement from the front fold.
d. If placket width is 3cm (1¼") finished, take half the amount off the CF bodice (1.5cm-⅝") before adding your seam allowance. Buttons and buttonholes are used on this placket opening, but are optional.
e. The bra is cut on the bias. See *Fig. 12/B* for details.
f. Close waist dart on back bodice and draw in back shoulder panels throught dart. The back armholes are altered slightly as shown in *Fig. 12/C.*
h. Mark in other panels and reshape the CB seam, removing unwanted fulness at the waist. Label and put in grainlines and notches as on *Fig. 12/D.*

Note

1. *Make-up*: Shoulder strap panels, and under bra pieces are made in plain silk, in contrast to the allover lace. Using an allover lace doesn't require matching up on these small areas.
2. Seams are trimmed with bias-cut silk binding and then stitched on the right side of the garment.
3. Rigilene boning is inserted between the seams.

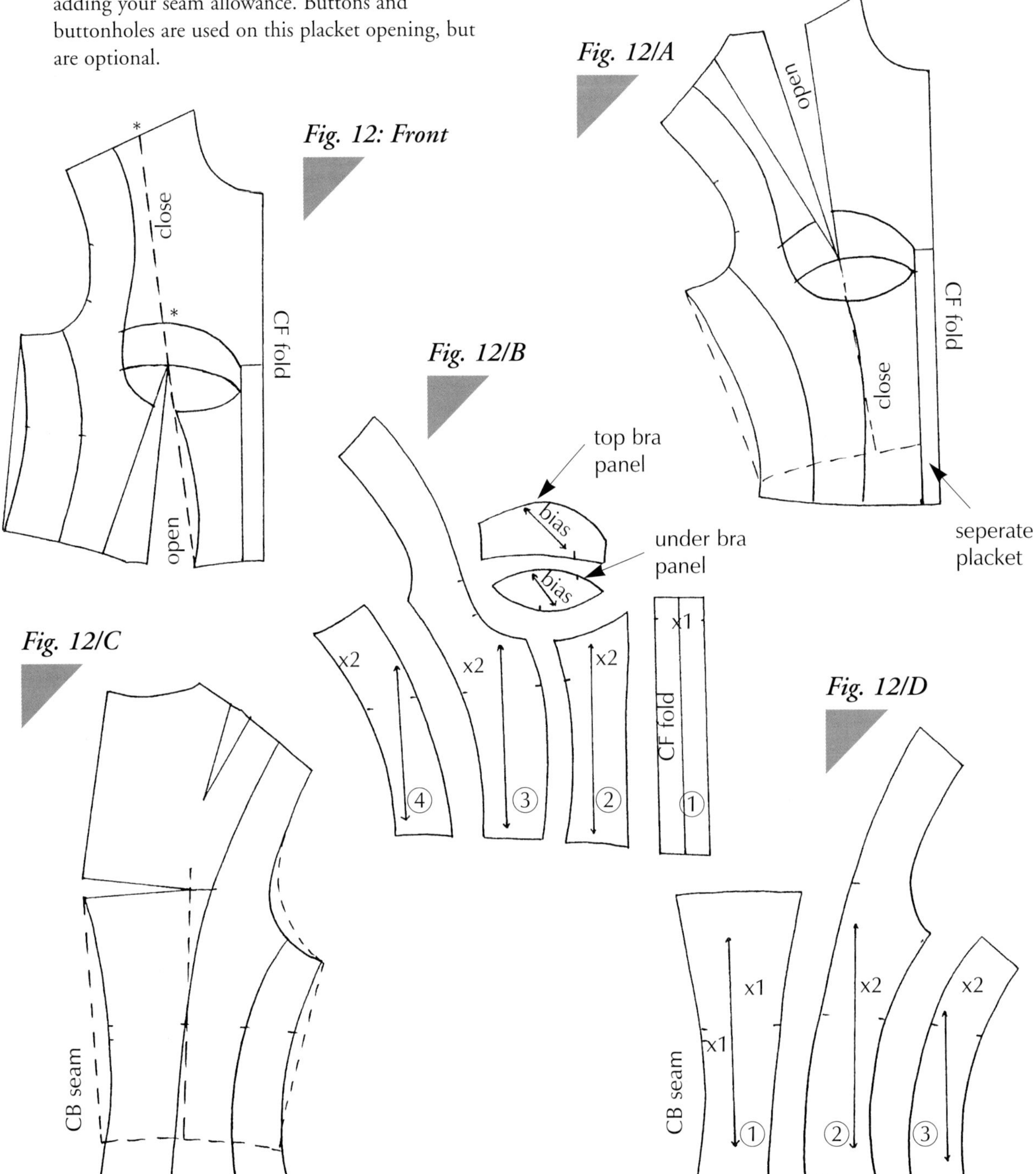

Components

Fig. 13: Decorative features for the bodice allow you to use your creativity as far as the bridal gown is concerned. However, if the bodice is worn as part of an ensemble, then the fabric and sometimes the seams may be sufficient in this respect, as seen above.

Fastenings for openings

Hooks and eyes

In the 18th century a boned bodice was fastened by means of metal eyelets and hooks or just metal hooks on which ribbon was fastened and pulled round, forming a lattice effect at the back. This operation took a very long time to do up since bodices were worn very tightly. Today, there are several ways in which one can fasten a back or front opening so they take a lot less time to do up. In this section, an example of the use of metal loops and hooks attached to tape, is demonstrated on a *left and right back bodice,* i.e. the centre-back panels are drafted with one side slightly wider than the other.

Fig. 14: Bodice panel (for left side facing you):

1. Open out the fold on the *loop* strip before it is stitched on the inner edge that is placed towards the seam edge of the placket. The narrower part of the strip shields the metal loops from rubbing against the skin.
2. Cut a placket width of 10cm - 4" (5cm-2") on the fold. Pin and tack the inner edge of the tape 1cm (3/8") away from the raw edge of the *opened placket* (on the right side of the fabric). Once in place, stitch both sides of the tape flat onto this side of the placket. The full width of the placket is also lined with an interfacing.
3. Fold the placket in half and neaten both top and bottom edges before attaching it to the CB panels. The tape is caught in the top and bottom seams. Now turn the placket onto the right side with raw seams inside. The *loops* on the tape are visible on this side.
4. Prepare the panels with a medium or heavyweight interfacing (woven or iron-on). This decision would depend on the fabric quality used. A woven interfacing would be better to use on velvets, for example. Then stitch the panels together and insert boning between the seams.
5. Cut out the lining and stitch these together. Open up the seams and iron flat. They are stitched 1.5cm (5/8") away from the edges of both front and back bodices of the top and under layers. Place the seams together for both layers with *right sides facing.*
6. Once the panels are prepared, bag out the lining and the top layers with the placket inserted between.

Note: This side of the bodice is made to the foundation pattern. However, when the right side of the back bodice is stitched together, make sure the hooks on the tape are lined up with the loops on the left side. See linings and interfacings in this text for more detail.

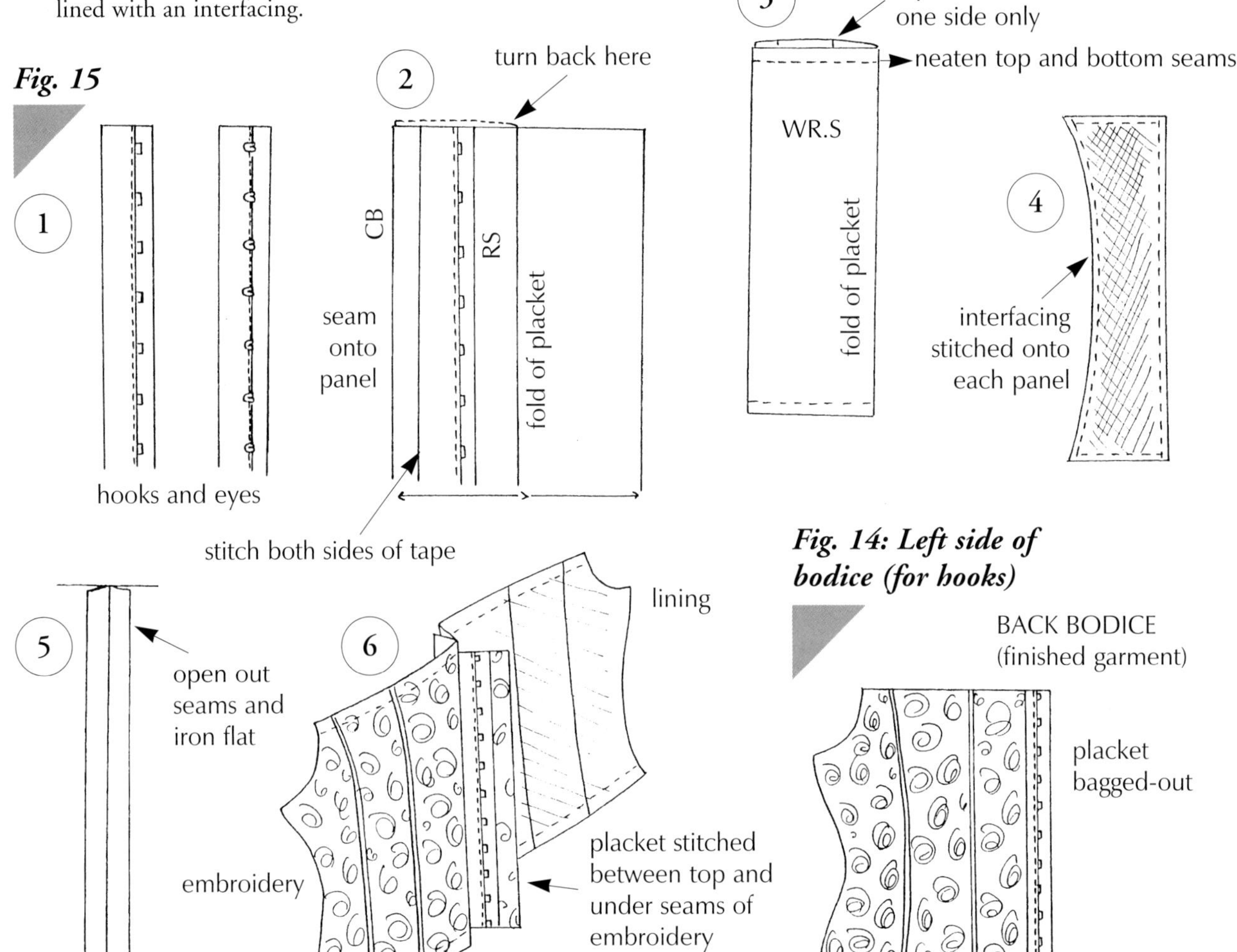

Fig. 15 Bodice panel - right side facing:

1. The CB panel on this side (the right side facing) is increased by 4cm (1½") from the CB fold line to the raw edge. This allows the tape to be stitched onto the grown-on placket. At this stage the top layer panels are backed with interfacing.
2. Position the *hook* side of the tape onto the grown-on placket of the CB panel, 1cm (⅜") away from the raw edge and stitch flat both sides of the tape. *Do ensure that the hooks are lined up with the loops on the placket side.*
3. Attach lining to raw edge of placket and fold the grown-on placket width onto the underside. Neaten the top and bottom edge of the placket 1cm (⅜") from the raw edges with the tape caught inside these seams. See illustration.
4. The seams of the bodice are stitched together on the seamlines and opened out and ironed to lie flat. Stitch these seams down to form a channel and thread boning through them. Bar tack the ends to secure the boning just above where the seam line is.
5. Prepare the lining panels and bag-out the grown-on facing seam with the lining and top egde of bodice.

Note: The front bodice has been prepared in the same way as that of the back top and under bodice layers The lining of the CB panel is reduced by the amount increased onto the grown-on placket (4cm-1½"), and add seam allowance.

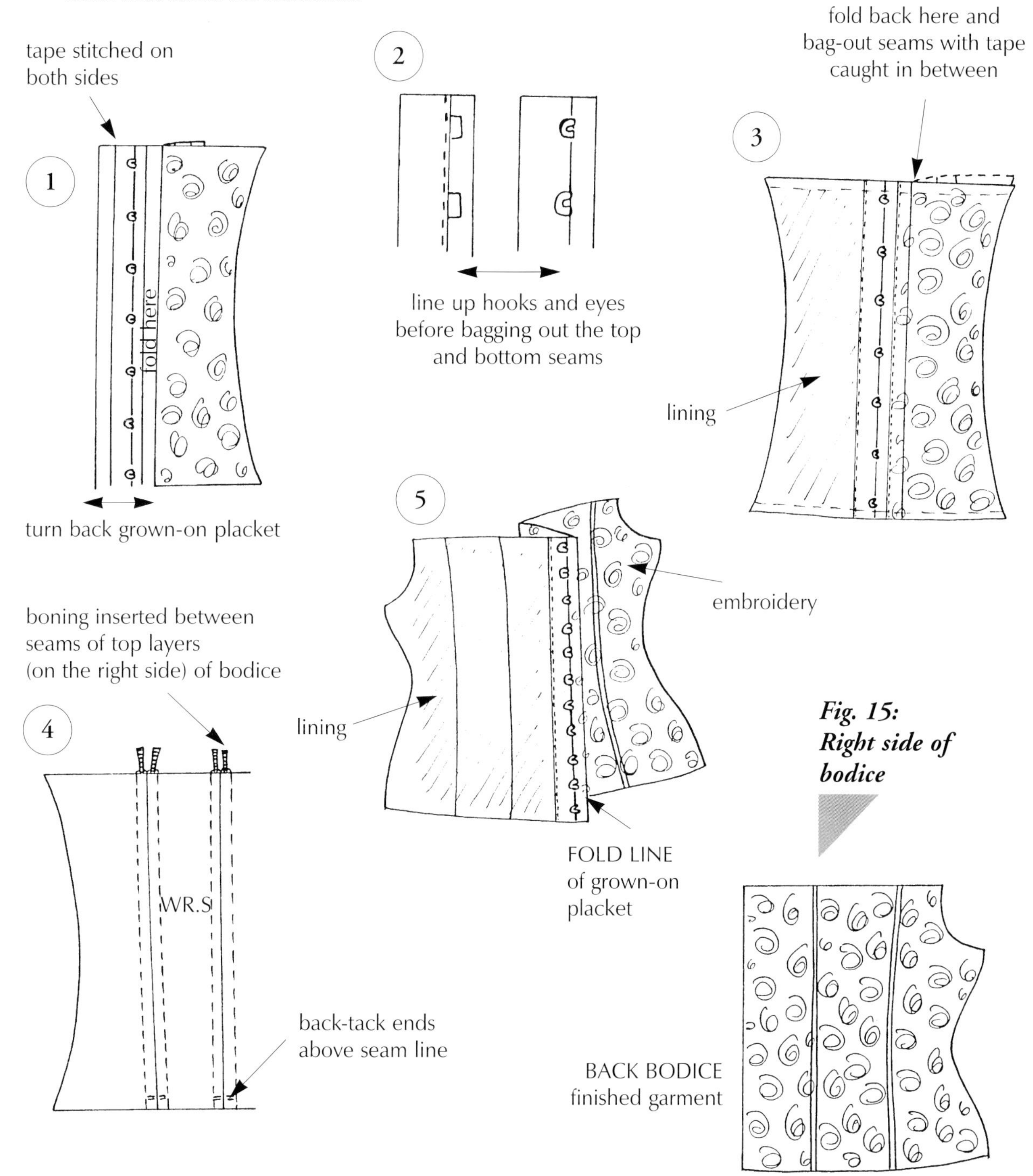

Fig. 15: Right side of bodice

Loops and buttons

Fig. 16: Preparation for rouleau loops and covered buttons

1. The diameter of the button depends on several things. The length and position of the opening, which could be a sleeve opening, small back opening or a CF opening will obviously be significant (***Fig. 16/A***). The quality of fabric and style of the garment will also determine the size used. Once this is established, cut out circles from the square pieces measured from the button moulds.
2. The rouleau loops are made from bias-cut binding and its width depends on the fabric used. Fabric that frays easily is not recommended for these loops. Position the buttons onto the opposite panel if this will help when stitching in your loops. They are placed close together, the first one just below the fitting line as seen on ***Fig. 16/B***.
3. Cut a wide enough strip 2.5cm (1") to accommodate a length of *cord* that is sandwiched between the two fabric edges (R.S.facing). Use a *zip foot,* or *hand stitch* across the top as close to the cord as possible (***Fig. 16/C***). Do not iron onto the finished strips.
4. Stitch one end to secure the cord to the fabric, and pull the cord through from the other end with a threader (***Fig. 16/D***). The raw seams are automatically caught inside the rouleau strip.
5. Once completed, cut the loops into short strips. This reduces the bulk between seams. Pin and tack them along the stitch line next to each other, with the loop edges facing the seam edge (***Fig.16/E***).
6. All loops are stitched between seams, the width of seam being approximately 1.5cm ($^{3}/_{8}$"). Turn and fold the seam back. The loops are now facing the button positions marked on the opposite panel. (***Fig. 16/F***).

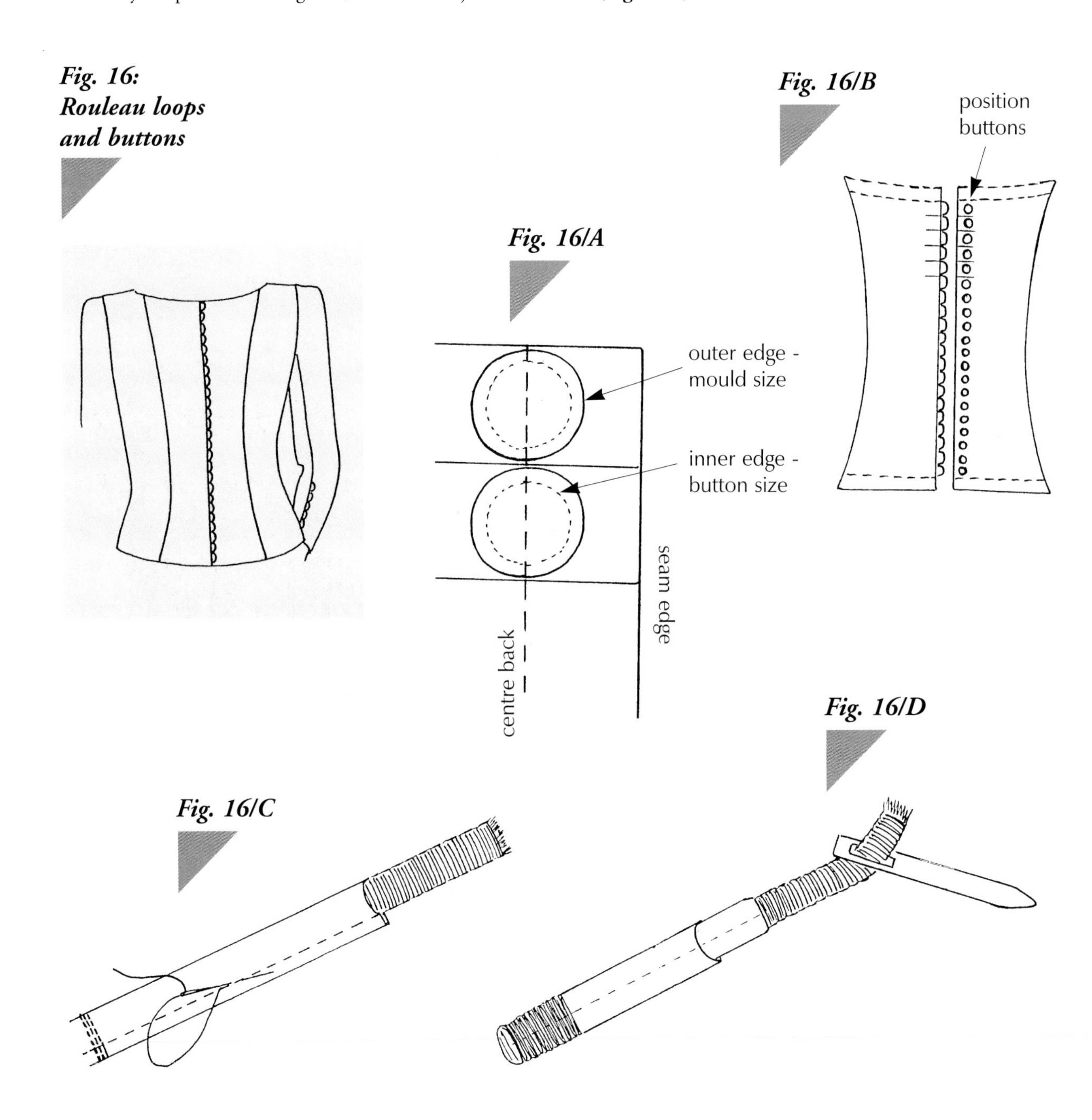

Fig. 16/E

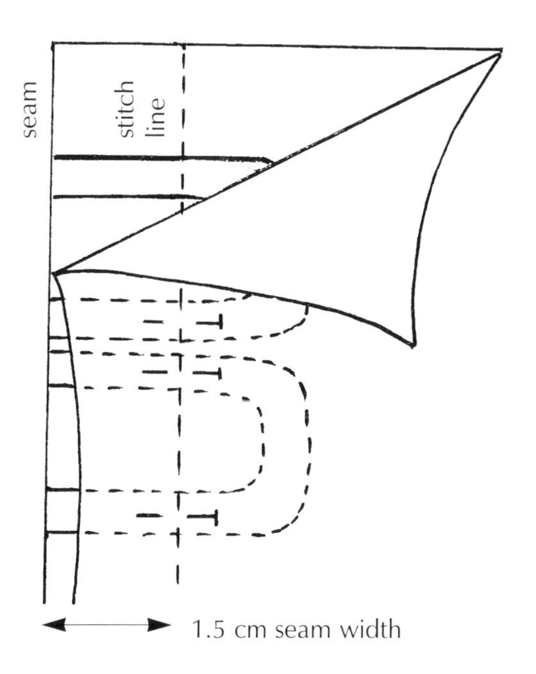

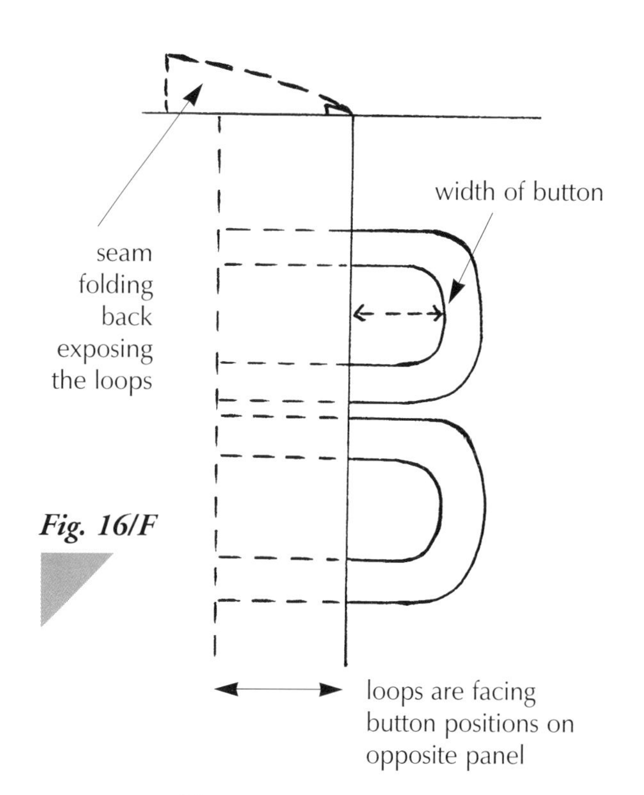

Fig. 16/F

Trimmings

Assembling lace from pattern to garment

There is a wide-ranging choice of lace and trim available to use for one's silhouette. Sometimes different widths of lace for the same design are used, or a large motif for the front panel, or perhaps an all-over lace with a scalloped edge.

Assembling lace onto your panels is not difficult in itself, except when trying to match up the lace patterns into pairs for repeats for several garments of different sizes. In this section I've expanded on the method used to assemble lace (*Fig. 17)* with the lace seen in its true shape in *Fig. 17/A*.

Fig. 17: An allover lace bodice

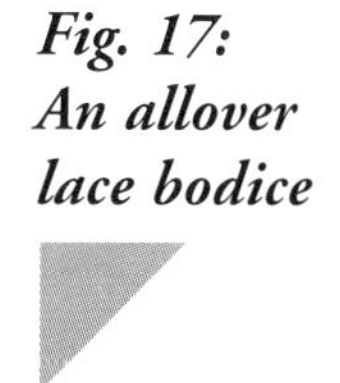

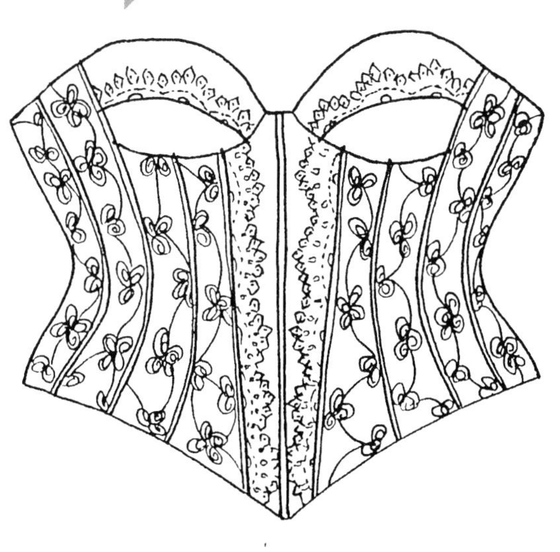

Fig. 17/A: Design scallops on a lace edging

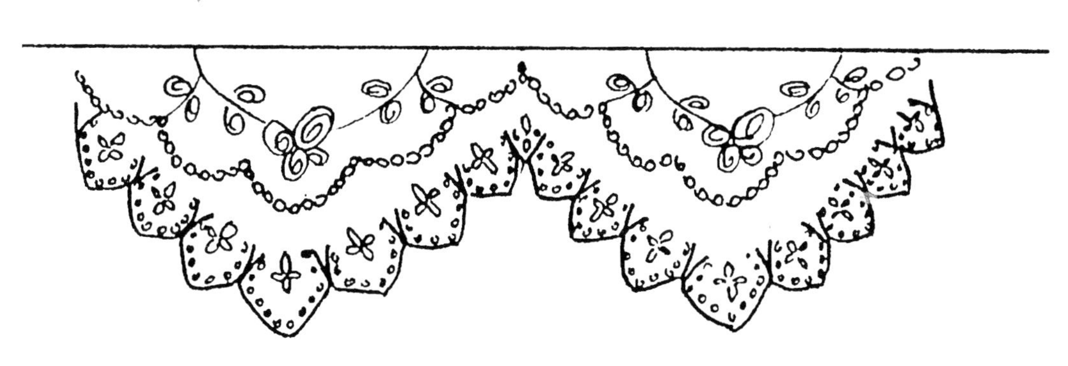

On the scalloped width of lace

1. Once your pattern is made, take the centre-front and bra pattern pieces and pin them onto the lace edging with matching scallops facing the centre-front. Cut out the lace to your pattern pieces.
2. Pin tracing paper over the lace pieces and make a rubbing of the design onto the tracing paper. Make sure you've recorded the image accurately or use a photocopier or fax machine if there is one to hand.
3. Now tack each lace panel onto the top layer of your fabric and ensure that the scallops match on both sides of the *CF and bra pieces* as seen on ***Fig. 17/B*** and ***Fig. 17/C***. Stitch around the edges of each piece, before attaching them to the rest of the garment.
4. Seam allowances on most lace edgings have a width of 1cm (3/8"). Tack the lace 0.5cm (1/4") away from the raw edge of lace onto the stitch line of the seams on your patterns, which has a width of 1.5cm (5/8"). Now stitch the seams together.
5. Seams are opened out flat and stitched on the raw edges to form a channel on either side of the stitch line.
6. Insert your boning through each channel. Alternatively use binding instead.

- ***Polyester rigilene***: Each silhouette in this text can be boned with a boning of your choice. The quality you use is determined by the thickness of the fabric and styling. Rigilene, the type most commonly used, is threaded through a channel or tacked between seams. It consists of narrow nylon strips fused together between nylon gauze. Each end, when cut, is quite sharp and this has to be encased between seams and bar-tacked along the top and bottom, to prevent it from prodding the flesh. The widths supplied range from 8mm (1/4") to 16mm (1/2") and what one chooses to use varies according to preference and design.

Fig. 17/B: Centre-front panels

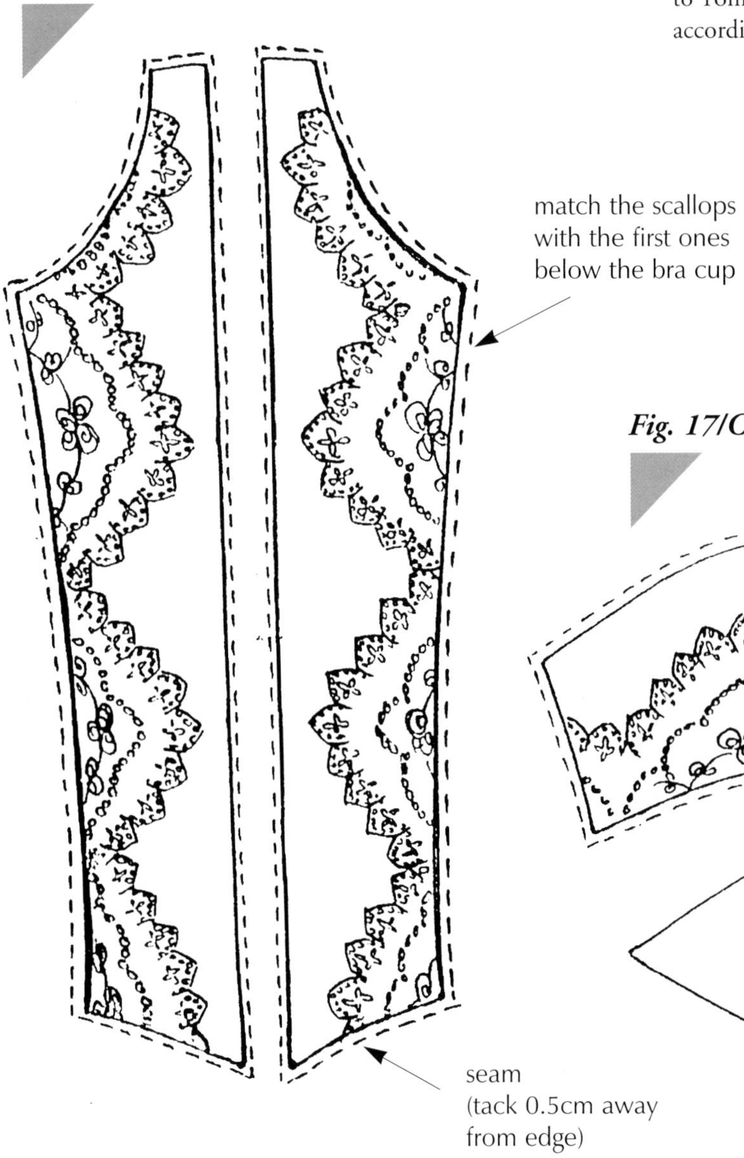

Fig. 17/C: Bra panels

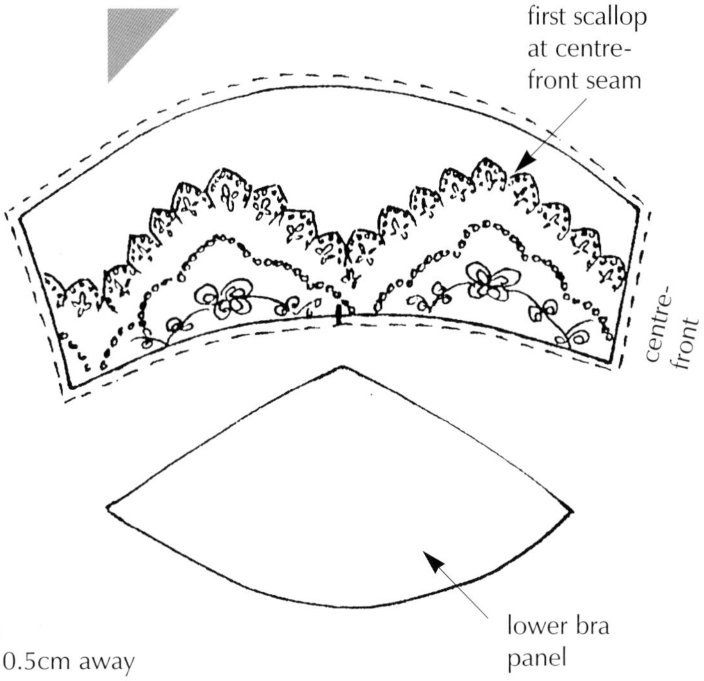

- *Paying attention to detail:* Seams are very important in the construction of the boned bodice. The treatment of them can be concentrated either on the outside or inside of the garment. When stitched on the outside of the garment the raw edges are concealed completely with bias-cut binding or braided trimmings, creating a feature of the seams. Neatening the edges of seams and easing in seams on the inside would depend on the quality of fabric used to create a smooth finish, see (*Fig. 12*). When seams are not used to decorate, the raw edges are covered with a lining. Necklines, with top stitching or lace edgings, trimming openings, and paying attention to back fastenings are all very important to the make-up of your design. See more about seams in Part 9 under Materials and Decorations.

Neatening edges: Figs 18 - 20

Figs 18 and 19 illustrates where one cuts into the seams, where there is strain on the curve of the seam, so that the seam lies flat and doesn't pucker on the stitch line.

Fig 20 illustrates neatening seams on armholes with binding.

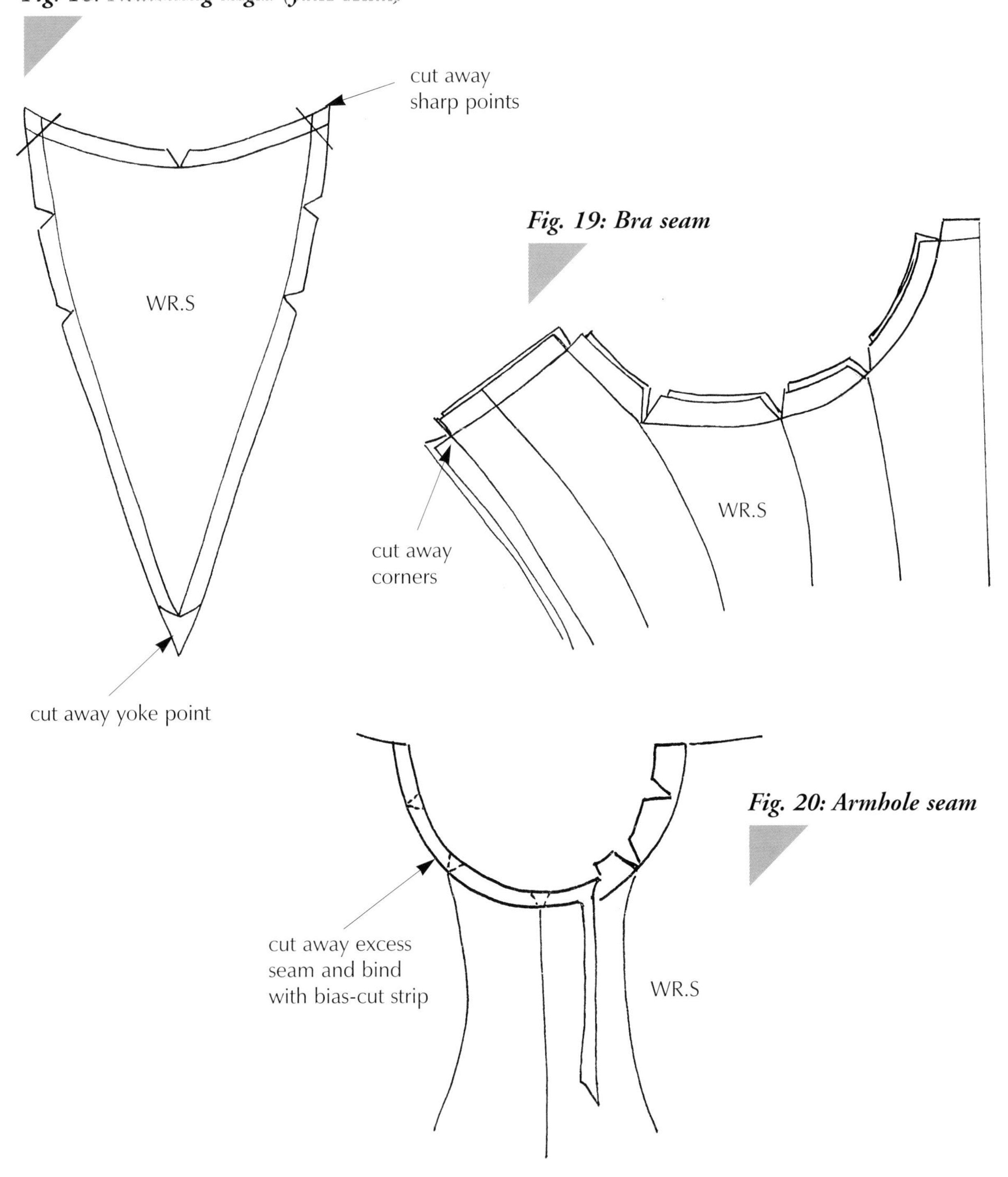

Fig. 18: Neatening edges (yoke seam)

Fig. 19: Bra seam

Fig. 20: Armhole seam

- *Seam allowances:* Seams are normally 1.5cm (5/8") wide on most fabrics. This allows for fraying on loosely woven fabrics. It also provides sufficient width to cut into curved seams. Where the seams do fray a lot, the width is useful for turning back raw edges to neaten them. It's also a useful width to channel boning through. Unless, of course, the fabric used has some stretch in it, then a separate channel is stitched over your seams. Where the fabric is soft and stretches, a 0.5cm (1/4") width can be used providing you use an overlocker (a three-thread domestic or industrial machine that stitches stretch fabric).

- *Underlinings:* The bodice consists of *several layers* to strengthen the garment. An under layer of a coarse netting or a very heavyweight cotton or canvas is used between the lining and the main fabric. These middle thicknesses vary according to the style and quality of your top fabric. It's always difficult to know how an interfacing will perform. The best thing to do is to try out a piece first. When an underlining is attached to the top layer of the bodice, it gives the bodice a crisp clean finish. However, on stretch fabrics, the top layer could ruck up. With woven interfacing, it's best to use on qualities with a piled surface like velvet, for instance. Each panel is pinned and tacked with this interfacing before the seams are stitched together. Pay particular attention to the grain, as it should be cut in the same direction as the fabric grain lines. If instead, an iron-on staflex is used, be careful not to iron it on the top layer of very thin fabrics but to put it on the facings instead. Vilene, fusible or non-fusible, can be cut in any direction.

- *Linings:* These fabrics are softer than the main fabrics and usually have a sheen to the right side. Once the bodice panels are basted together with the underlining, the lining is cut to the main pattern and stitched so that all the seams are *bagged-out.* This means that the top and under layers are encased with raw seamed edges placed together, i.e. with seams facing.

- Linings are kept separate from the main body of the garment and are attached only at neck edges, waist seams and some armholes. If cut on the bias, the seams are pinned and tacked together first to prevent distortion. Lay the panels flat and do not handle them too much since the seams tend to stretch.

Skirt shapes and trains

PART 7

Skirt shapes

It is important to choose a skirt shape that *enhances the figure but also complements the bodice of the dress.* Proportions should be worked out at the design stage: avoid large bows on large hips, for example, unless your client is about average height or taller. The four examples as seen in this text are shapes that have been chosen to demonstrate their popularity and suitability for almost all brides. Three out of the four skirt shapes are attached to the bodice of the dress. The separate skirt shape is worn with a jacket.

The traditional full skirt will always have a place in modern society, especially for the very young bride. However, in recent times, the trend has been towards the straighter silhouette. Panels and gores are by far the most successful style lines on skirt shapes.
To advance the hang and drape of the skirt and train, fabrics with body such as taffettas, dupions, and dutchess satins are examples used for the very full skirt and the elaborate train. Lightweight crepe satins and chiffons are some of the fluid fabrics appropriate for draping and ruching. Velvets are suitable for A-line or straight silhouettes.

For *bought patterns* the waist, hip and high hip measurements are crucial to the fit of your pattern. ***Fig. 1:*** There are normally *two darts on the back* and *one on the front* of a drafted pattern. For A-line skirts and striding widths, allow approximately 3-5cm (1¼"-2") on each side seam at the hem to nothing at high hip.

Fig. 1: Skirt back

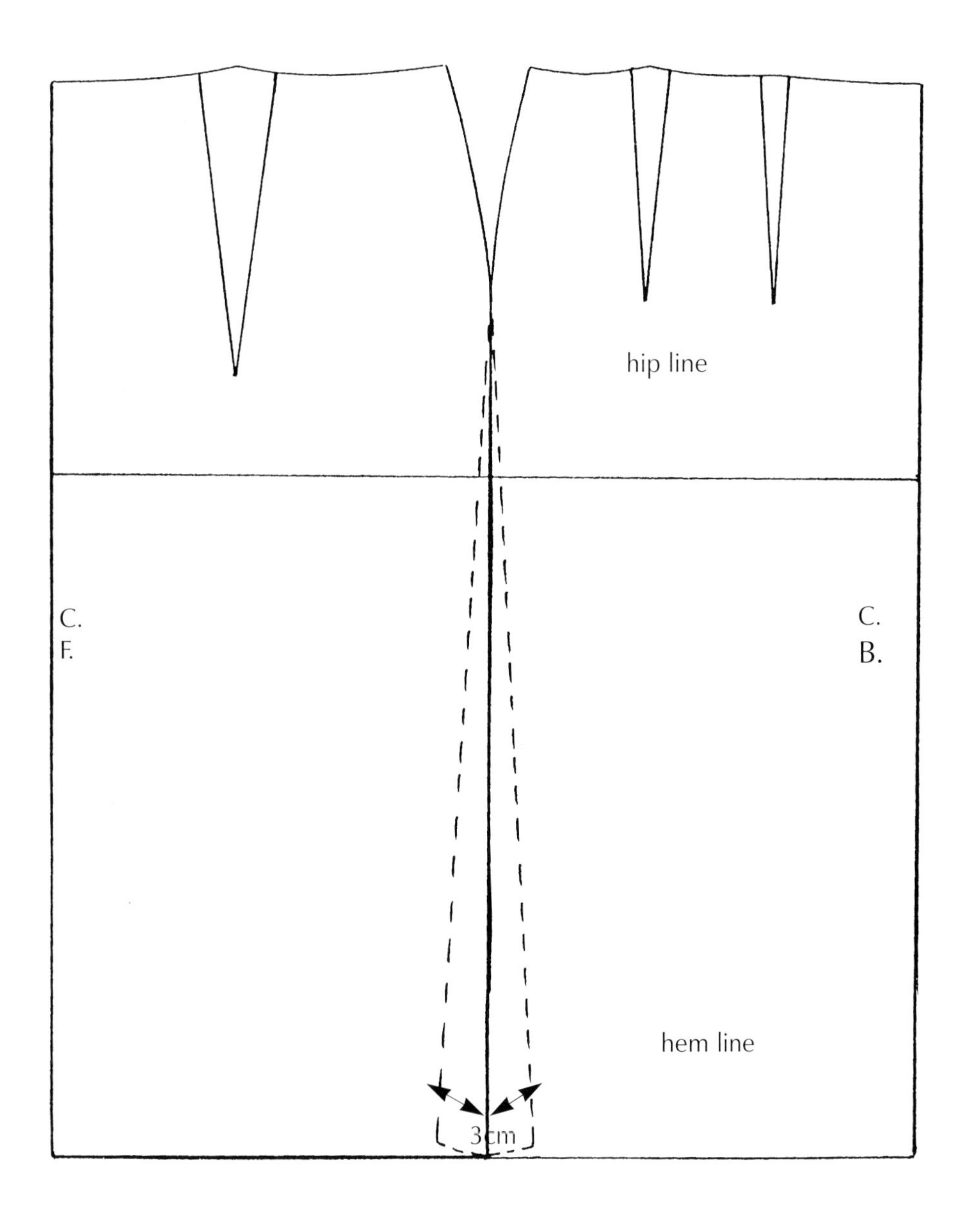

Adjustments to the skirt block

For most bridal patterns the skirt darts are seldom used as they are because *waist seams* are either below or above the waist. However, adjustments to the waist darts and hip measurements should be made before designing your new shape: on bought patterns, alteration lines are normally indicated and are placed away from the darts. I've used the back skirt block to demonstrate these methods. You may want to take more out of the front than the back or vice versa. A toile should be made up to perfect the shape, before re-adapting your silhouette into something new.

Fig. 2: Adjustments to the waist line can be made either by taking fulness out (by altering the darts) when *too loose,* and adding into the waist when *too tight.* To reduce the waist measurement at **b,** widen the darts, and at **a** adjust the side seam curve. *Alternatively,* the centre-back and front can be reduced but make sure the hip measurement is accurate and the darts are where you want them to be.

Fig. 2/A: For extra fulness at the waist and hips, cut through line **c-d** and mark in the required amount.

Fig. 2/B: To increase or reduce the length of the skirt, cut through your pattern below the knee at **e** to the required amount, as illustrated.

Fig. 2:
To reduce and increase waist measurements

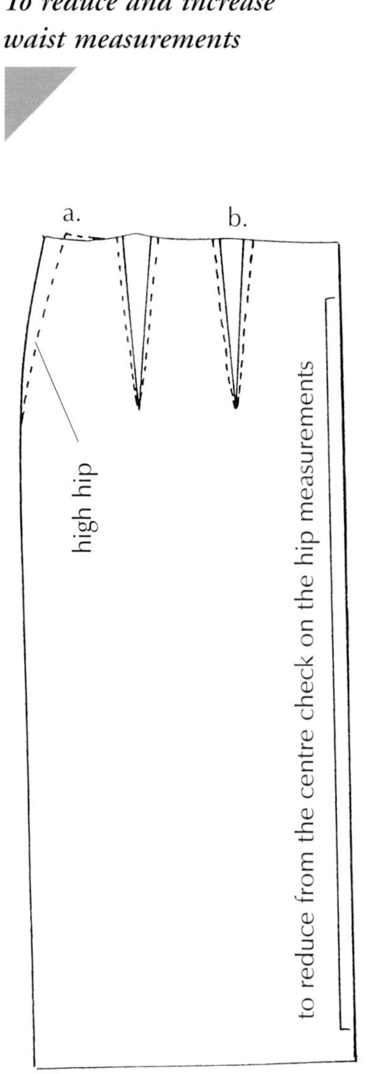

Fig. 2/A

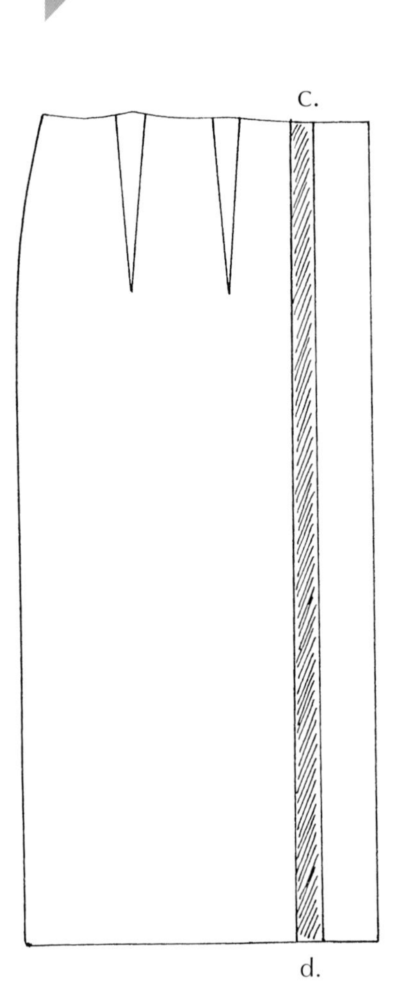

Fig. 2/B

Low-waisted (with full skirt)

The dropped waistline *accentuates the torso* making the silhouette from nape to high hip look longer and slimmer. The bodice shape is invariably panelled and quite fitted and often has a low-cut front and back neckline. It therefore seems natural to have a full skirt bellowing out from beneath it. Although the CF extends to a point, the back is fairly straight. This combination of style lines is very flattering to the wearer and therefore very popular. *Fig. 3:* For this shape I've used a dress block (see under this heading).

Fig. 3/A:* Close up shoulder and waist dart and put it in the armhole. Mark in all the style lines, including the new waist position on the skirt block. *Establish how long the skirt length is to be before closing up the waist dart on the skirt, and opening it up at the hemline. *Fig. 3/B:* Where there is unwanted fulness **(a) at the waist dart, place into the nearest panelled seams or bust dart. Reshape **(b)** by filling in uneven curves at the dropped waist and bodice panels. *Fig. 3/C:* *Slash through skirt into equal panels and spread them evenly across your paper allowing for a full gathered skirt and extra fulness at hemline. Mark in grain lines and notches. Do the same for the back skirt pattern.

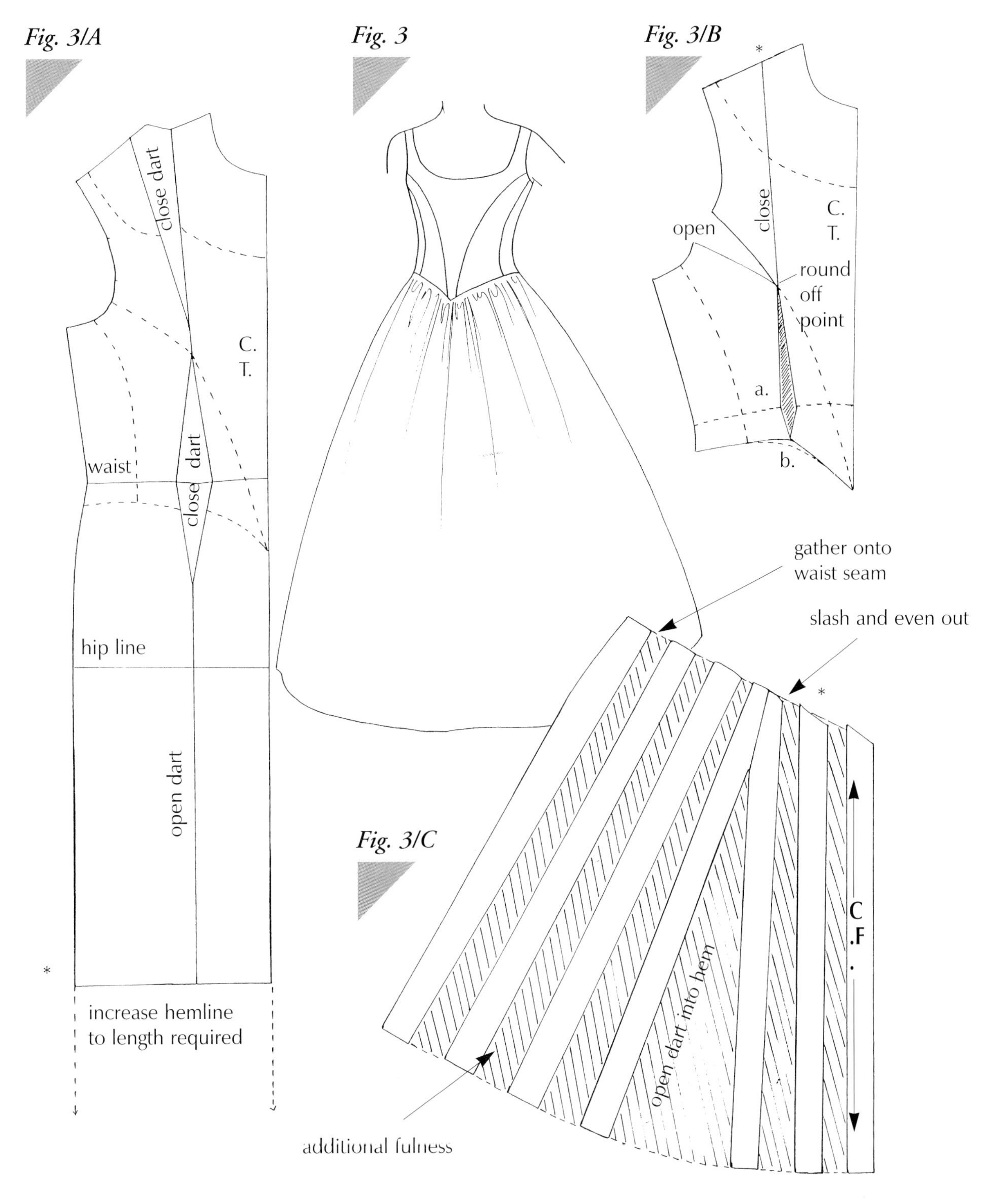

Creating a dress block

Since many of the fitted styles have dropped waist shapes, *creating a block is the obvious choice to make.* To achieve the desired silhouette, adjustments to the fitted bodice block and skirt block have to be made. These blocks will vary according to your size and figure. By attaching the bodice to the skirt one creates a one-piece pattern. On *bought patterns,* make sure that the *bodice darts are at the waist* and not at the armhole or side seams, and that they are accurate. The bodice front and back darts remain virtually the same on college blocks except for the length of the back waist dart, should it extend beyond the chestline. The skirt darts are made to fit the waist darts on the bodice so make sure the *waist measurements are correct* on both blocks before repositioning the darts.

Fig. 4: Place back and front bodices on the chest and hip lines. See that CF and CB are on the straight grain. *Ignore waist darts on skirt.* *Measure from **a-b** at centre-front to bust point on bodice and from **c-d** at centre-front at waist towards centre of dart. Use these corresponding measurements for the skirt dart **e-f.**

*Mark upwards from hip **g-h** to dart point, approximately 9cm ($3\frac{1}{2}$"). Apply the same method for the back. Reduce the length of the dart at **i** on the back bodice to the chestline by moving the dart point.

*Mark upwards from hip line to dart point on back skirt to approximately 6cm ($2\frac{1}{4}$") at **j-k**, so that the dart measures the same as the bodice dart. For striding width at **l** on hem, add up to 5cm (2") from high hip on side seams.

Fig. 4

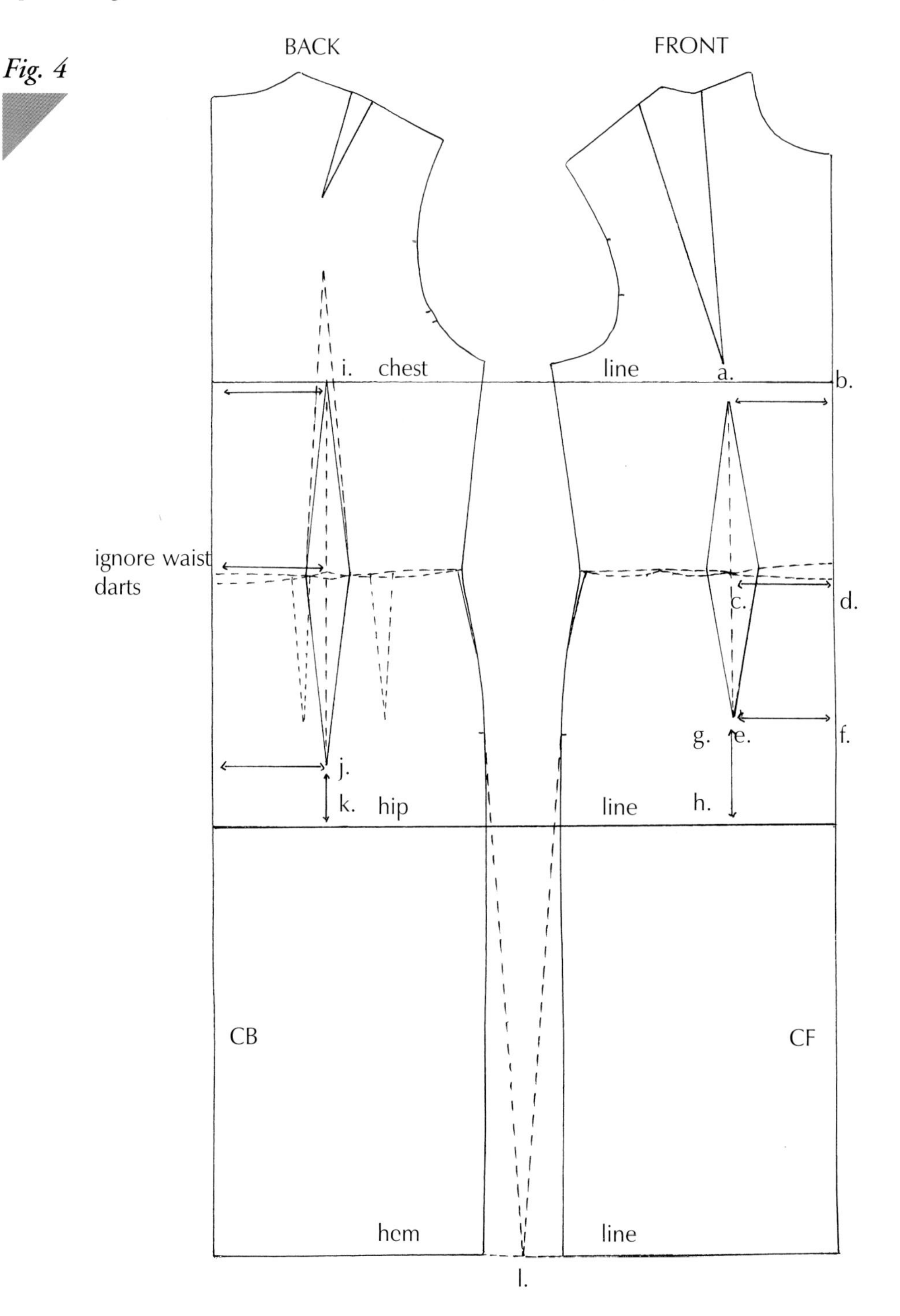

Panelled (for the empire line):

The *princess line* has always been an attractive feature of the dress for many brides. The seams start from the shoulder line and extend down to the hemline. Its slim-line skirt curves at the waist and accentuates the contours of the hips. The cut of the seams is made to enhance the figure and to reduce excess fabric where it is not needed. Variations on this silhouette, as seen on ***Fig.*** *5* where the seam lines are drawn from the armhole, are very popular too, and were worn especially during the *Georgian and Regency* periods. The panelled skirt at CB extends into a simple train, but an effective one, where the fulness starts from the hip or at the bodice seam if so desired, and trails down to a comfortable length on the ground.

Fig. 5: This high-waisted *empire line,* with its seam line cut right under the bust, is usually quite tightly fitted and low, exposing the cleavage to its fullest potential. ***Fig. 5/A:*** Close the shoulder dart and put it in the armhole, then raise the waist seam to just under the bust. This shape has four panels: two front and back, drawn through the waist darts. *For extra fulness in each panel, extend from nothing at dart point on front skirt to the amount required at hem and at the side seams from the hip line to hem length. * *The front hemline is reshaped;* draw in a curved line downwards from CF towards the front side seam. Separate the panels as in ***Figs 5/B-5/C*** and make sure they match on the seamlines of the side front panels and the curves are smoothed out at the waist and hemline.

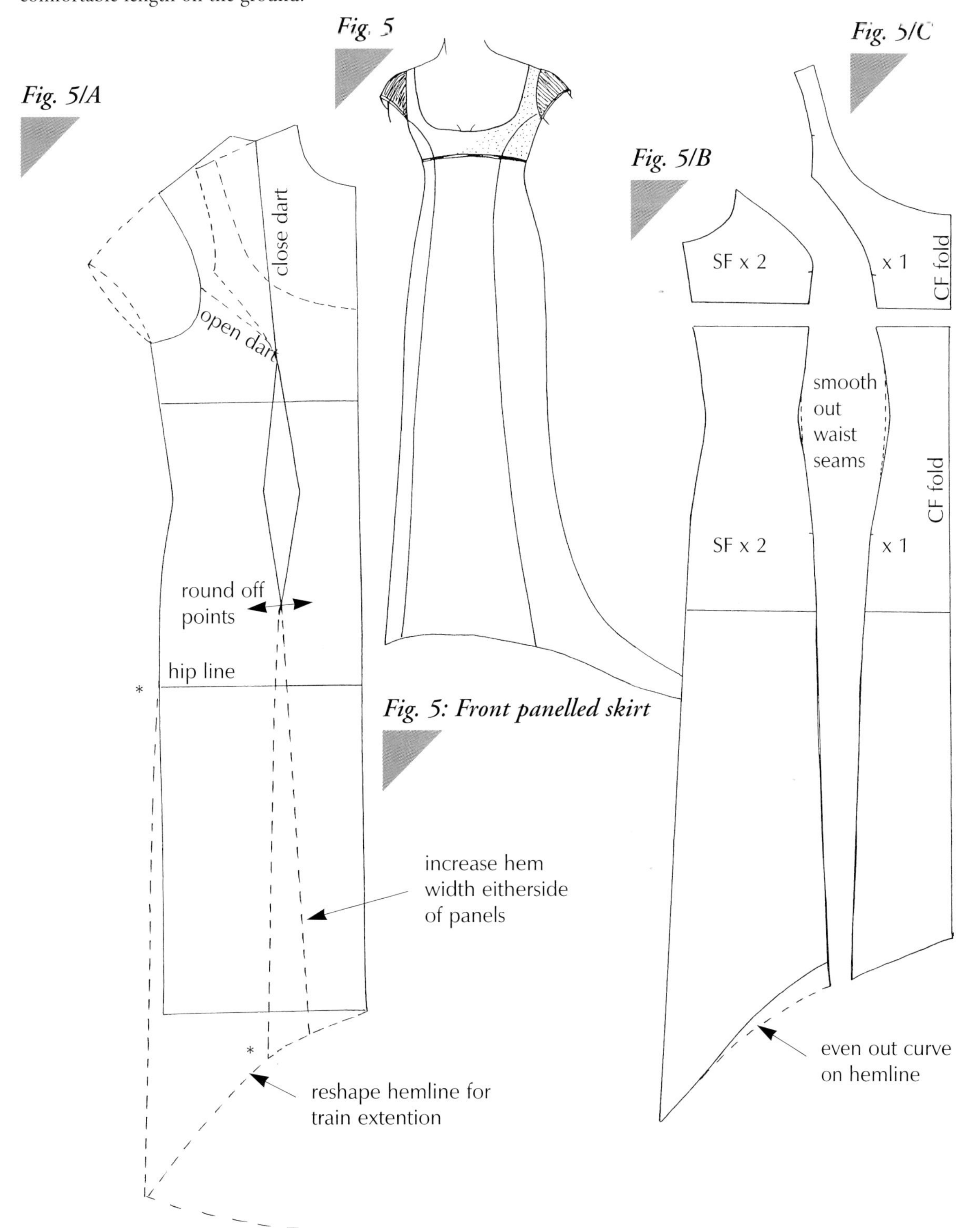

Fig. 5: Front panelled skirt

Panelled skirt: back view

For the Georgian period, the dress had fulness on the centre-back panel beneath the bodice seam, which was either gathered or pleated. Keep to the authenticity of the style by using small covered buttons for the back opening, even though it may not be visible to the eye on the skirt panels. The cap sleeves have pleated fabric stitched onto a flat patterned shape, starting from the armhole seams towards the sleeve edges, where they are pleated and then bound. See cap sleeve draft in Part 5.

Fig. 6: The CB back panels graduate in length to form a train. On this silhouette it isn't very long but it can be extended if you want. Ignore the shoulder dart and round off the points on the waist dart when drawing in your back panels.

Fig. 6/A: Allow an extra 20cm (8") or more on each panel for gathers or pleats, depending on the look you want to achieve, and take it down to the hem length. This amount should fit comfortably into the centre-back yoke panel.

Fig. 6/B: Make sure the side back panels fit together at the notches and especially at the hemline so that the hem edge has a smooth and even curve.

Fig. 6: Skirt panels for the back

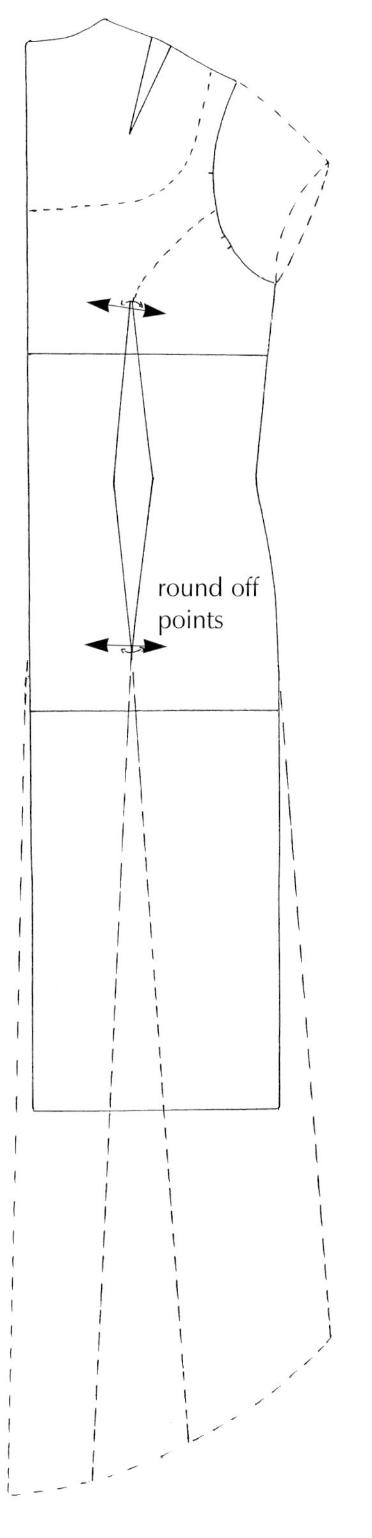

Fig. 6/A

Fig. 6/B

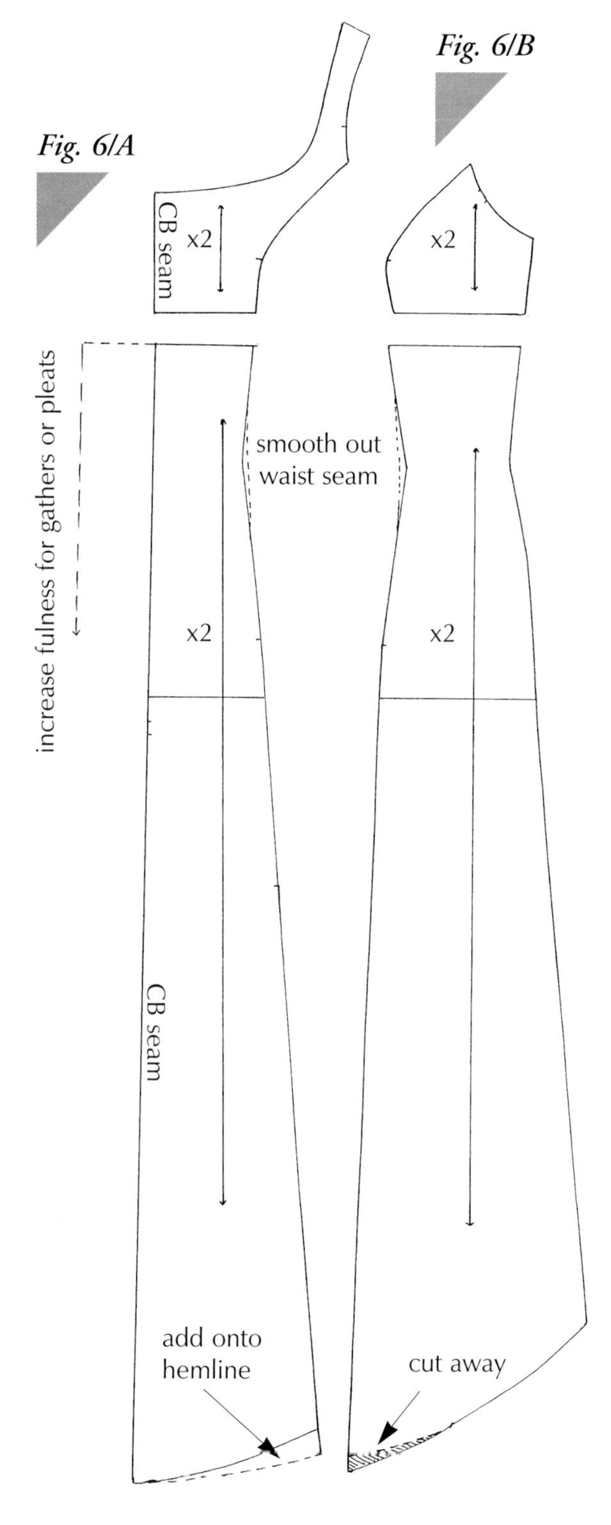

Ruching and draping

Skirt styles with *ruching* or *draping* at the hips or on the buttocks can be flattering on practically any shape providing the skirt enhances the figure and the fulness is well balanced.

The style illustrated is part of a three-piece Thai silk riding outfit (*Fig.7*). The silhouette has a draped front skirt which is attached to a shaped front yoke. The ruched sash extends from the front shape at the side waist seam, and drapes over the hips to form pleats at the centre-back opening.

Fig. 7

Fig. 8: The dimensions of the drape in this silhouette are concentrated across the high hip position, which is slightly different from that of the photograph. *Two darts are used for the front skirt in this draft.* *To shape the hemline of the skirt, place the side seams of the back and front blocks together on the hip line. See that the CF and CB lines are on the straight grain.
* Determine how long the skirt is and mark down from thigh to hemline to the new position where the train ends at centre-back. See under trains for dimensions. Curve upwards from this new line towards the centre-front.

Fig. 8/A:
Draw in style lines: at **a-b** measure 5cm (2") from front side seam towards darts. From **b-c**, mark downwards towards the high hip measurement and cut through. *Place this piece onto the back hip curve. Where it overlaps, add that amount to seam edge!* Mark from **d-e** at centre-front, the width of the front yoke. To complete the shape **e-b,** the front darts are closed and placed into the side seam at **f.** To increase the fulness for your draping, slash through from **c** to CF at **g.** (*Fig.9*). *Shorten* the *back waist dart* to finish under the draped sash. Mark in the width of the sash at CB from **h-i,** and across to **j** at high hip (*Fig.10/A*).

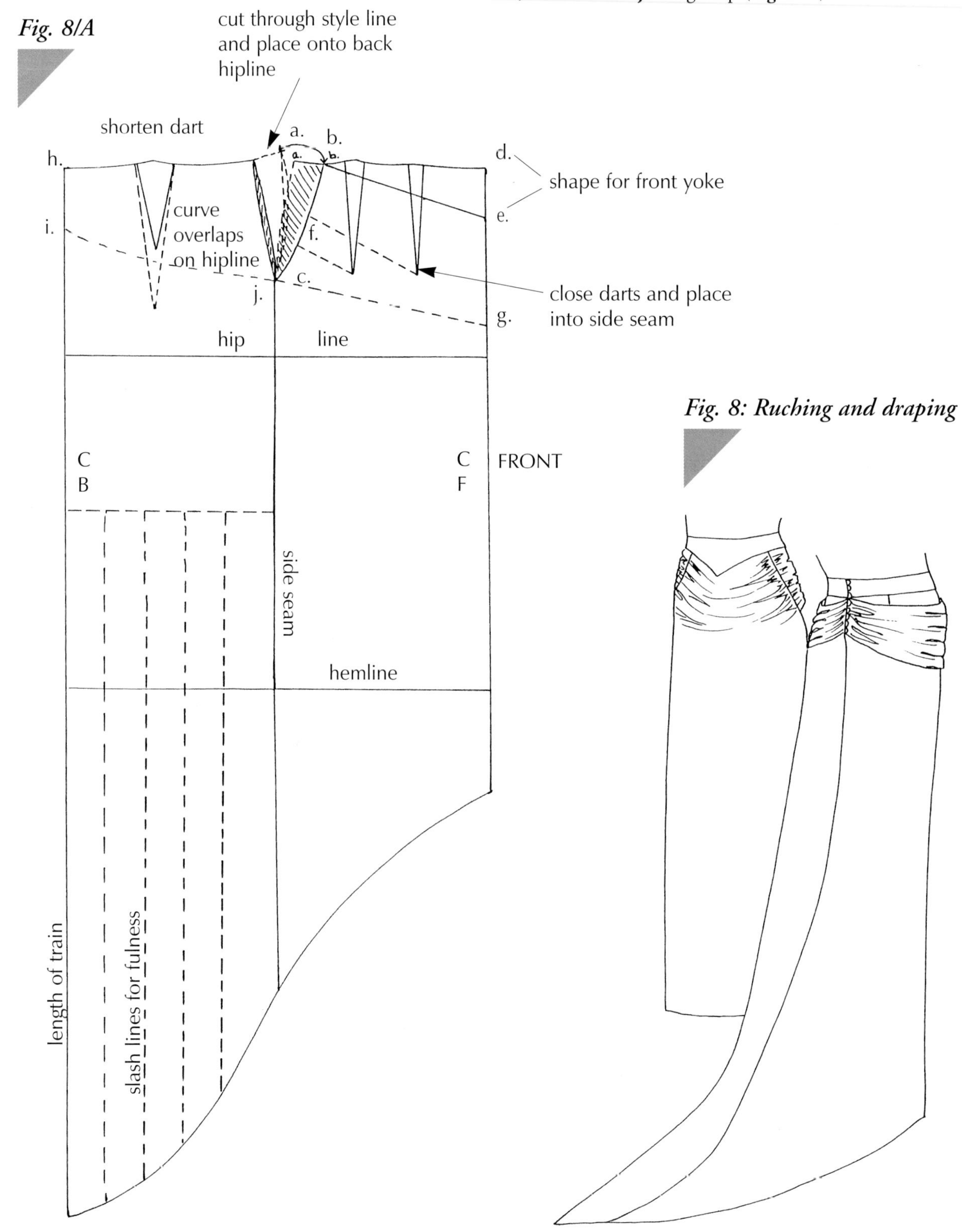

Fig. 8: Ruching and draping

The front draping: Fig. 9

Both darts are closed at the waist and opened into the side seam. For a fuller drape, open up to the centre-front (see diagram).*Mark in new centre-front fold line from CF yoke seam to hemline. It increases the fulness across the hips but not by much. Pleat or ruch the amount into the new side front seam. Ensure that these pleats match those of the back sash. The yoke for *Fig. 9/A* is cut on the fold at the waist and at CF. The width of the back waist band is added to the yoke. Mark in the notches which correspond to that of the front skirt.

Back view and draping

- *Fig. 10:* The side seam takes on a new shape at the high hip position. The fulness of the train takes shape from below the thigh. * Slash through the lines marked on the pattern and add the amount required, then smooth out the uneven hemline and CB seam. Leave dart in place at waist.
- Trace off the shape from the back skirt across the hips and make a *separate pattern piece* (***Fig. 10/A***). Close the waist dart and use this pattern as a foundation pattern for the lining of the drape before drawing in slash lines to increase its fulness. Mark in the notch for the actual side seam and see that it matches the notch on front yoke pattern. Cut out on the bias.
- *Fig. 10/B:* Slash through and allow fulness for pleating at both centre-back and new side seam positions. The back skirt waist band is cut to waist measurement and approximately 3cm (1¼") folded and used as a finished width to match the side seams of the front yoke. Before attaching the draped pattern piece to the side front seam, it is bias-cut and ruched onto a flat piece of lining made from the foundation pattern, before it is stitched into the side front seam of the skirt.

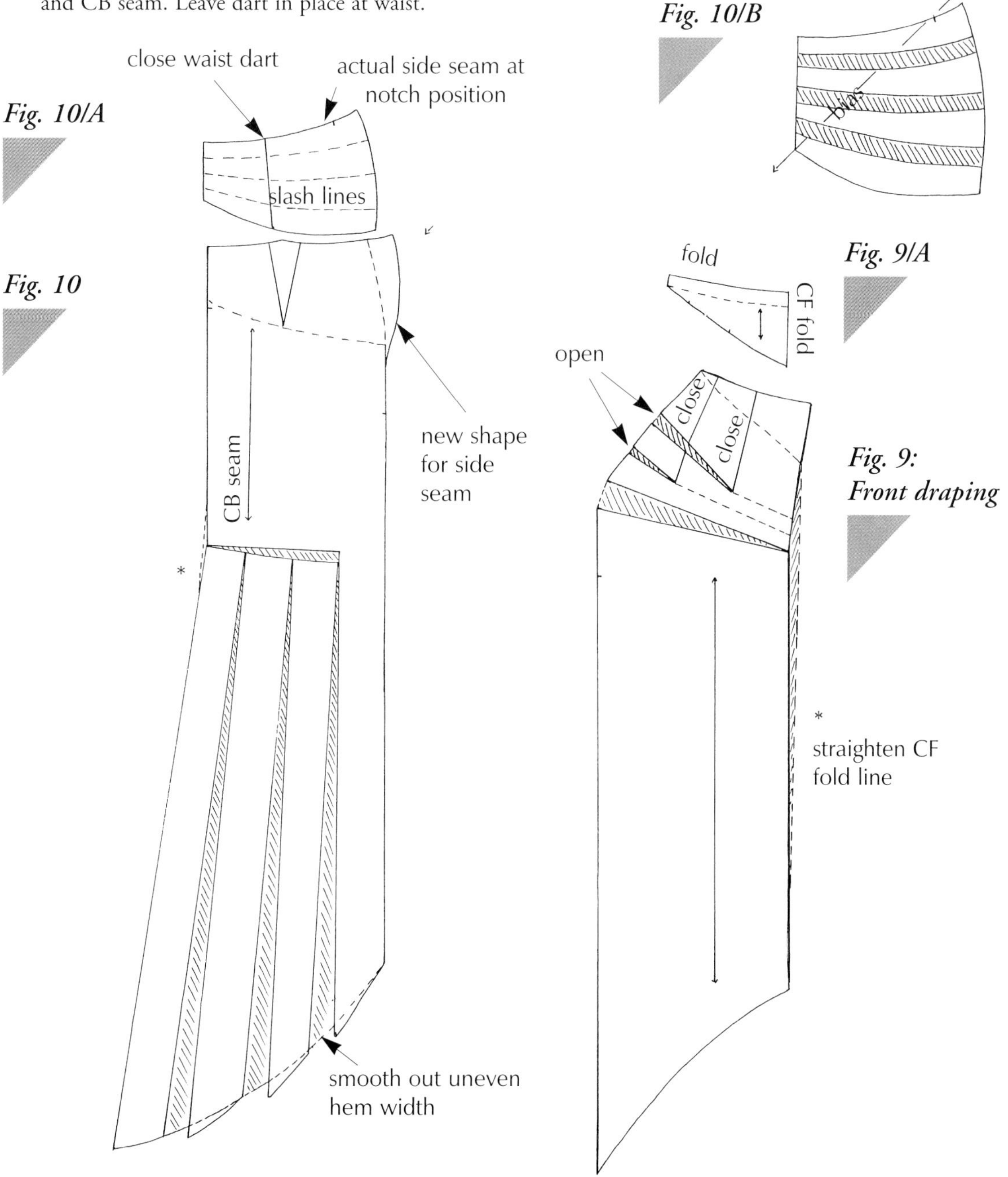

Layered (and cut on the bias)

This silhouette is normally made in soft fluid fabrics like chiffon and crêpe georgette, where the fabric is layered and cut on the bias. The centre-back opening is shaped and has rouleau loops secured with a draw-string that ties at the top edge of the back yoke. For each panel, the side seams are sewn together using french seams (*see under trimmings in Part 9).* Only the *under layer* for the centre-back has an open seam. The normal width for chiffon is 90cm and this restriction makes it difficult to spread out the pattern panels for the larger pieces to their fullest potential. To match up the side seams, *number each end, at the hem of every panel* on your sketch, and then apply this to your pattern pieces, as seen on ***Figs 11-11/A***. The complete front and back blocks are required to plan the layout of these panels. Close the *darts at bodice seam* on the top skirt panels and put them into the hem width. For the under layers use the darts as they are for a fitted under skirt or ignore the darts for a looser fit.

Fig.11: Front

FRONT
① ①
②
③
②
③

Fig. 11/C: Front bodice

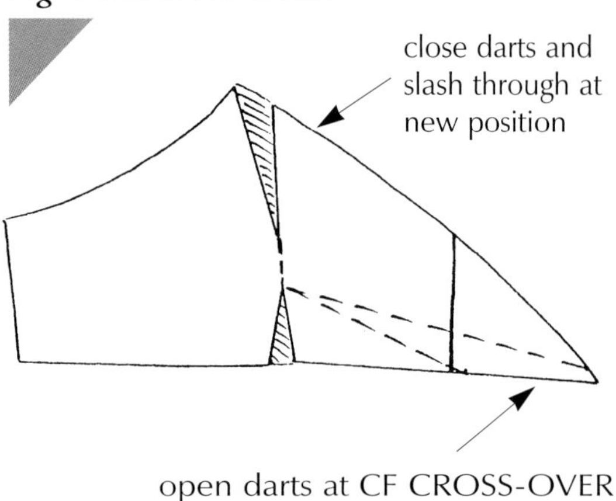

Fig. 11/E: Back bodice

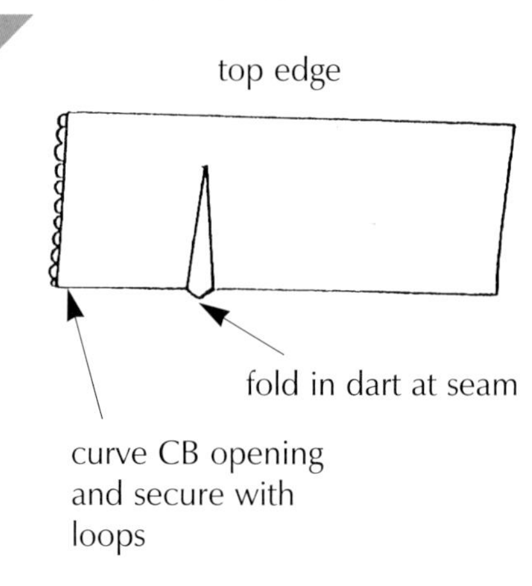

Fig. 11/D

smooth out
uneven
neck edge
close
CF
smooth out uneven fulness and
gather or fold in pleats at CF

Fig. 11/A: Back

BACK

1. 1.

2.

3.

2.

3.

top and under layer

Pattern preparation

Fig. 11/B: Put the front and back blocks together at one side seam. Line up the chest and hip lines and see that the CF & CB is on the straight grain.*Mark in your new hem length and style lines for both the bodice and skirt panels. Then *number from 1 to 3,* where the shape *begins* on the hemline and *where it finishes* on each panel.

For the bodice (*Fig. 11/C*) close up darts and open them at the CF in the usual way. Smooth out uneven seams on both neck edge and at the CF. Gather or pleat fulness at the cross-over bodice (*Fig. 11/D*).

Darts at the back bodice remain as they are. The back opening is curved and finished with loops and covered buttons as seen on *Fig. 11/E*. The under skirt has some fulness and can be cut on either the straight grain or on the bias. For the top layers it would depend on the width of fabric whether they can be cut on the bias.
**Skirt darts,* as mentioned earlier, are left in position for the lining of the under layer, but can be put into the hem width for the top layer or have the amount taken out of the side seams.

Fig. 11/B

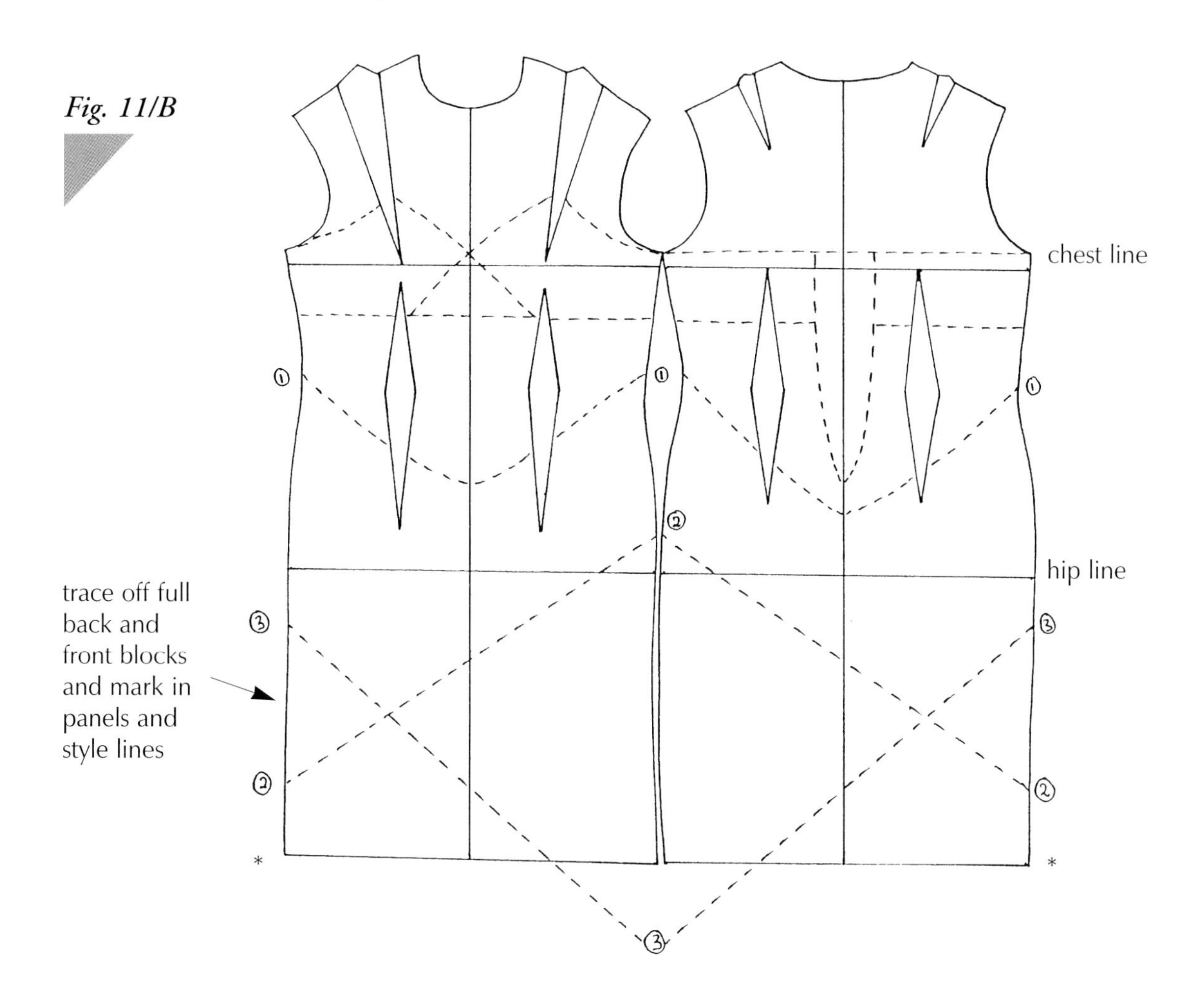

Tracing off the panels

The fulness on these panels are increased from the *hemline to the bodice seam.*

- For **layer (1)** *(Fig. 12)* slash through to nothing at the bodice seam, and spread out the pattern evenly to a half circle. The dart width on the bodice seam, for this pattern, is taken out of the side seams. For a better drape, cut on the bias. The CB opening narrows when slashed and spread out.
- **Layers (2) and (3)** will be controlled by the width of the fabric as to how much fulness goes into the hemline. They are also cut on the bias, should the fabric width be wide enough.

Note

The same principle applies to the back skirt layers, and ensure that the side seams match up.

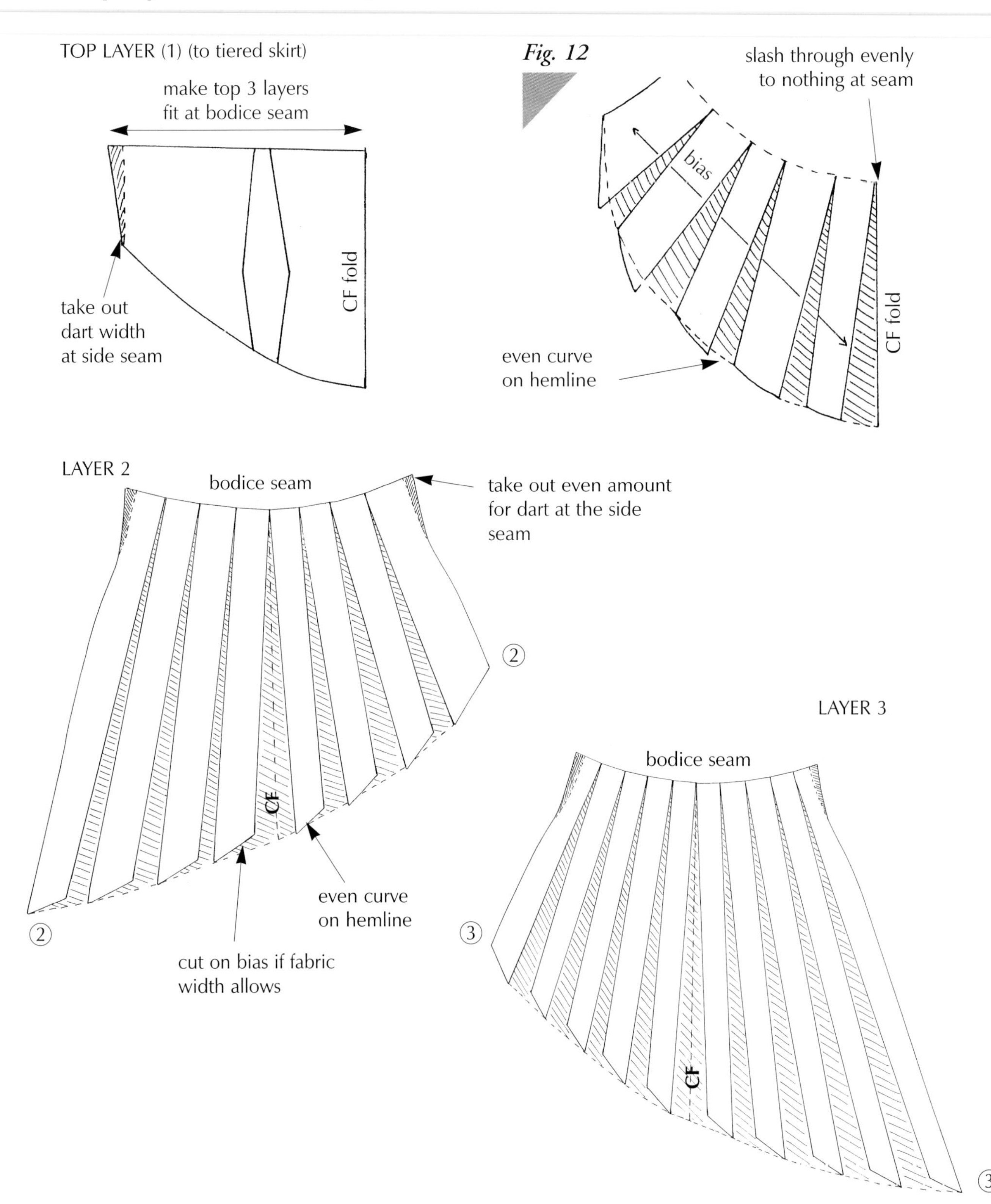

Trains

A train can be symbolic in demonstrating wealth and affluence. This was clearly demonstrated in the nineteenth century when society journals sought to increase their sales by photographing and publicising society weddings. A novel experience, and one that the aristocracy used to their advantage. Royal brides, even in recent times, would wear many metres of silk-embroidered tulle for their veils over extravagant trains: an effective way of showing off their wealth when walking down the aisle! The veil can exceed the length of the train for some brides.

I will demonstrate that the design of the train complements the design of the dress for both simple or more complicated shapes. The method adopted for any style whether the train is attached or detached from the dress, is to measure down from **a** at the centre-back bodice seam (*Fig. 13*) to **b** at hem length of the skirt at floor level, and outwards to the desired length of the train at **c.** Some heavy weight fabrics, or style lines increase the fulness of the train over the hips. This can be remedied if the fulness needs to be reduced, by reshaping at **d** at the centre-back seam. *Weighted hems* apply to dresses of heavyweight quality. A bonded interfacing used on the under side of the hem could be ironed or stitched on.

Fig. 13

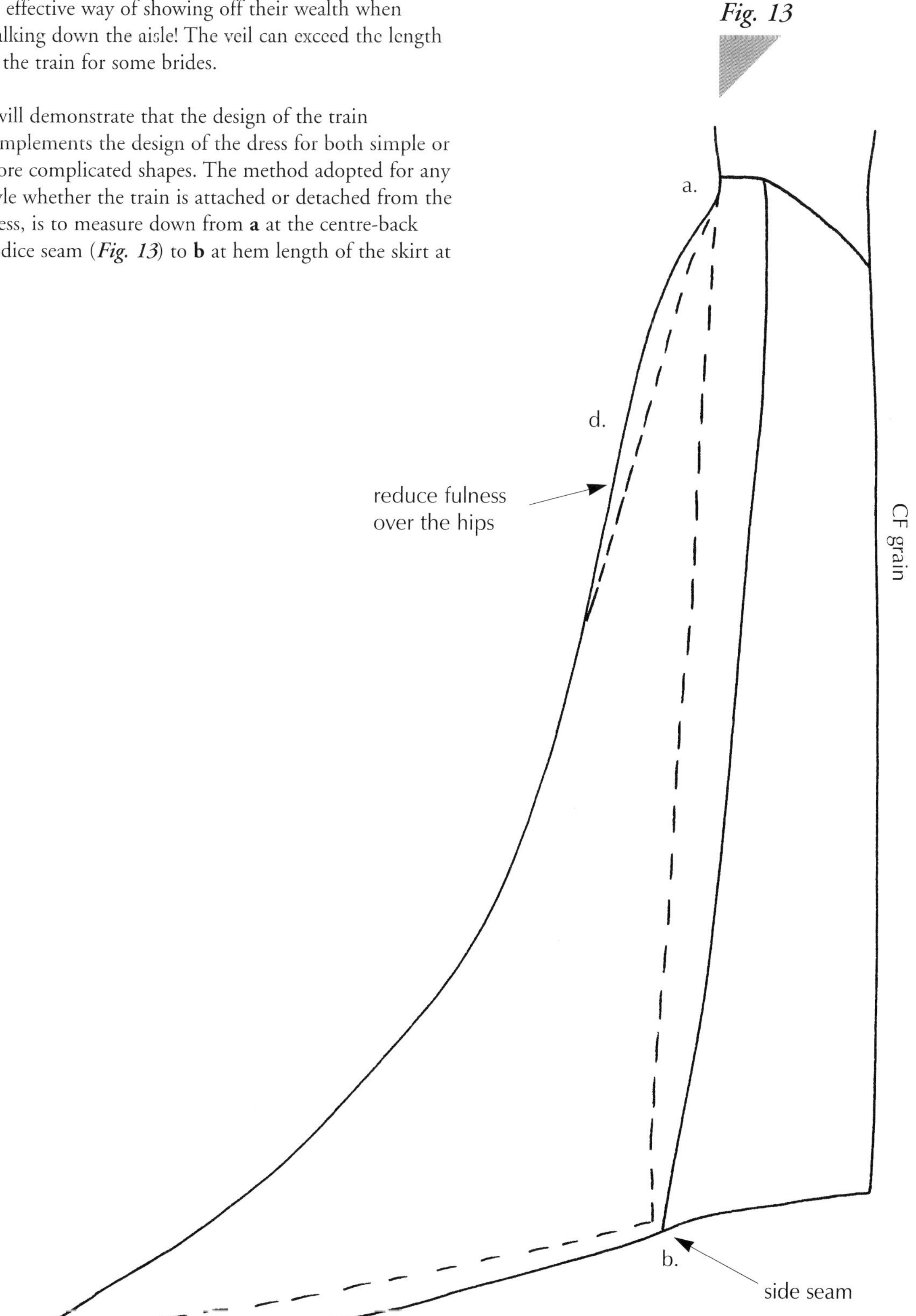

A fitted train

A train that is attached to the back of the dress and forms part of the overall design, normally has two or more panels with a centre-back seam that has a zip opening or loops and buttons. The length varies according to the style and normally increases in width at the hemline. Once the shape has been drawn on paper, make sure you notch through both bodice and skirt pattern pieces, indicating where your fulness is being created. Measure how long the train is to be and the depth of the CB opening, and curve out the new hemline. The lining in this instance is cut from the same pattern (***Fig. 14***).

Fig. 14/A
On this pattern, the fulness starts *between notches* **a-b** from 2.5 cm (1") away from the centre-back edge to 4cm (1 1/2") away from the side seam on both panels. Calculate how much fulness is required and *add the amount onto the CB seam.* Close the waist dart at **c** and open it into the hem width. At the hemline at **d**, allow an extra 10cm (4") or more on the back and front side panels at **e**, fanning it out to give the wearer plenty of ease when moving about. A hemwidth of 5cm (2") at **f** is sufficient and is folded back and hand stitched down. To increase the weight of the hem on medium to heavyweight fabrics, iron on or sew in a thick weight of interlining to the width of the hem allowance.

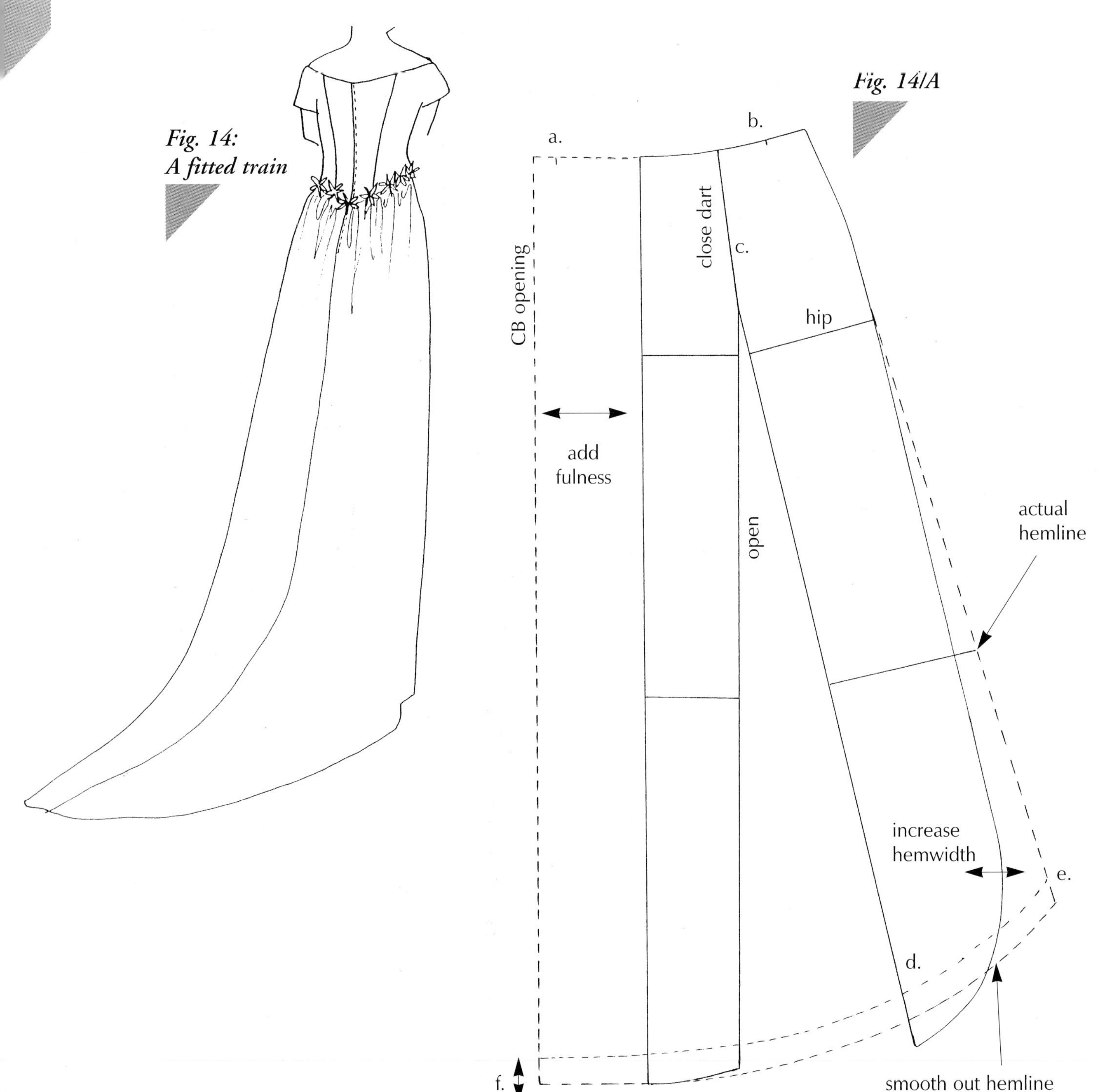

Fig. 14: A fitted train

Fig. 14/A

A detachable train

This type of train has some advantage in that at receptions where there is dancing, one can move around with ease and feel more comfortable without it.

The train is attached to the centre-back seam by loops and buttons, or by hooks and eyes and sometimes press studs. Whatever is used, make sure that they are well-secured to the back of the garment.

*A band of ruched netting (which is optional) is stitched between the lining and the top layer of fabric. This increases the fulness of the train in the hollow of the CB and enhances the shape of the silhouette.

At a glance, the train in this photograph looks as though it's attached to the skirt. The silhouette should always have a uniqueness about it.

Fig. 15

Fig. 16: There are three parts to this pattern. It is an adaptation from the style shown in ***Fig. 15***, and has a bow stitched above the sash.

Fig. 16/A: The net padding piece is made from a firm and coarse netting that would provide a bustle effect for the CB waist.

Note: To make a netting strip, make the strip approximately 16cm (6 ¼") long and three times the width across the back. Gather up the two rows of tacking stitches and stitch between the two layers: one of lining and the other of fabric. The waist seam of the train for these layers have already been gathered to the correct measurement. To neaten the seam edge, bind it with a 4cm (1¼") bias cut strip. If you plan to use rouleau loops, make sure to encase these between the seam of your lining and the bias strip.

Fig. 16/B: **(A)** The full-length train has a *top layer* and an *underlayer* or lining, and is cut with a straight edge across the top to a gathered width. This measurement fits into the required amount taken across the hollow of the CB. The hemline of the lining is optional. It can be straight or curved to the shape of the top layer as illustrated.

Fig. 16/B

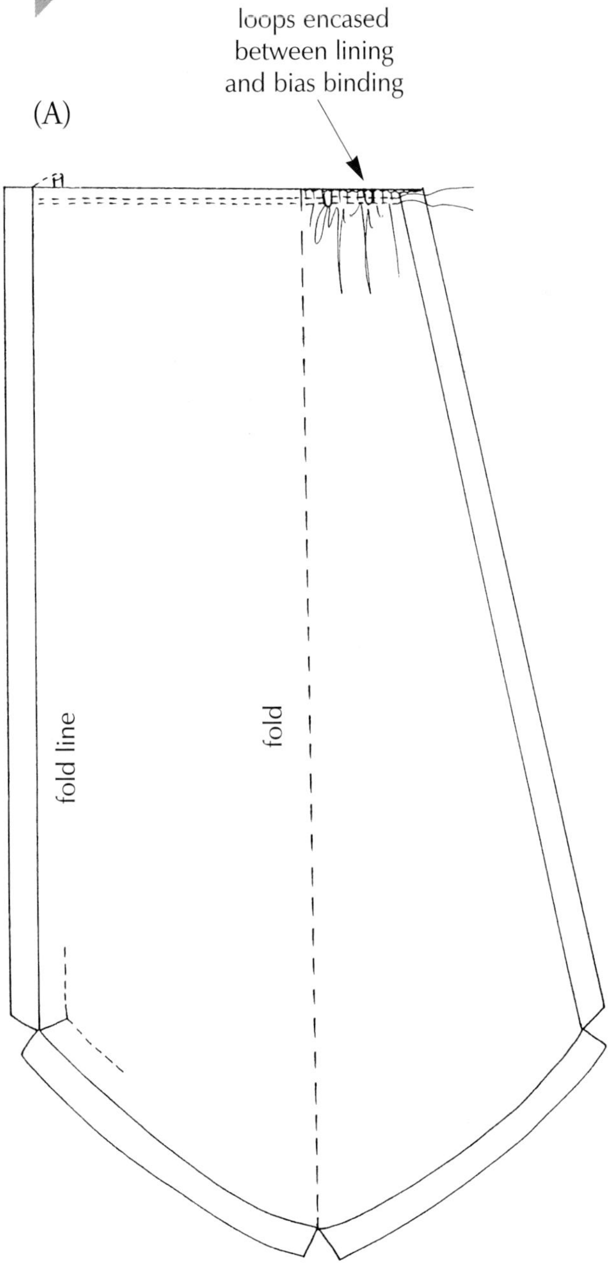

(A)

loops encased between lining and bias binding

fold line

fold

Fig. 16/A: Net padding piece

net padding stitched between top and under layers

Fig. 16: Detatchable train

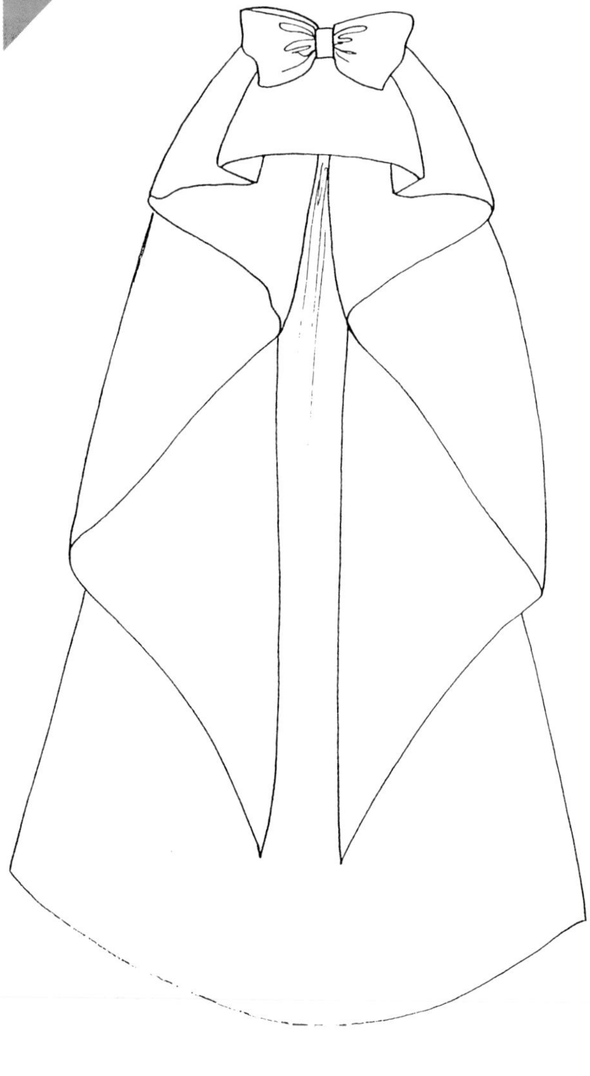

Fig. 16/C:
The draped ***overlay or sash,*** is cut on the bias. It is lined with a netting to increase its volume. Measure how long you want the sash to be, then measure how wide you want it. This would include how many folds or pleats you want for your drape.

Note
You may be restricted by the width of your fabric. Once you have drafted your pattern, toile the sash first, to achieve the drape you want, and notch the positions. *Do not iron your sash flat.*

Fig. 16/D: The bow is stitched above the sash and is made to fit across the full width of the train.

a. Make an oblong shape that is turned inside out once stitched along seam lines. The width of the bow should be at least 20cm (8") folded double. Mitre the corners before turning the right side out. This shape is also lined with netting and is not ironed flat.
b. Make up a narrow band cut approximately 8cm (3") x 10cm (4"). Fold along the length and seam together.
c. Pull the bow through this band which keeps it in position. Tuck in the raw edges and hand stitch.

Fig. 16/C: Sash

Fig. 16/D: Bow

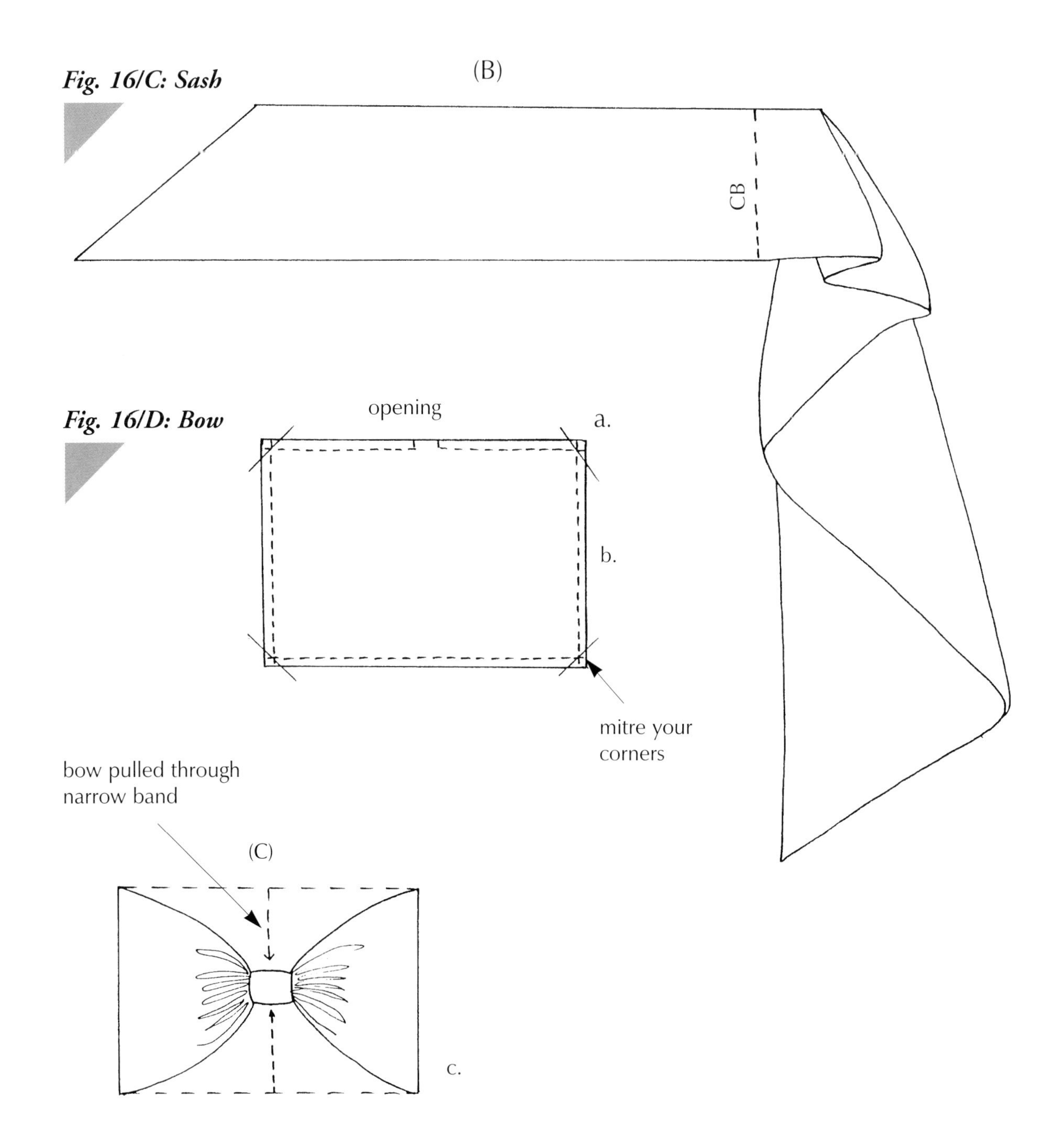

Bustles

Bustles are not commonly worn but do feature in the more extravant designer-label bridal gown, where the style has been made to suit the wearer. In the nineteenth century, corsets virtually shaped the contours of the figure. The dress was drawn up at the back in folds and pleats. The crinolette replaced the crinoline: *a cage-shaped* item (see illustrations in underskirts) which was attached at the waist and which fitted over the under garments by means of a waistband or ribbon ties. Wooden strips were first used and then horsehair frills and also a cushion effect, that would perfect the bustle. They were designed to maximise the fullness below the folds and to distort the silhouette.

These days, however, one can achieve similar effects without strapping oneself in, as illustrated under boned bodices. The desired silhouette has to have clear structural lines which fit well and curve beautifully over the figure, and the hips in particular. ***Fig. 17***: the bustle in this photograph demonstrates an advanced method for the fitted train. There are two panels either side of the CB of the train. The lining is discussed in Part 8 under 'Underskirts'.

Fig. 17

Fig. 18/A: illustrates the draft of the two sections showing the *CB panels* which are draped and ruched to form the bustle. I've used a single dart for this draft. **a.** Close waist dart and place it into the CB opening. **b.***The train drops from the CB hip line to a suitable length as required and is reshaped at the hemline.

The side back panels are two flat panels either side of the CB, which are shaped at **c** to increase the fulness at the hem.

Note: Divide these panels to your choice, but do not make the bustle width too wide across the back. Allow the side seams of the bustle to match your bodice seams. The drape from the front is extended towards the side back panel and caught in the seam.

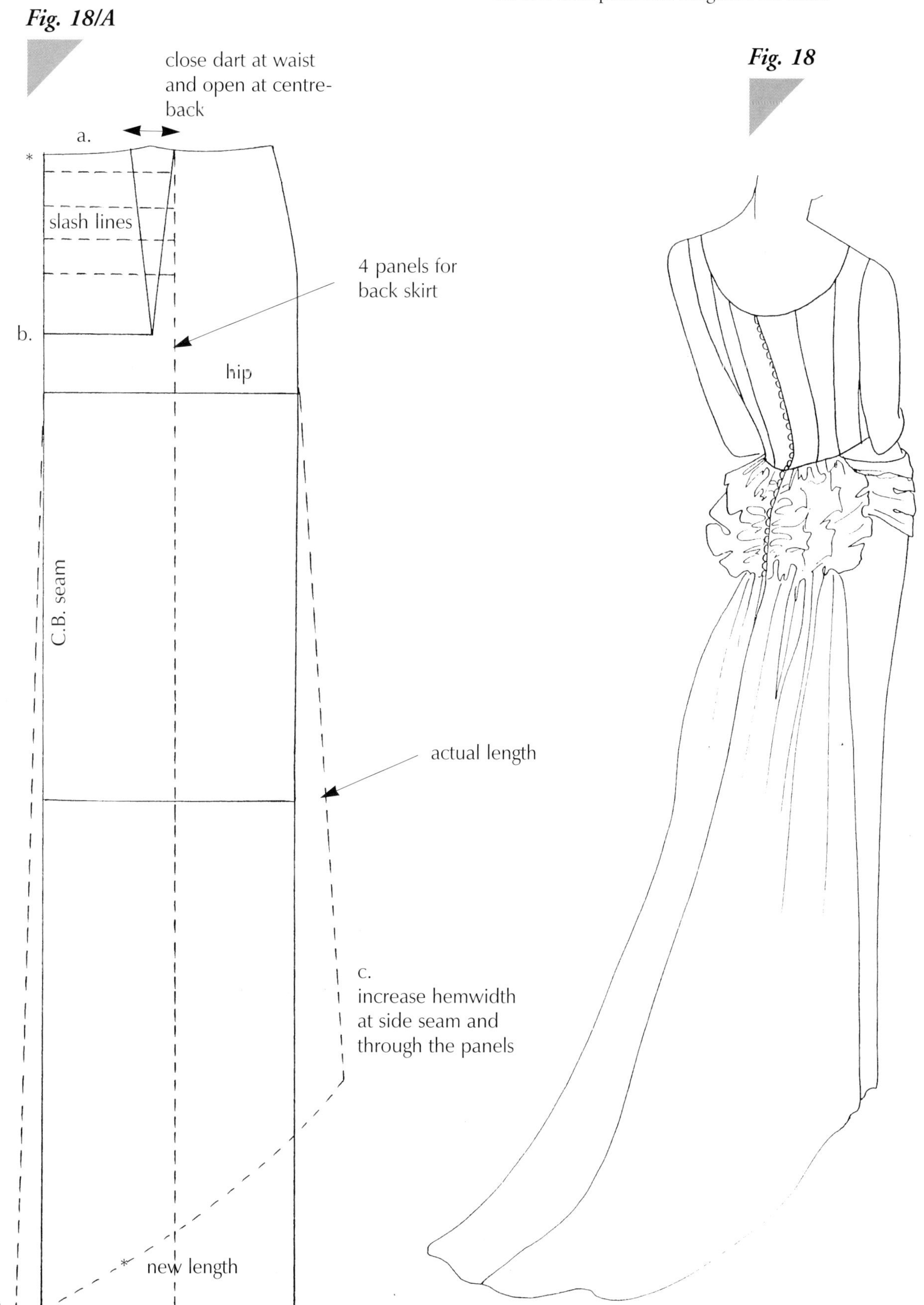

Fig. 19: The pattern layout for the CB panel
Close the waist dart into the CB seam. Measure how far down the bustle position is to be and slash through evenly from this point to nothing at opposite seam, through to waist seam. Reshape the curved CB seam to the required fulness for the bustle. Increase the width of the hemline at the CB and side seam from the hip position.

Fig. 19/A: Trace off the pattern and slash through the opposing side to nothing at CB seam to the required fulness.

Note: You can slash through the entire panel for the bustle, eliminating the second method. However, I find following through these various stages, retains the shape of the pattern far better but either way is acceptable.

Fig. 19/B: This side back panel is cut to the foundation pattern and increased at the hemline to match the corresponding seams. Mark in your notches to tie in with the draped yoke when positioned into that seam.

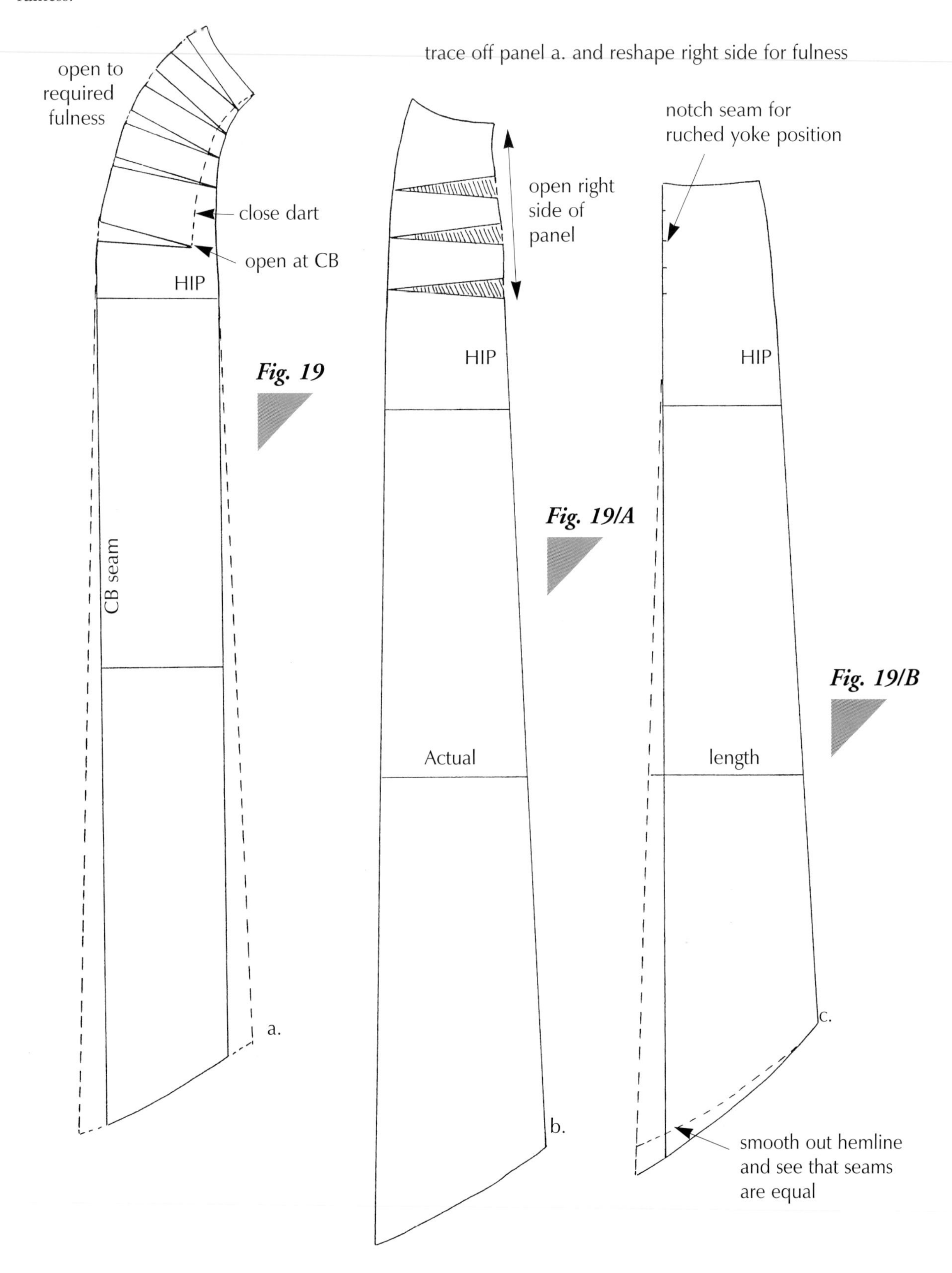

Underskirts

PART 8

Hooped petticoats

In the past, underskirts were not only worn as a fashion statement of the period, but they were also made to keep the wearer warm. However, the primary function of some of the *undergarments* during the Victorian period, were to shape the figure by exaggerating or diminishing it, especially at the waistline and hips. Where the underskirt became visible from beneath the dress, it was trimmed with lace, embroidery, or broderie anglaise. Sometimes several layers were given this treatment to increase the fulness of the skirt. Over this, a hooped petticoat was worn and made from many types of materials. Steel strips, in one method, were covered by coarse linen and some hoops were made with horsehair.

Today, its primary function is to be worn as an additional layer under the bridal gown to increase its fulness and to prevent irritation against the skin from coarse netting. Very seldom do we see the petticoat worn as a feature, except perhaps when the dress interprets a period style. All bridal gowns are lined, with some having three or more layers, and others having one, as discussed in this text. Hooped petticoats are made in polyester cotton or nylon, with a stiff polyester rigilene strip encased between bias-cut binding. Various styles can be bought or hired from bridal shops. When making one yourself, decide which type would suit your dress shape. A *fully gathered waist* on the dress, could have an elasticated waist seam. To prevent unnessary bulging at the waist on *low-waisted* fitted bodices, allow the gathers to fall from a yoke seam on the net petticoat. The yoke (or basque) is normally made to waist and hip measurement.

Fig.1-2 illustrates two styles of hooped petticoats. The first one is tiered with three hoops, worn mainly under skirts with full gathers from the waist. The second one has one hoop at the hemline, worn mainly under skirts which have no gathers that fit at the waist or under the bust and which bellow at the hemwidth. However there are no fixed rules about these things. What looks good on the day is what matters.

Fig. 1: Three hoops

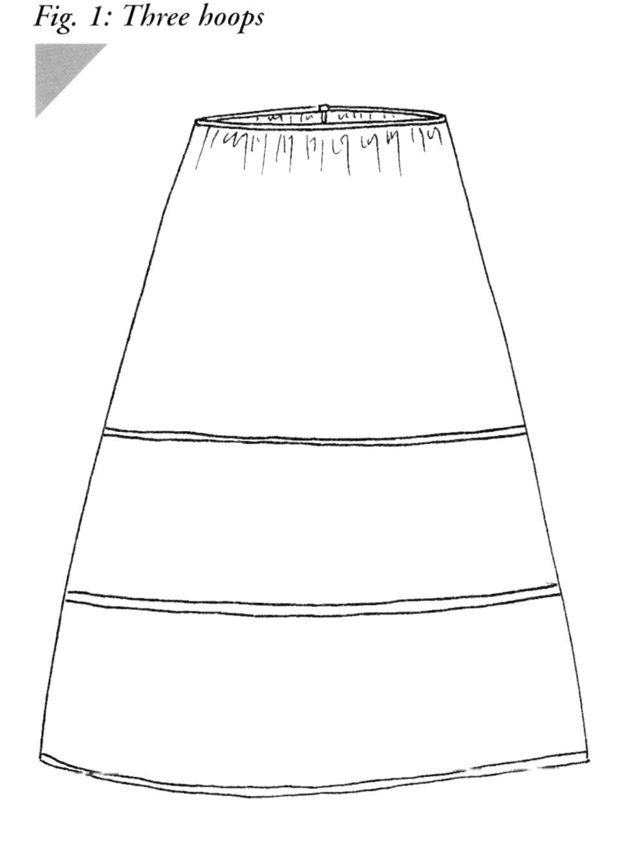

Fig. 1: One hoop at hemline

Preparation (for the three-tiered hooped petticoat)

Fig. 3: **a-b** is approximately one-and-a-half times the hip measurement. **a-c** is the required length and **c-d,** the new hip measurement + 30cm (11¾") approximately for the hemwidth. Allow a 3cm (1¼") turnback on the waistline (**e-f**) for an elastic channel (the width is 1.5cm) (⅝"), and thread through to the actual waist measurement.

Fig. 4: Stitch a bias cut binding across each seam of the tiers, including the hemline. The finished width is approximately 1.5cm (⅝"). Secure one seam end 1.5cm (⅝") away from the raw edge to the actual seam line, by bar-tacking that position. When threading the rigilene through, it stops short and doesn't penetrate the turning. Bar-tack the other end once this is done. When the seam edges are neatened, they are opened out and ironed flat.

Fig. 3

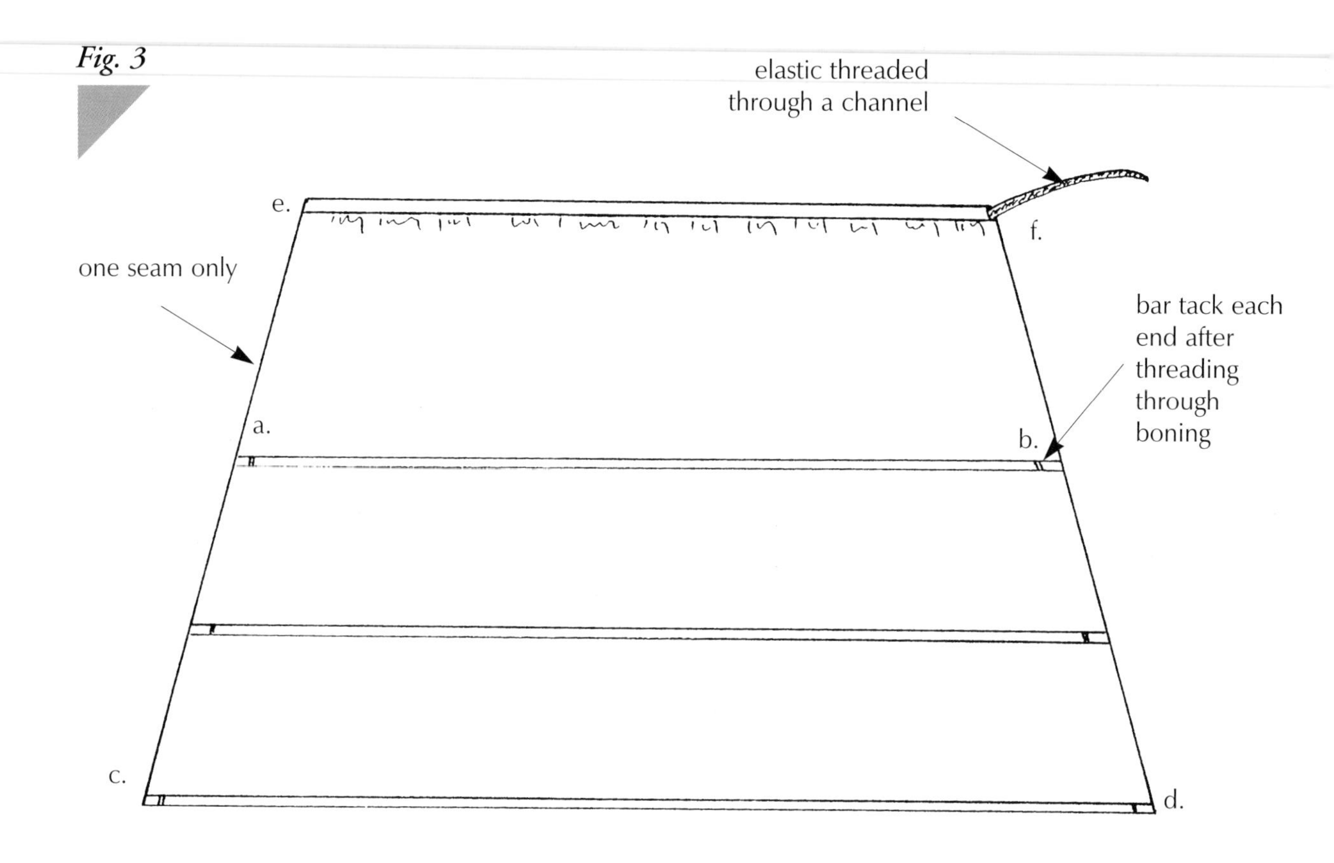

Fig. 4

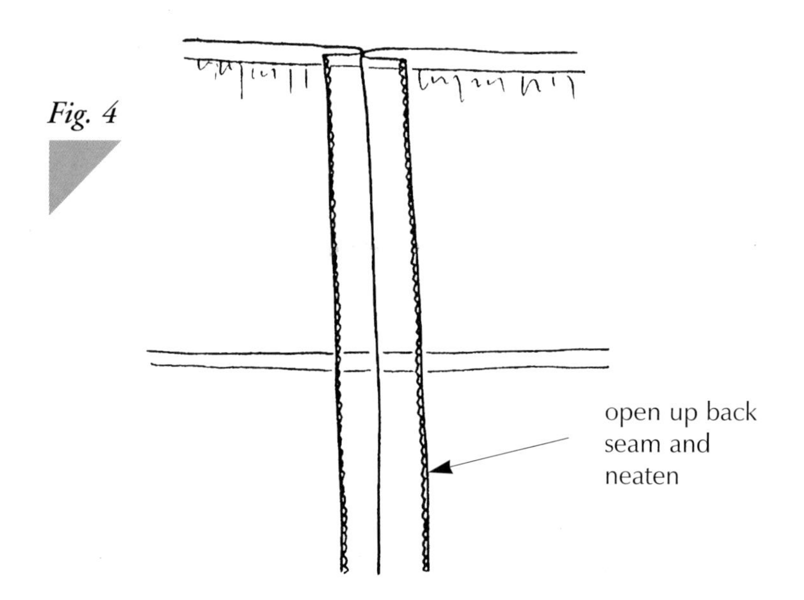

Tiered petticoats

An underskirt of several layers of netting produces a similar effect to the hoop but with a much softer look and feel to the garment. It would depend largely on the effect the wearer wants to achieve. When making your own, a muslin or anti-static lining should be sewn beneath the netting and worn against the skin to prevent irritation. However, a softer, silkier netting can work as effectively against the skin.

The anti-static lining on most net petticoats is made with a flat front and back yoke on which a tiered skirt of netting is hung. Gathers fall from the high hip or hip measurement into several rows of tiers depending on the length of the dress. The *waistband* is sometimes made to waist measurement by using a satin finish ribbon (approximately 2.5cm/1" wide) with a satin bound opening at the back fastened with two small buttons, as seen on ***Fig.*** *7/A,* or it is drawn in with elastic. The second tier is always made up to three times in diameter of the first tier, and gathered onto the edge of the first tier, as shown in the example below (***Fig.*** *5*). Once you have these layers of netting sewn together, use a *matching colour* satin ribbon to match the lining and netting, and neaten the top edge of the netting by stitching the flat part to the yoke seam of the lining. For the shape in ***Fig.*** *6* only one layer of netting is sewn onto the hemline of the petticoat, commonly worn under bridesmaids' dresses.

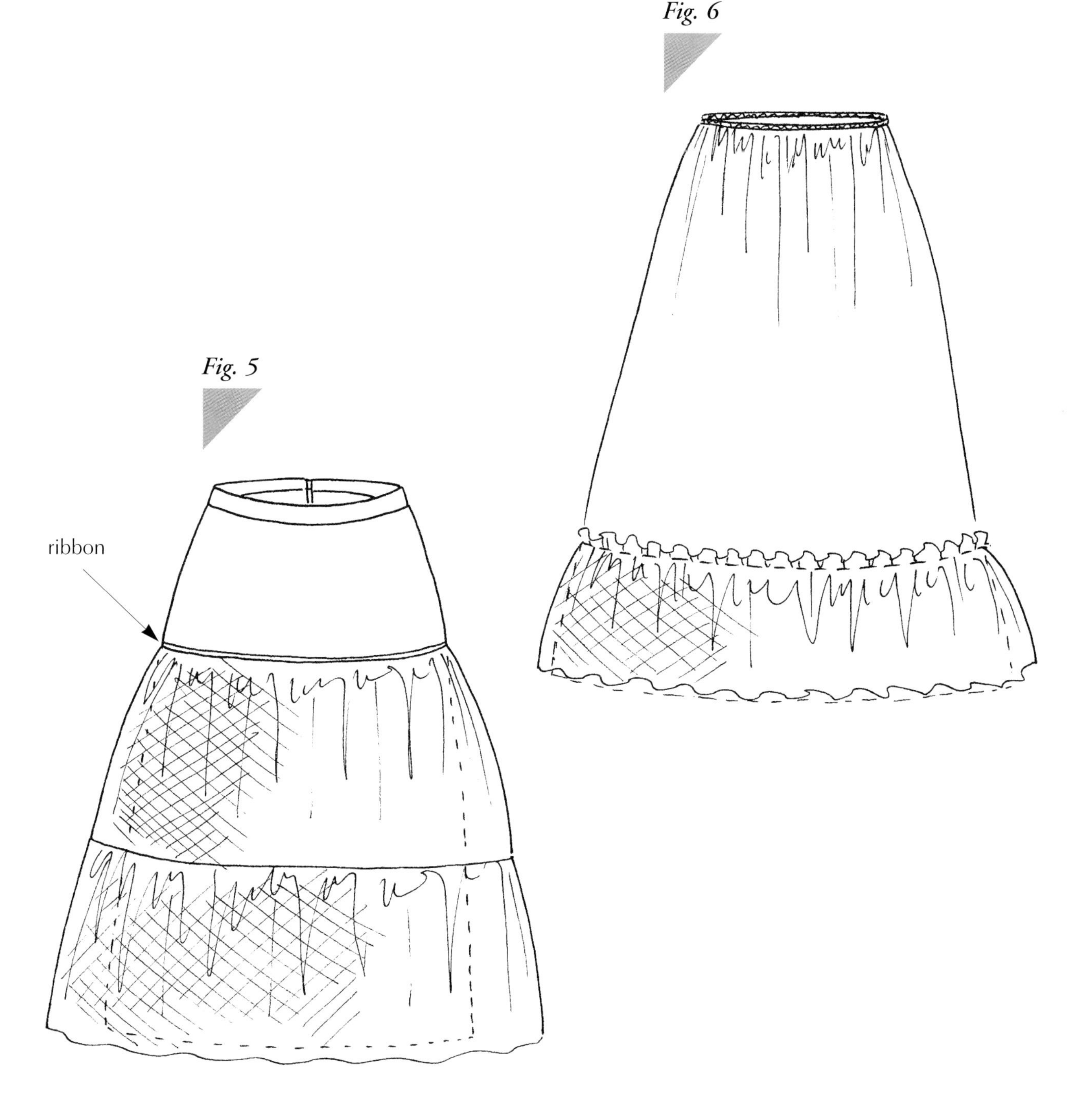

Preparation (on the three-tiered skirt)

Measure down **a-b** from the waist to approximately 18cm (7") or to where your hip measurement is. The yoke or basque is made to waist and hip measurements, with some ease of movement on the hip. Each tier **b-c** is cut equally from the yoke seam down to the hemline. With each panel, *gather 3x1* (three times as much) to the measurement it is stitched onto. The layers of tiers are optional and the lining is always A-line shaped from waist to hem. Neaten the hem edge with a narrow lace trim, ribbon or a zig-zag stitch (*Fig.7*).

Fig. 8: The petticoat is opened out flat and a channel, with a finished width of 1.5cm(5/8") for the elastic, is attached to the waist line. The elastic is cut to the actual waist measurement. The depth of frill at the hem edge is optional and is made *3x1* for gathers. Two rows of tacking stitches are sewn below a heading of the frill, which is made approximately 2.5cm wide (1"). This actually increases the fulness of the frill under the top layer. Before attaching the frill to the petticoat, neaten the raw edges on either side with a zig zag stitch as seen in *Fig. 8/A.*

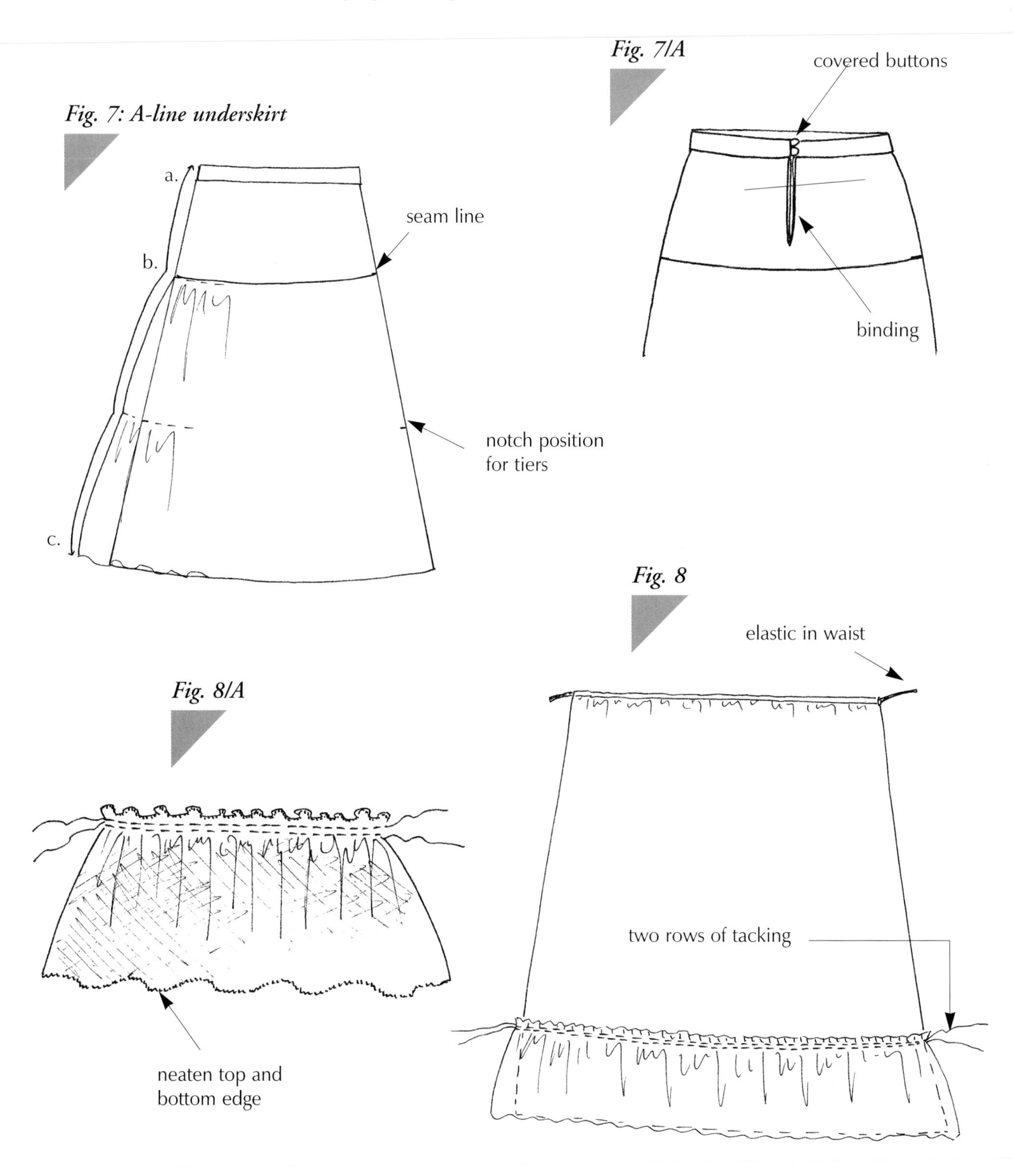

Underskirts for trains

For most styles, an *underlining* is as important as a *lining*. For example, to have *three layers* on a very full skirt is not uncommon. This would include the *top layer*, the fabric of your choice; an under layer (or underlining) of netting which is attached to the top layer to reinforce it and give the skirt body; and the *lining* which hangs loose and is only attached at the waist seam and along the CB opening. Not all dresses need the underlining, especially when the dress is in soft, fluid fabric. However, when the train forms part of the dress, there are two ways to create fulness to the underskirt. One can either wear a hooped petticoat with train, or make a tiered layer of netting, which is attached to the lining at the waist, and has tiers starting mid-way between hip and knee.

Figs 9 - 9/A: To do the second version, the first layer is normally a flat piece of netting taken from the lining pattern, starting from the waistline and hanging free. Thereafter, one would adopt the same principle as on tiered skirts, of applying two or more widths of tiers to form the required layers of netting. Then neaten the hem edge with a narrow ribbon of your choice and matching colour.

Fig. 9: Side view of underskirt with train

Fig. 9/A: Back view

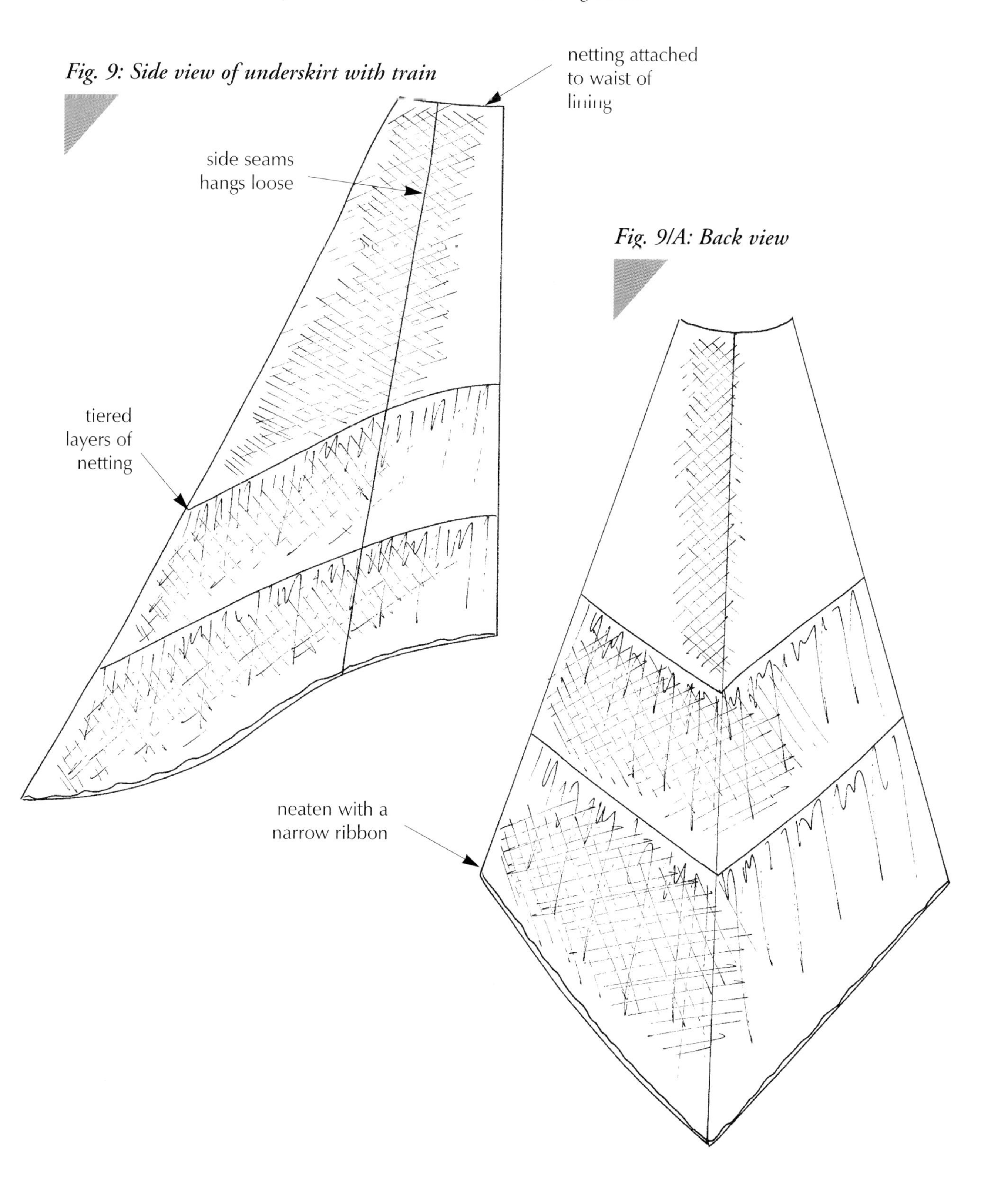

For a *hooped train* (***Fig. 10***) *reshape* the skirt from *waist* to *hemline,* taking a measurement from ground level. Use the hip measurement, where you have allowed plenty of ease, as a guide to how wide you want the hemline to be (at least twice that of the new hip measurement). This shape has *only one seam* at the centre-back of the petticoat. The tiered widths for your hoops are made according to personal taste as seen in ***Fig. 10/A***. From **a-b** at the waist seam, the CB seam is lengthened by the required amount at **c-d.** Remember to reshape the angle for the train (to suit your style of dress), starting at the point from the hem width at c-d, and draw a line to **a-b**.

Note
To make up this style, use the method described in ***Fig. 3***, under'Hooped Petticoats'.

Fig. 10: Hooped petticoat with train

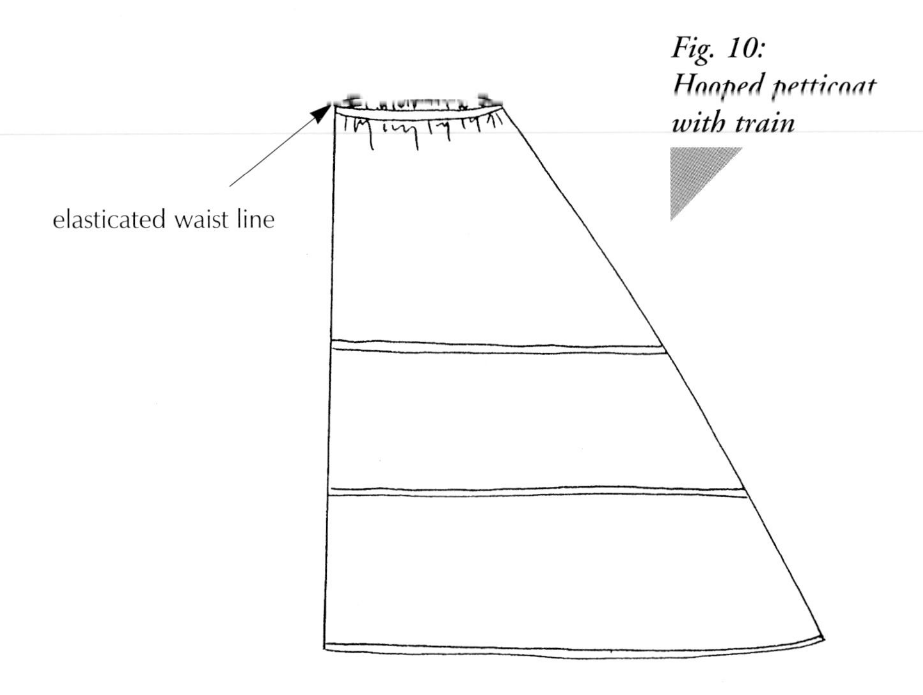

Fig. 10/A

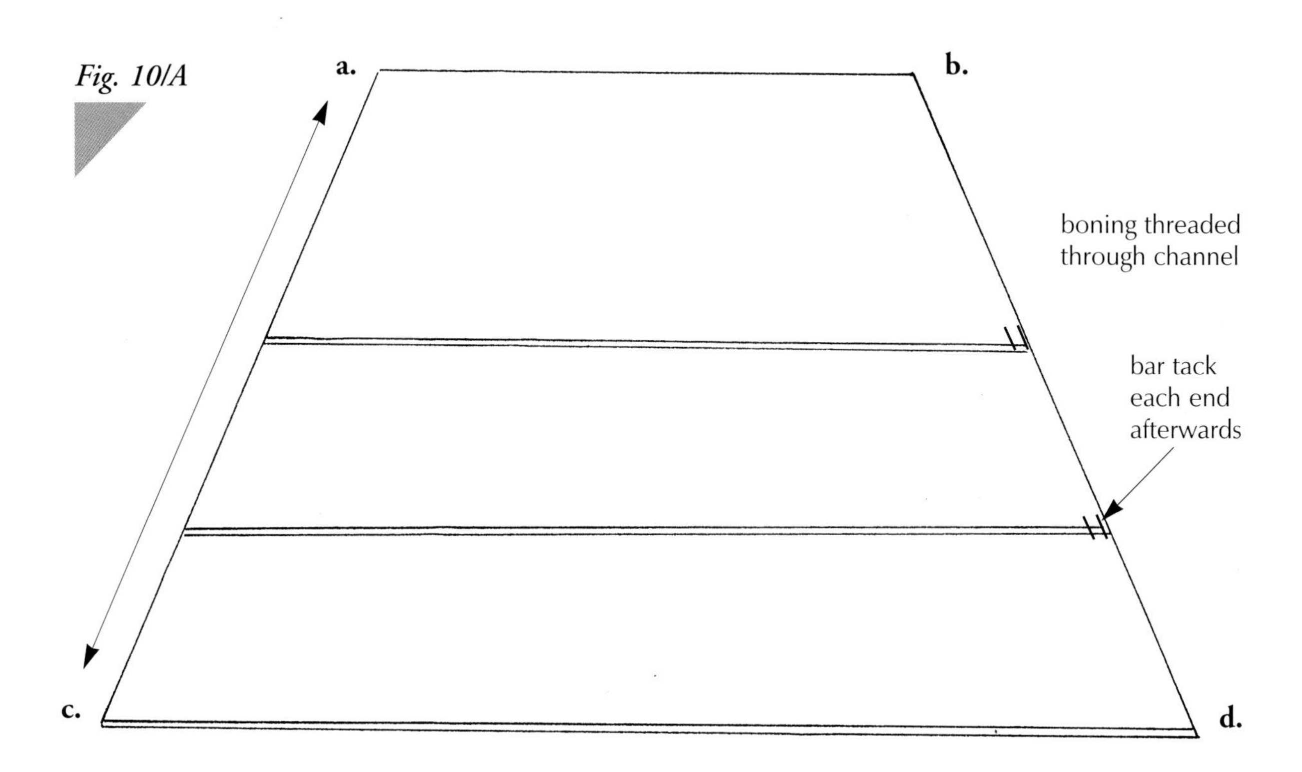

Underskirts for bustles

Reshaping the underskirt for a bustle

There are several different methods used to increase fulness at the centre-back of the skirt. In this text we deal with the following:

Fig. 11 is the underskirt which is the lining of the silhouette shown in *Fig. 18* in Part 7. This shape is normally made to the measurements of the foundation pattern and is either gathered, or hung straight from the waist and only attached at the CB opening. See illustration *Fig.18/A* in Part 7.

Fig. 12 is the cushion effect which is stitched between the lining and the top layers, and where the skirt opening is at the side seam.

Figs 13-14: the *Crinolette* attachments to the waist in the late 1800s were made from wire strands and horsehair (as discussed in Part 7 under 'Bustles').

These are two illustrations among many, loosely based on what the original shapes looked like from which so many of the creative inspirations for bustles come from.

Preparing for the lining: Fig. 11

a. Before preparing to reshape the top skirt pattern, trace the CB back panel to where the dart is of the foundation pattern. The second part of the pattern is left unchanged.
b. Add the required amount for gathers between notches on the waist seam. Ignore the waist dart and use it as part of your gathers.
c. The CB panels are attached to the side back panels of the lining, which are not gathered and hang loose from the waist. These panels are also attached to the CB opening as far down as the bottom of the opening, and secure the bustle.
d. The hem length of the lining is made approximately 4cm shorter than the actual skirt.

Fig. 11: CB lining pattern

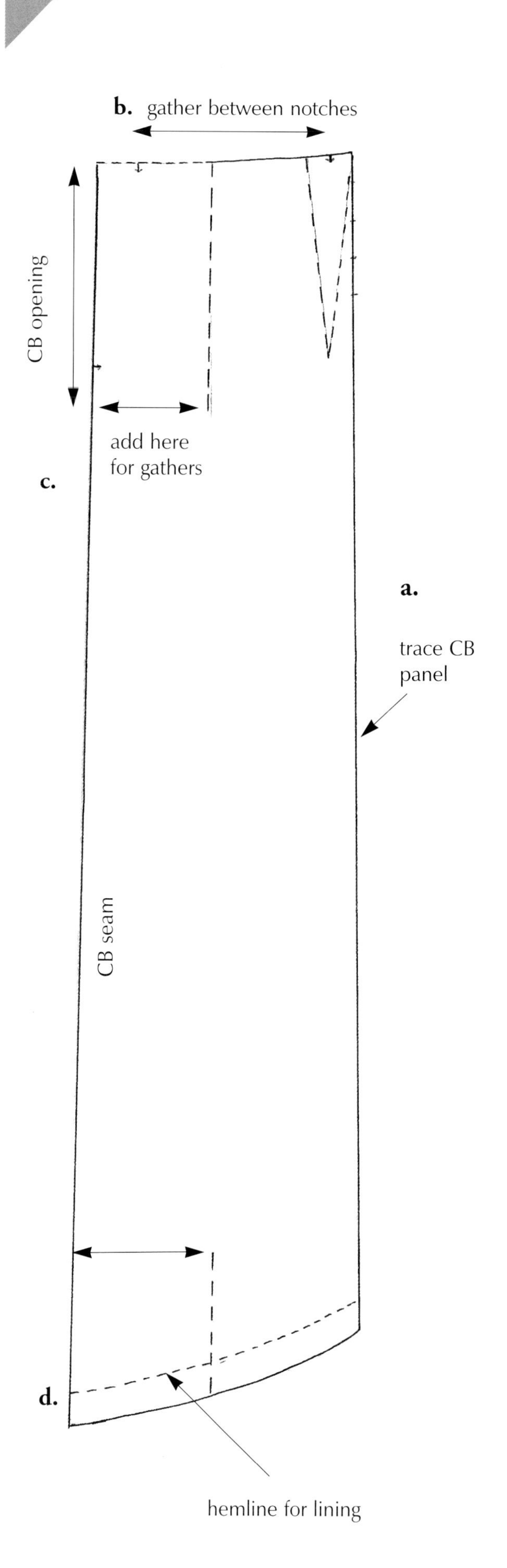

Preparing the bustle cushion

a. Measure the CB waist line from **a-b** and subtract a minimum of 2.5cm (1") from either side of the side seams in ***Fig. 12/A***, since the bustle will not be stitched into these seams.

b. Use white calico for the top layer, which is firm and has a slight sheen to it. Cut out a pattern to the measurement achieved from **a-b** and the finished length required for the cushion. Double the amount in length, with the fold line on **c**.

c. For the under layer of netting in ***Fig. 12/B*** decide how full you want the bustle or cushion to be and how deep you want the tiers to be (two in this example).

d. Once this has been established and the first half of the pattern is divided into two sections, notch each of these positions where the netting is to be stitched. Use this measurement to achieve the length for the gathers (3x1) on each section.

e. Gather and stitch each panel onto the calico. Fold up the second part of the calico to meet the top edge encasing the netting, forming a cushion shape for the bustle, as seen in ***Fig. 12.***

f. Close up the sides of the cushion and stitch the top edge between the top and bottom layers of the skirt at the waist seam.

g. This side view (***Fig.12/C***) illustrates what the cushion effect should produce on the garment.

Note: with a centre-back opening as on this style, two cushioned examples are required and placed on either side of this opening.

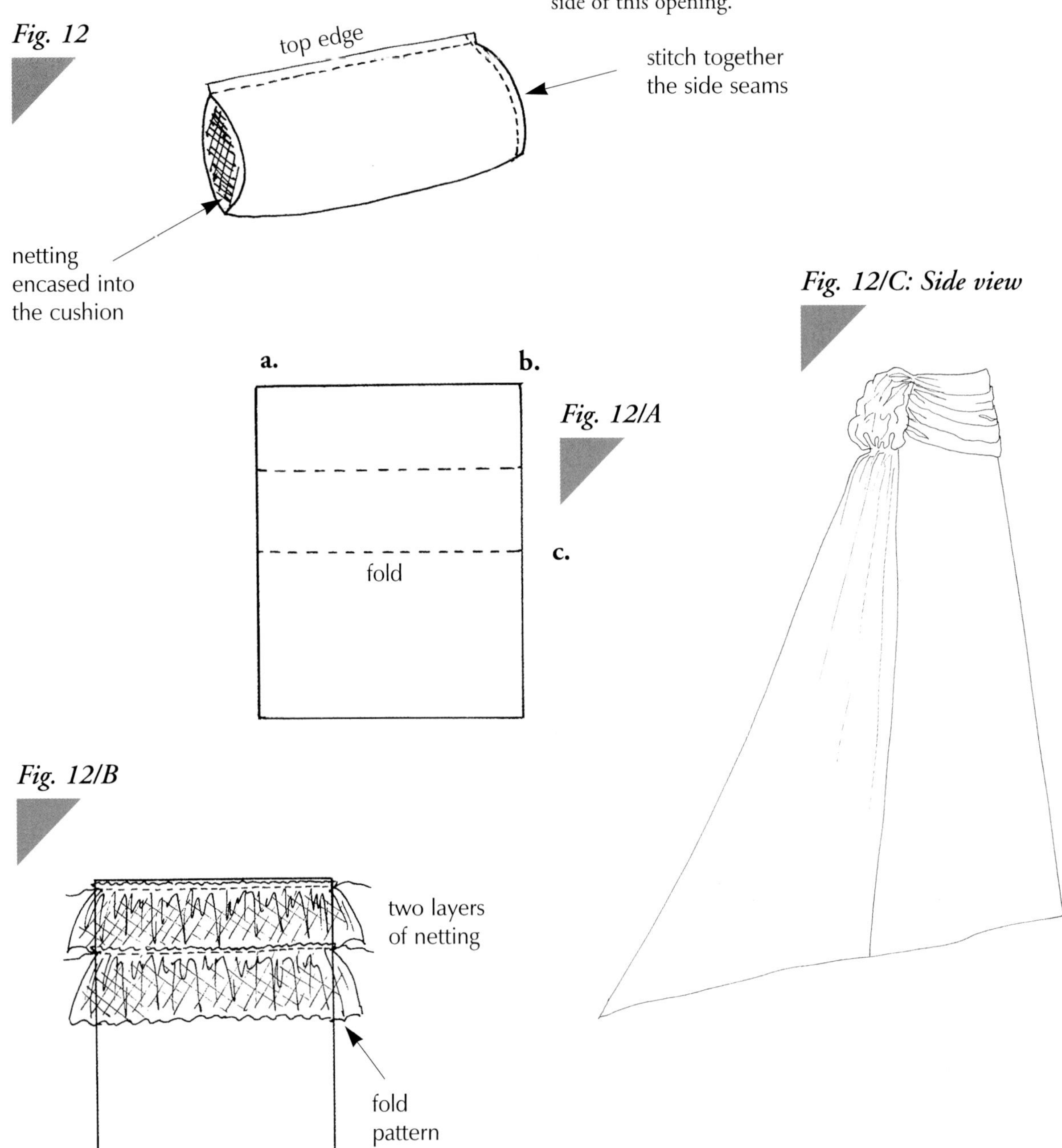

Figs 13-14: Two sorts of crinolettes worn during this period (circa mid-1800s).

Materials used for underskirts

Netting: The standard petticoat dress net is approximately 137cm (54") wide and comes in a variety of colours. Unlike other nettings, this quality is made from a stiff coarse nylon where the holes, as in other qualities of this type, are stretched into place and heat-sealed. It is also cheaper than other nettings. Tulle is used for the softer finish for underskirts and to line the top layers of the dress.

Linings: The most likely quality to use for a lining is a soft fine fabric, either silk habotai or a polyester satin. A taffetta lining is a firm quality used for skirt shapes with volume. For linings which are likely to fray, trim the edges with pinking shears or neaten with a zigzag stitch or overlock neaten. Be sure to keep the seams as flat as possible. Puckered seams look untidy and unprofessional. Where possible, do not bind the seams on the underskirt. Indentations will show onto the right side of the fabric when ironed. Change your needles often since well-worn ones can snare fine fabrics.

Ribbons: This trim is 100% polyester and is machine-washable. Used mainly to neaten seams and hem edges of the underskirt. Satin ribbons in cream or ivory are the popular colours for the bridal gown. The single satin finish, with the sheen only on one side, is suitable to use. For bridesmaids' dresses, a double satin finish may be preferable and is available in several colours and different widths, ranging from 3mm($^1/_8$") to 75mm(3"). Picot satin ribbon has tiny loops on the edges. It is a double satin ribbon used primarily for bridesmaids' dresses and comes mainly in narrow widths.

Lace edgings: A scalloped lace trim is used to neaten some petticoat edges. Make sure the heading of the lace is wide enough and strong enough to be stitched along the edge. Qualities available are shiny viscose, broderie anglaise, cotton leavers, through to cotton barmen lace. The latter has an open weave, and the heading of the lace is very delicate.

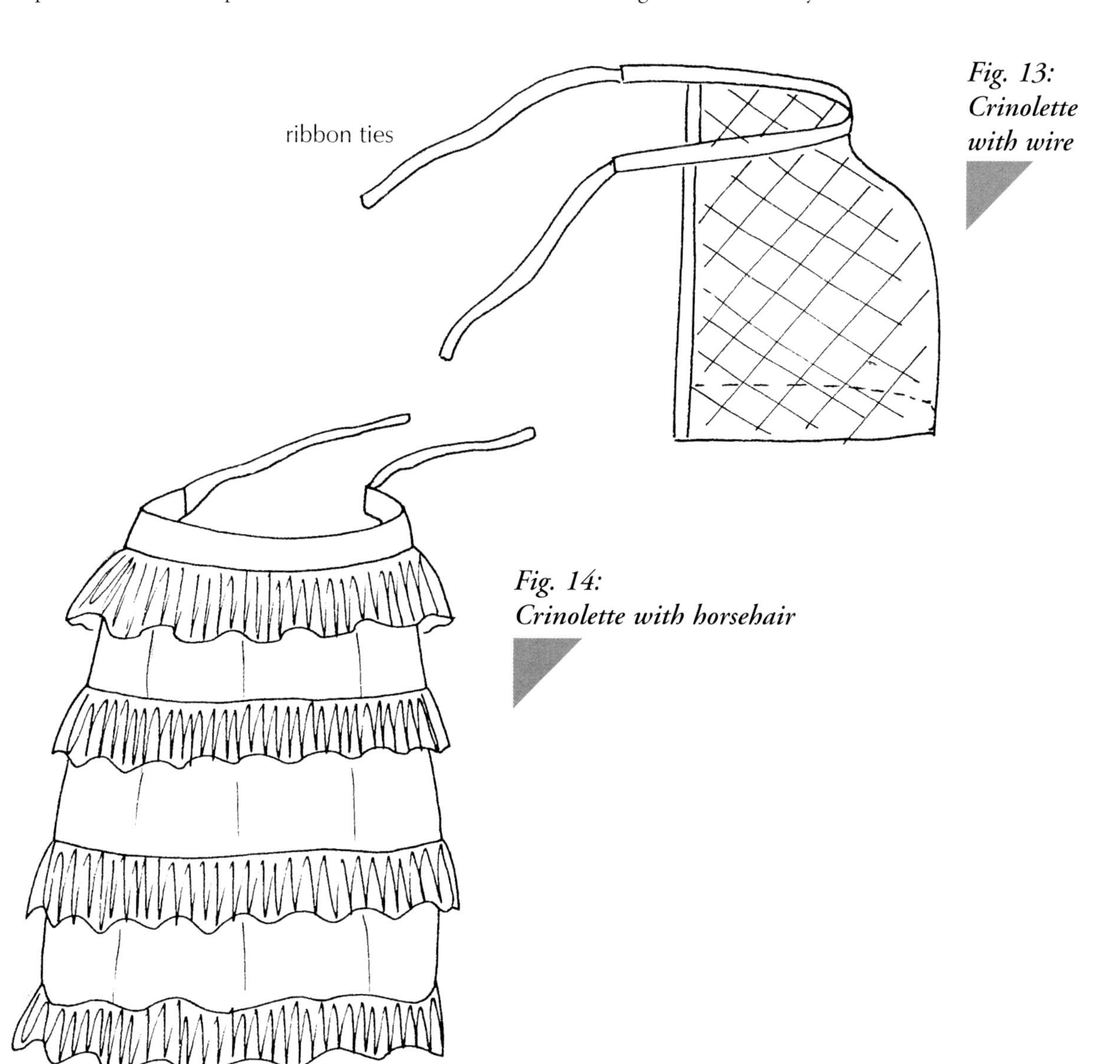

Fig. 13: Crinolette with wire

Fig. 14: Crinolette with horsehair

Materials and decorations

PART 9

Trimmings for necklines, panels, collars, cuffs and trains

There are several popular types of trimmings used on the bridalgown, some of which have been discussed in other chapters. The following name but a few: *piping, bindings, embroidery and lace edgings, bows, loops and buttons, scalloped edgings.* The overall appearance of the dress or the head-dress is particularly enhanced by the trim or method used for these areas. A practical way by which one can achieve a good effect with trimmings is by using contrasting fabrics. For instance, the rose design, used more than any other, can be expensive to buy as a ready-made trim. Bindings and pipings can also be made rather than bought. For this chapter, try out some of the methods illustrated in calico before going ahead with using the real fabric.

For a simple rose design or rosette, ***Fig. 1*** shows a photograph of roses set into a centre-front panelled bodice, with the use of contrasting fabrics and beading, to create an unusual finish to the design.

Fig. 1

Rosettes: Fig. 2

1. Decide how wide you want the folded strip to be as this will determine the depth of the finished sample.
2. The length is calculated to approximately three times the finished fulness of the actual rosette and is cut on the bias.
3. Curve each end and stitch with a tacking stitch, 1cm away from the raw edge.
4. Draw up the stitch and gather to the required fulness.
5. Cut a circle of fabric to the required measurement and hand-stitch the gathered strip onto this patch as in ***Fig. 2/A***. Tuck in all the frayed edges, then attach the finished item to the desired area of the garment.

Note

Fig. 2/B: For a more elaborate rose, fill the centre area with another contrasting fabric like netting or fancy ribbon and add to this some large beads or sequins.

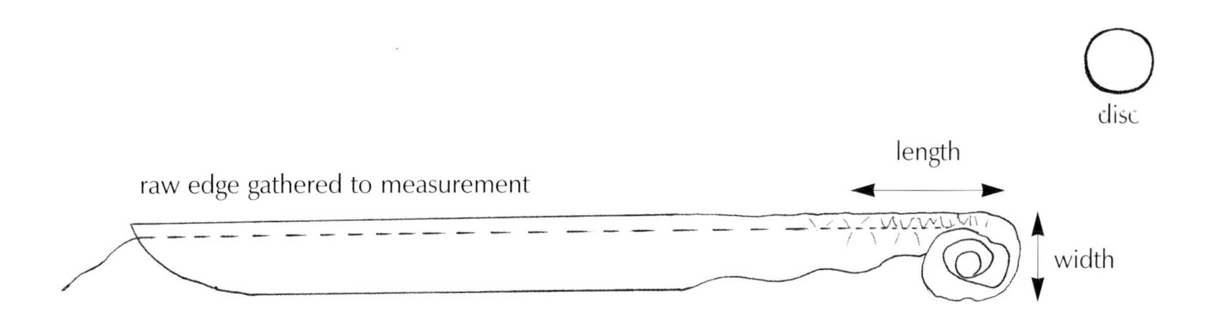

Fig. 2: Rosette

Fig. 2/A

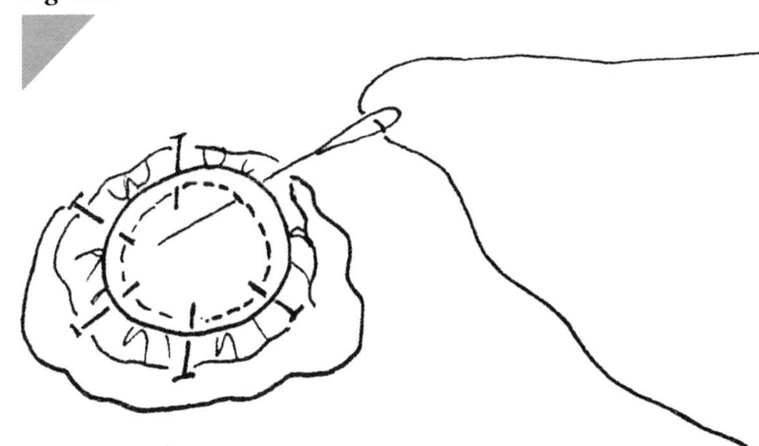

Fig. 2/B

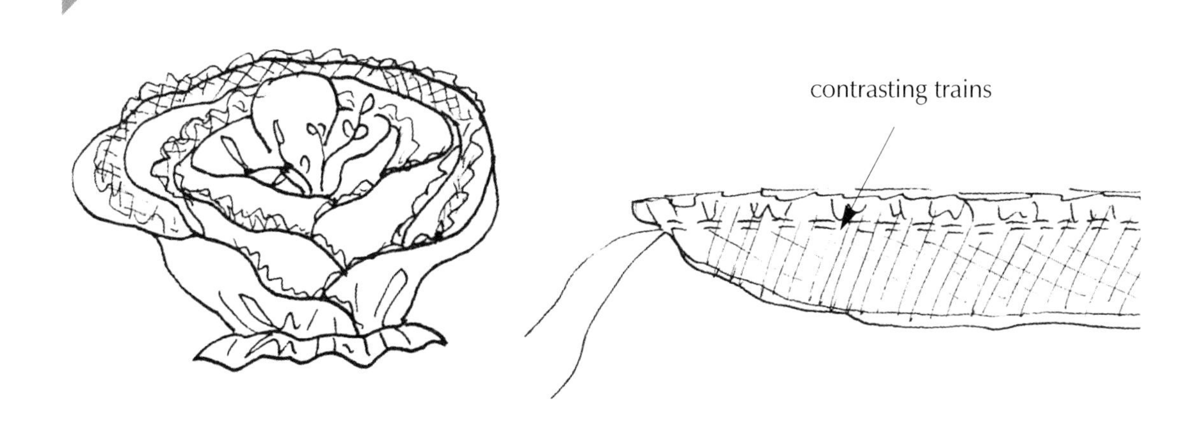

Scallops

Fig. 3 shows a scalloped hem edge as a decorative feature to a sleeve style.

a. Measure the hemwidth of your pattern piece and decide how wide these scallops are to be.
b. Divide your pattern piece into halves and quarters, so that all the scallops allocated will fit into the hemwidth.
c. Make a *template* of one scallop by folding your paper in half and measuring the depth against the width. Curve the scallop equally on either side of the fold working from the centre to seam edge.
d. Make sure in your calculations, that this template fits into the pattern width and that the side seams have an equal scallop either side of the stitch line.
e. Add 1cm (3/8") seam on the outer edge of the scallop and mitre these seams when attaching a facing as seen on the segment illustrated in this section.

Note
This method applies to other features such as necklines and hemlines. The interfacing used would depend on the quality of fabric.

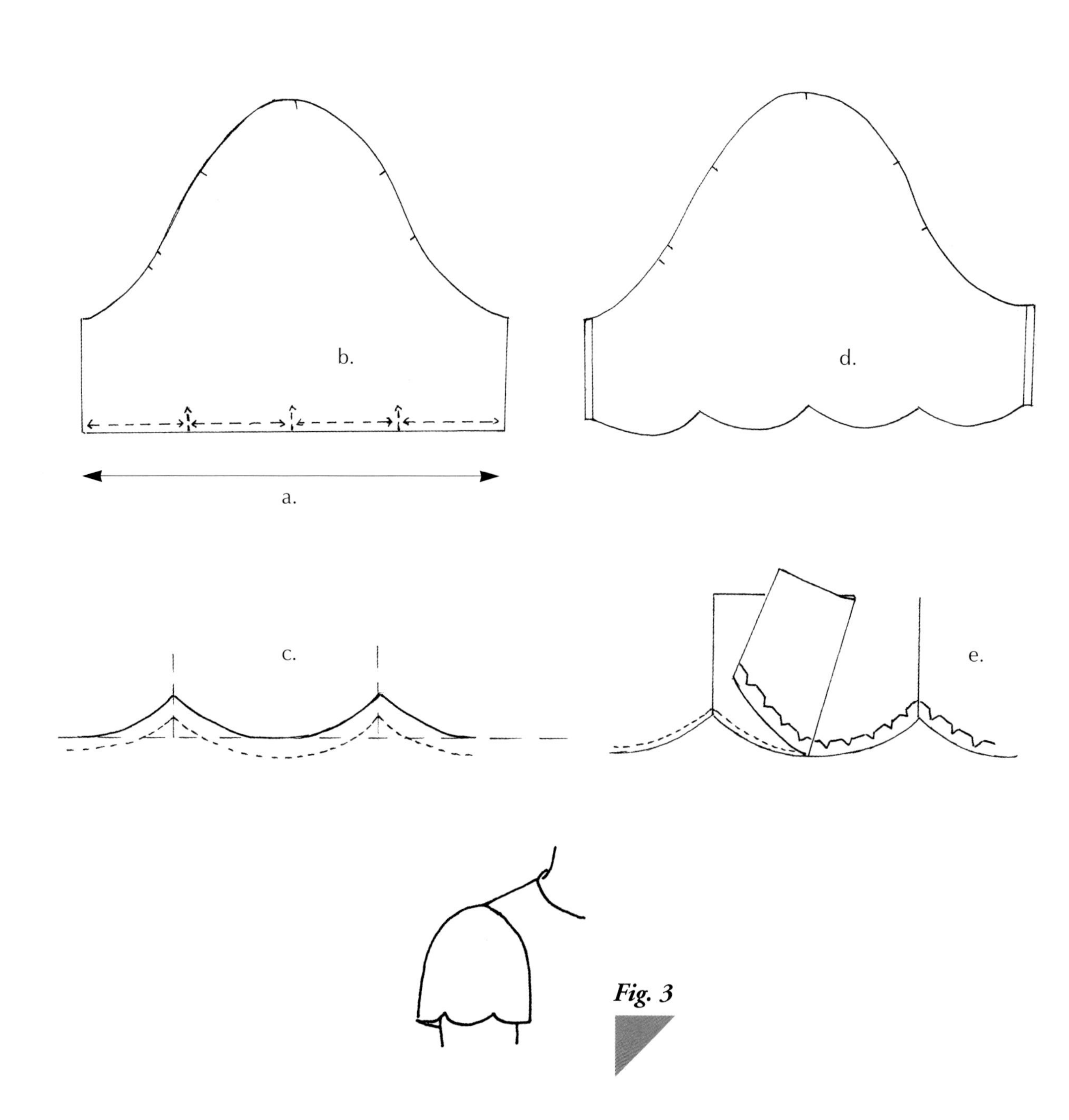

Fig. 3

Piping

This trim has a heading which is made from cord sandwiched between a folded piece of fabric, or a heading consisting of either a braided trim or beading. Either way, the trim is divided into two parts, the top half is decorative and the bottom half is the seam allowance made approximately 1cm (3/8") wide. Its function is twofold: it is normally stitched *between* seams but also along *single raw edges*. ***Fig.4*** is a square of fabric cut into bias strip widths of 4cm (1½").

Figs 4-4/A

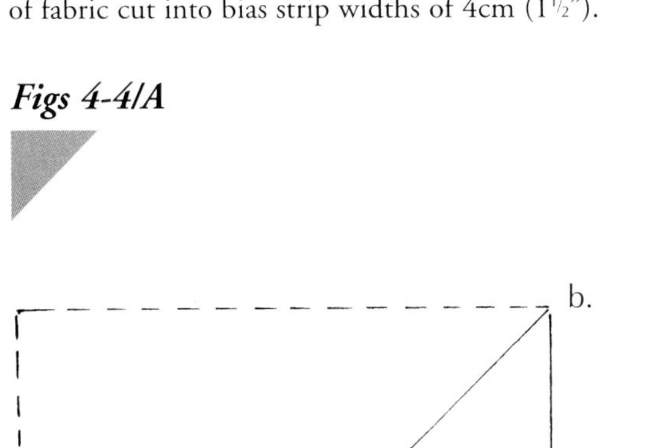

1. The selvedge is folded over at right angles to the fabric.
2. Cut through the fold from ***a-b***, so that the blade of the scissors cuts right up against the fold (***Fig. 4/A***).
3. The two pieces of fabric are pinned together and the width required is marked along the raw edge and then cut into strips. Join together these strips by placing the right sides together at right angles (45%) and stitching them 1cm (3/8") away from the raw edge (***Fig. 4/B***). For a 4cm (1½") strip, a cord width with a diameter of approximately 8mm (¼") is used.
4. Fold the strips in half and insert a length of polyester cotton cord of a width suited to your taste. Pin and stitch the fabric closely to the edge of the cord (***Fig. 4/C***). This bias-cut trim enables you to use it effectively on curved seams.

Fig. 4/B

RS

bias-cut strips joined together at right angles

WR.S

Fig. 4/C

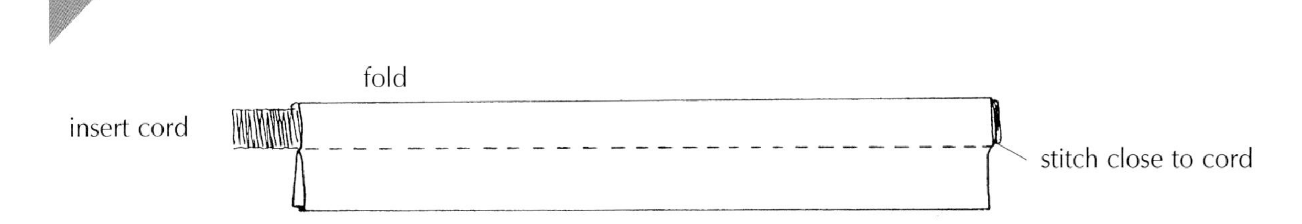

Bindings on necklines, armholes and general openings

The difference between this bias-cut trim and piping is that it is stitched flat over a raw edge or seam. The width is discretionary and the fabric type should either be the same as, or complementary to the garment. The same principle applies for each of the items mentioned above, two of which are demonstrated here, as seen in *Figs 5 - 6.*

Binding armholes: Fig. 5

For a seam which covers three or more thicknesses, especially on boned bodices, use a bias-cut binding in main fabric. Measure the seam width, then double the amount for your binding, plus the seam allowance. Cut away any frayed edges, then first stitch one side of your binding onto the right side of the armhole. Fold over the binding, tuck in your seam allowance and hand stitch the other side of your binding onto the inner side of the armhole. (***Fig.5/A***).

Fig. 5

RS garment

Binding necklines: Fig. 6

This 'V' shaped neckline is cut into at the CF to the fitting line, so that when your bias binding is stitched onto this fitting line it doesn't pucker at the point. The strips should be cut to a narrow width of 3cm (just under 1¼").

Fig. 6: Binding

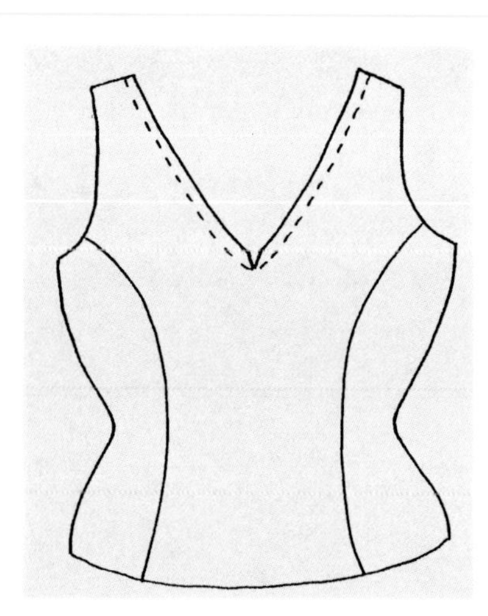

Fig. 5/A

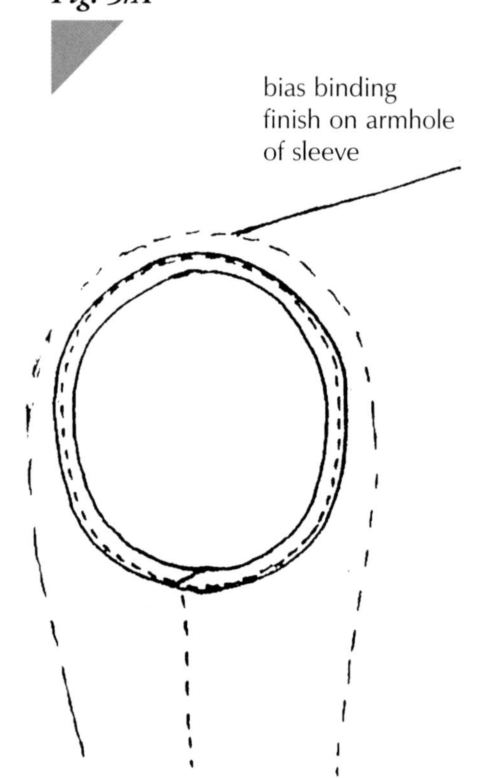

1. To join up strips of the same widths, put the right sides together at a 45% angle and stitch 1cm (3/8") away from the raw edge in much the same way as your preparation for piping.
2. Open up the seams onto the wrong side and iron flat.
3. The bias strip is stretched slightly onto the fitting line when stitched onto the neckline, and the neck edge is pulled out to almost a straight line as seen on ***Fig. 6/A***.
4. Make sure the *fabric is of a soft quality. Anything stiff will not bend around your curves.*
5. Cut away the seam width to half the amount so that the finished width of your binding is quite narrow. Hand-stitch along the folded edge (***Fig. 6/B***).

Seams

French seams: Fig 7

French seams are used for fine and sheer quality fabrics where seams are likely to show on the right side of garments. Seams are generally straight and not curved because of the method of application. It is important to tack these seams together first, especially for those cut on the bias.

1. For the first row, tack the seam on the *right side* of the garment away from the fitted line, i.e.stitch 0.4mm (1/8") away from the raw edge, using a *fine* needle.
2. Trim away frayed edges and iron the seam flat.
3. Turn the garment over onto the *wrong side* and tack and stitch the second row next to the raw edge, along the fitted line as seen in ***Fig. 7/A.*** Make sure these edges have been cleared of unwanted threads.
4. The finished seam width should be approximately 0.7mm (1/4") wide.

Fig. 6/A

Fig. 6/B

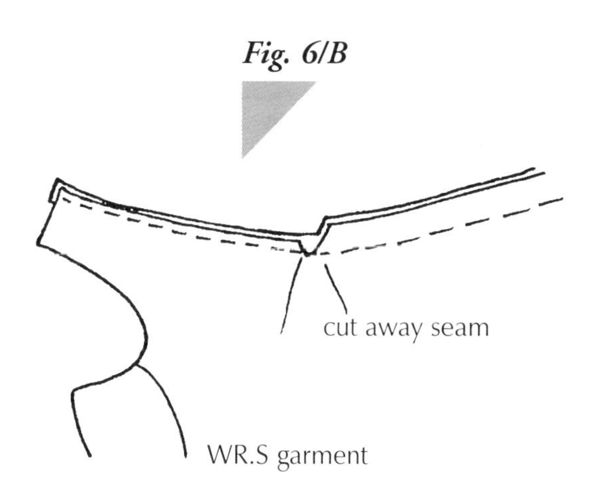

Fig. 7: French seams

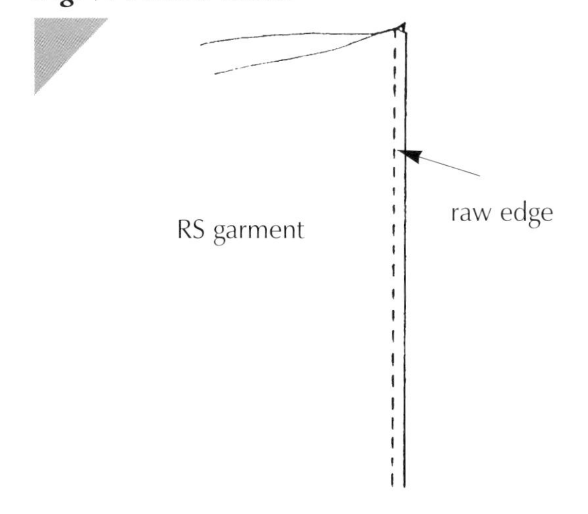

Fig. 7/A

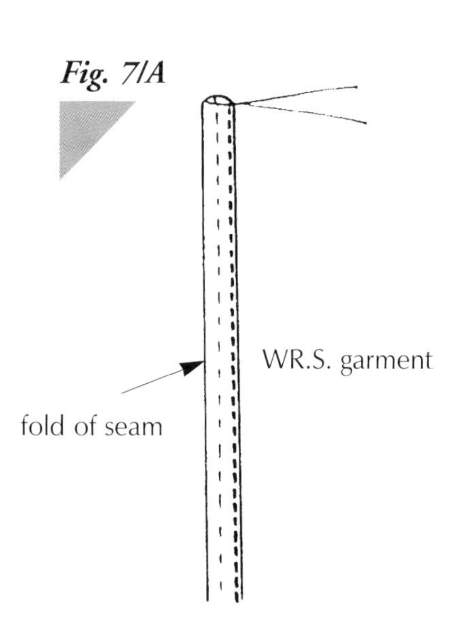

Neatening plain seams

Fig. 8: A seam width is normally 1.5cm ($^5/_8$") wide. It is important to ensure on bridal fabric that neatened edges *do not show on the right side once ironed.* A way to overcome this is to use *pinking shears* after cutting away any frayed edges. This method only works on firm fabrics.

Fig. 9: Another flat method is to *zigzag* raw edges. Once the seams are stitched through, open them and iron flat. Turn back the seam edge 0.5cm ($^1/_4$") and use a zigzag machine stitch with a suitable stitch width to cover the raw edge. This method is unsuitable for thin fabrics. For veils, using a narrow zigzagging stitch over raw edges of nettings and other textures can look very effective.

Embroidery features: collars, cuffs and yokes

For collars: Fig. 10

This design application has been discussed briefly under 'Boned Bodices' in Part 6. It is a method used in the fashion industry to produce samples for orders as part of their collections. These embroidery features are normally made to a specific design and measurement, worked out in advance for a particular shape. The design is traced out and transferred onto the pattern piece required. A template is copied from the original and sent away to the embroiderer to be made up, along with sufficient fabric and instructions for the method and design layout. This is sent off weeks before the collection is put together so that it arrives (hopefully) when the garment is ready to be made up.

Fig. 8: Pinking shears

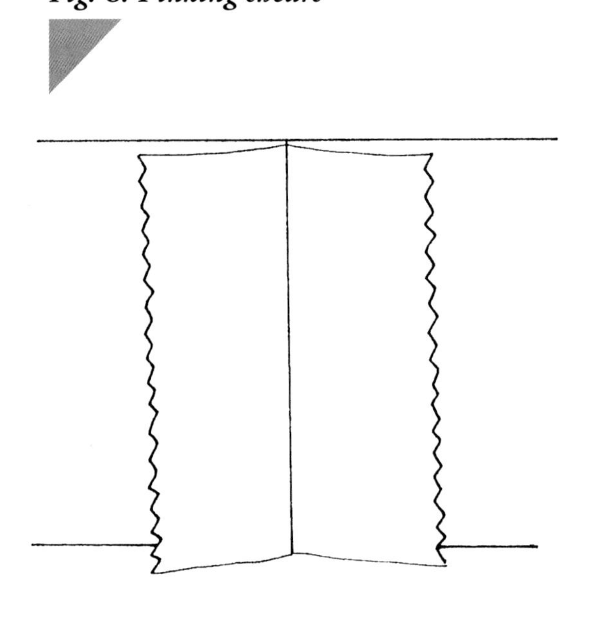

Fig. 9: Zigzag

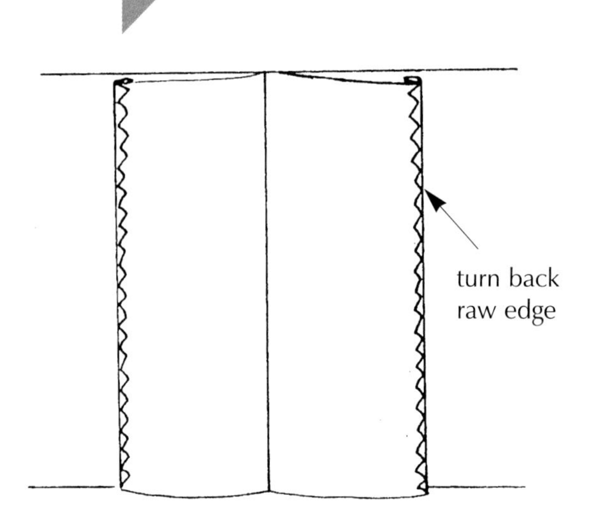

Fig. 10: Embroidery features

This method can be used for individual garments. It's an expensive but satisfying way in which to create your own design. Take the opportunity to find ideas as discussed in Part 3. Photocopy them, cut and paste pieces together, and draw from stencil designs until you are satisfied with the design of your choice. The alternative is to use a ready-made all-over embroidery design.

For those who have embroidery facilities on their machines, the next step would be to try a percentage of the design out on a swatch of fabric. This would determine the amount of stitches per square inch and colours you'd like chosen for the design.

Preparing the template

Mark out your collar pattern onto tracing paper. Lay the traced out pattern onto the embroidery design chosen and to the position required. Make sure your embroidery pattern matches on each end of the collar when it meets at the CF. (***Fig.10/B***). The design layout is marked within the perimeters of the seam allowance of 1.5cm (⅝") around the inner edge of your shape. Before it's embroidered onto your fabric, take a copy of the design by either rubbing a piece of wax over the tracing paper or take a photocopy. To secure the paper onto the fabric, pin or tack it on first of all. Allow sufficient fabric around your pattern piece for the embroiderer when it is being machine stitched. The paper is for position only and not to be stitched through.

For cuffs: Fig. 11

Apply the same method as above; matching the embroidery is optional. It is often easier to have one large piece of fabric sent off to be embroidered, especially if the designs are to be matched for both collars and cuffs. This prevents shading.

Fig. 10/A: Embroidery template

Fig. 10/B

Fig. 11: Sleeve cuff

For Necklines
Guipure Lace trimming (illustration): Fig. 12

Fig. 12 has a scalloped guipure lace edging used as a feature around this shaped neckline and waistline. The scalloped edging can be cut out to create a smaller edging if need be. (***Fig.13/A and B***) so that one part can be used for the neck edge, and the other part can be stitched onto the waist seam, (or sleeves and hem). This design is quite florid in its texture and application and is hand-stitched onto the finished garment, since the application of the scallops is effected onto the neck and waist, where part of the design hangs free, as seen in the illustration.

Fig. 13/A

Fig. 13/B

Fig. 13/A Guipure lace trim

Fig. 13/B

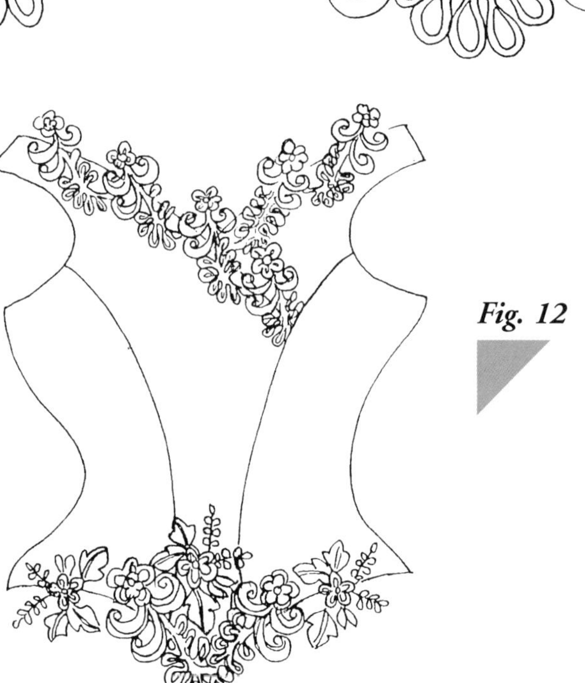

Fig. 12

Panelled yokes: embroidery appliqué lace yokes: Fig. 14

These individual motifs are sold in pairs for bodice panels which can be stitched on before or after the panels are assembled together. For styles such as these, the yokes are hand-stitched over the seams and can be unpicked when having the bodice dry cleaned. They come plain or with sequins, beads and cord.

The size and shape of the appliqué would determine the shape of the bodice. In each of these yokes the designs can be *changed* (***Fig. 14/A***) whereby the flower motifs can be stitched with the flower heads meeting at the CF, or, as in ***Fig. 14/B***, placed away from the centre-front. In the case of both shapes, the appliquéd yokes may extend beyond the waist seam depending on how low the neckline is and how deep the CF bodice is. If this is so, the yokes would need to be hand-stitched after the bodice has been stitched together.

Fig. 14: Appliqué yokes (on boned bodices)

Fig. 14/A: Flower heads meet at the C.F.

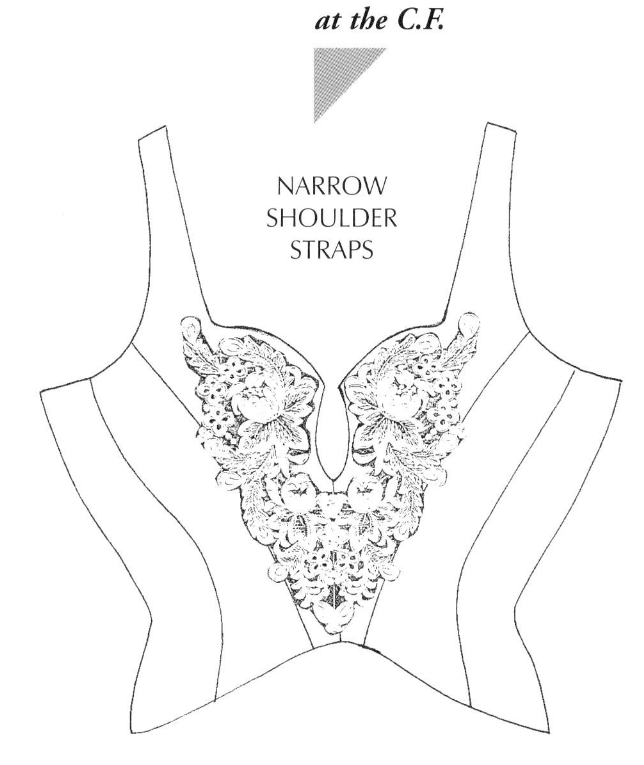

Fig. 14/B: Flower heads placed away from the CF

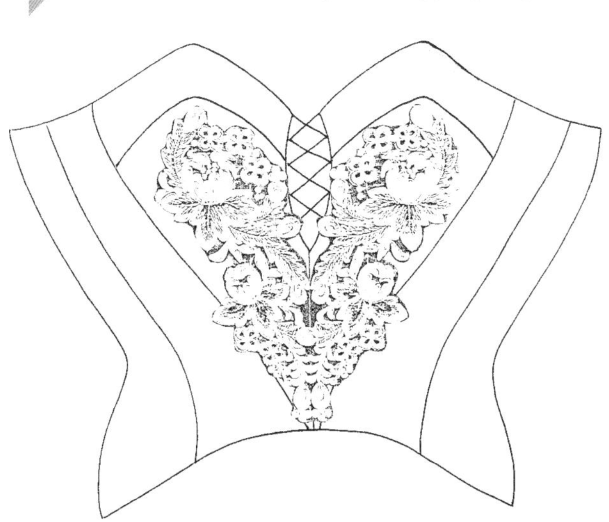

Beaded features: neckline and sleeves

Neckline: Fig. 15

The design is worked out before applying it to the pattern piece in very much the same way as the embroidery features discussed in *Fig. 11*. However, instead of sending the template away to be done, do this yourself. For shape *Fig. 15/A* first prepare the bodice panels with an interfacing, which can either be ironed-on or stitched onto the fabric (suitable for beading). The interfacing strengthens the neckline when the beading is stitched onto the fabric. Have a good selection of beading and sequins in the colours appropriate for the colour and texture of the fabric. The beaded design which is prepared for the CF panel is traced onto tissue paper and then tacked in position on the CF. Allow sufficient room for the seam allowance and fitting lines when the beads are ready to be hand-sewn onto your panel. The corners of your

Fig. 15/A: Centre front bodice panels

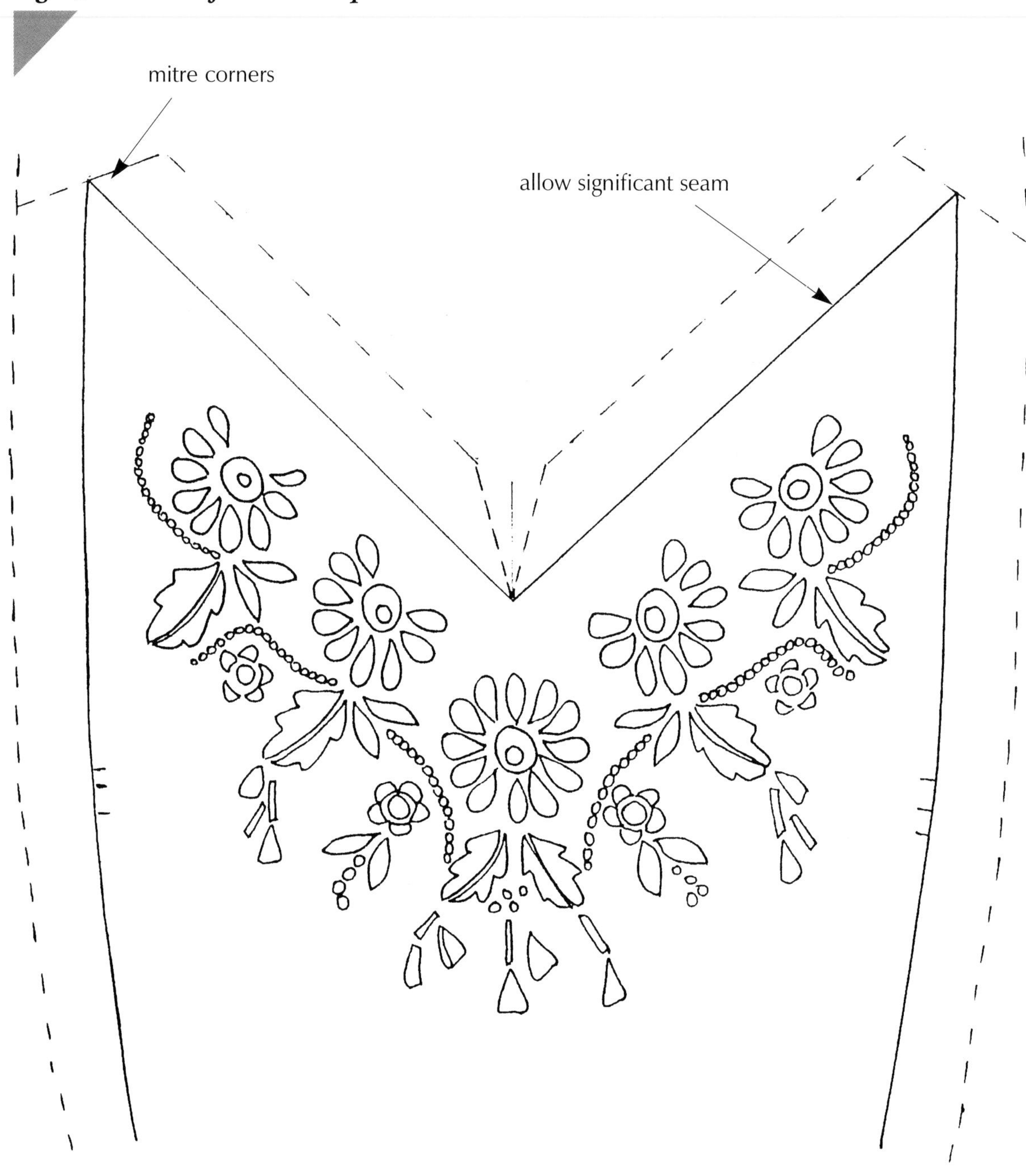

patterns are mitred as indicated on the illustrations. This helps to give the neckline and sleeves a clean finish. Use a beaded needle and strong cotton to sew through the tissue paper. Once your design is completed, tear the tissue paper away from under the beads. This is a simple way to stitch beading onto a shaped surface and one that I've often used. The photograph is such a design.

Sleeve edge: *Fig. 15/B*

Make up the pair of sleeves to the beaded design that matches your bodice. The corners of the sleeve pattern are mitred in the same way as those of the centre-front panel seen in *Fig. 15/B.*

Fig. 15: Neckline

Fig. 15/B: Sleeve (wrist section)

Accessories

PART 10

Accessories for bridalwear have become an industry in their own right. Designs from the most lavish to the very simple are now available to buy. However, it is possible to make your own with the correct materials and trimmings. Some trims are expensive but usually only a small quantity is needed to create the perfect look. Embellishments such as lace, silk flowers, beading and waddings can be glued or hand-stitched on. The accessories shown in this chapter represent but a few of the things which can be done by yourself. There are professional sources which can be approached for more ornate and elaborate accessories.

Head-dress selection

Firstly, decide what you want to do and then select the components suitable for your creation. The area to concentrate on is the centre of the head, above the nose and eyes. From this position work your way along either side, creating a mirror image of the design. The shape of the face, hair style, colour and design of the dress will to some extent determine what the style of the head-dress should be. Once this is achieved, the veil, if worn, will be your next project. With an elaborate head-dress, one would opt for a plain veil. The length and fulness is a personal decision, but do bear in mind the height and weight of the bride.

Fig. 1: Equipment

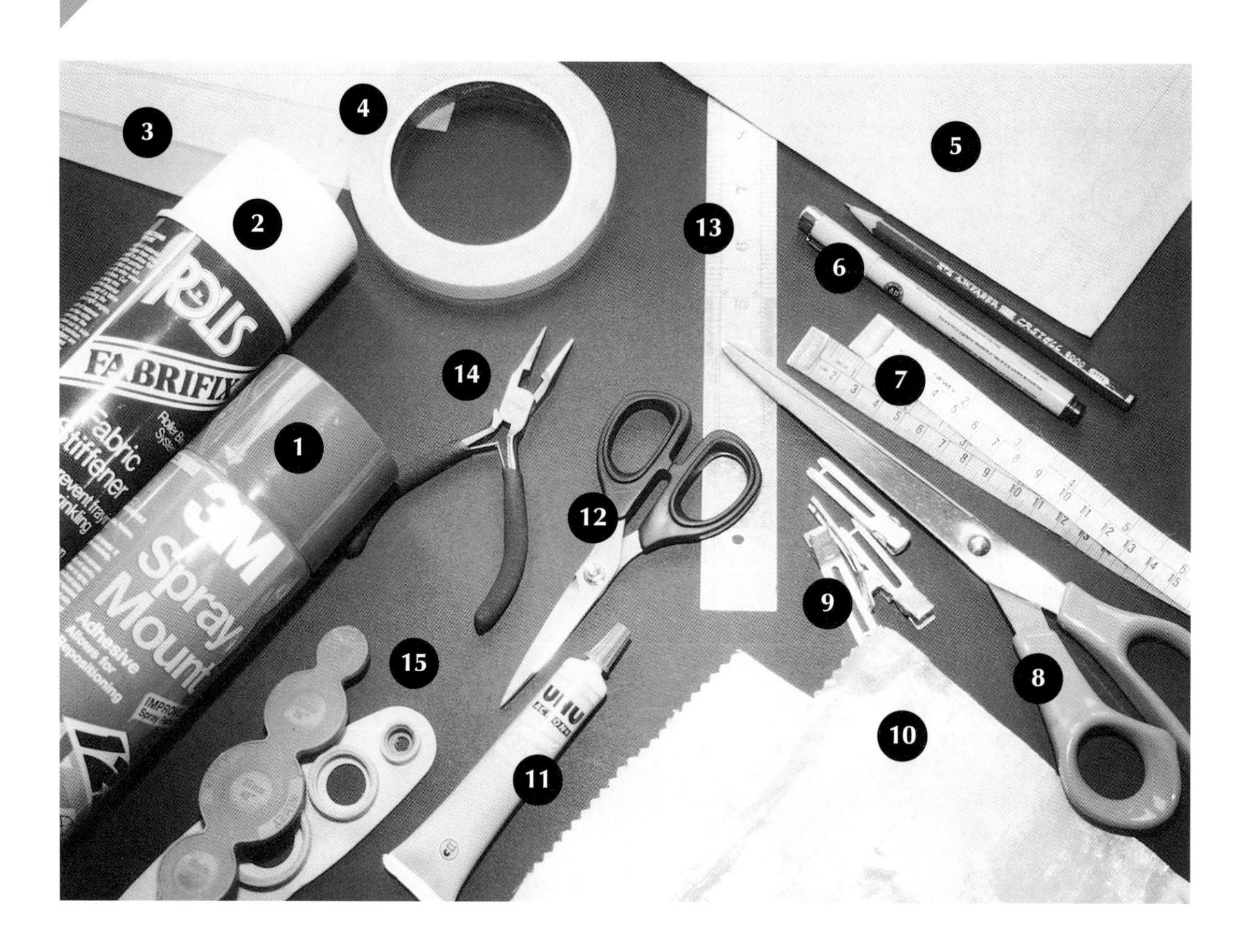

Equipment

Each head-dress has its own materials dealt with in different sections, but some of the tools mentioned below are used for general purposes when making head-dresses.

1. *Spray mount* is used to glue the fabric pieces together. Spray on the wrong side of the fabric and leave for a few seconds before pressing it down onto the other piece of fabric. It's also used to mount paper images onto card to form a collage.

2. *Fabric stiffener* hardens or firms up fabric that is too soft to use for head-dress decoration. For both these sprays, please follow the instructions, because the glue can be quite powerful when inhaling.

3. *Tracing paper* can be obtained from art supply shops. It is essential for making a template for any of the designs you do and want to keep as a copy, or when laying out the design to see how it fits onto the pattern piece.

4. *Double-sided tape* is useful when making flower stencils on card. Like spray mount, it's used to fuse two pieces of paper together.

5. *Card or an envelope* or anything that's firm enough can be used for tracing out stencil designs.

6. *Pen and pencil* for working out the designs. A soft leaded pencil is better to use for tracing onto tracing paper.

7. *A tape measure* in both metric and imperial measurements is useful for those who are not familiar with one or the other.

8. *Paper scissors,* length 23cm (9"), are used solely for this purpose.

9. *Hair clips or grips* for pressing decorative apparatus down onto your head-dress after squeezing glue onto the base of these pieces.

10. *Fabric* which looks and feels attractive. Anything that has surface interest or sheen and unusual colours should be considered. Always keep the bridal design in the forefront of your mind.

11. *Fabric glue* is used to fuse items together especially decorative flowers and trinkets. You wouldn't use spray mount for this purpose because the items are small and intricate.

12. *Fabric scissors,* length 13cm (5"), must have sharp pointed edges to the blades so that one can cut into intricate corners.

13. *A ruler or set square* is necessary to mark out the positions for your designs: it can be obtained in metric and imperial measurements.

14. *Cutting clippers* are very useful for shortening stems on leaves or cutting into wire used for coronettes or bouquets.

15. *Fabric moulding for buttons* as used on the appliqué head band design.

Beaded head-dress: 20s style

The materials used for this head-dress are straightforward: a square of plain silk, like dupion, provides a nice texture. It is a 20s style so keep the fabric as close to the period as possible. The same amount is used for both the wadding, (which is sandwiched in-between the lining and the top layer), and the satin lining that backs onto these layers to give the underside a clean finish. Put together beads and sequins of your choice keeping in mind the style of design. Use a needle thin enough for beadwork and a thickish cotton thread that would support the beads well and prevent them from dropping off. A simple design of this kind can be done by you; you won't need to be an expert to accomplish this level of bead work. Use an elastic width of 1cm, which is threaded through a bias-cut narrow band of silk to support the head-dress around the head circumference. The elastic is cut to measurement with a seam allowance of 1cm (3/8") each end. Use tracing paper and a pencil for the design layout.

To make a template: Fig. 3

a. Measure the head circumference and decide how wide the front piece is and how deep the centre front and sides are to be.
b. Draw in the design lines on tracing paper, including seam allowances of 1cm (½") width.
c. Make a template (*Fig. 3/A*) of the design and roughly draw in the beading application of your choice, by the selection of beads earmarked for each panel.
d. Cut the top layer of fabric and wadding to one and a half times the size of the pattern width and tack together. Pin the tracing paper in position onto this.
e. The top and under layer is stitched together through the lines marked in for the design. This gives the head piece a slightly padded effect.
f. Now hand stitch the beads onto the design through the stitch lines and between each panel. Cut the finished article to the pattern shape, adding seam around the outer shape.

Note
The lining is cut to the foundation pattern and stitched along the seam line for the top and bottom areas with the side pieces left raw. The seams are encased between the lining and the beaded top layer. To machine-stitch, a zip foot is easier to use. *Thread elastic* through the bias-cut channel and hand-stitch each end to the raw edges of the beaded piece. Once the head piece is completed, hand-stitch a row of pearl beads across the top.

Fig. 3

Fig. 3/A: Template for the design

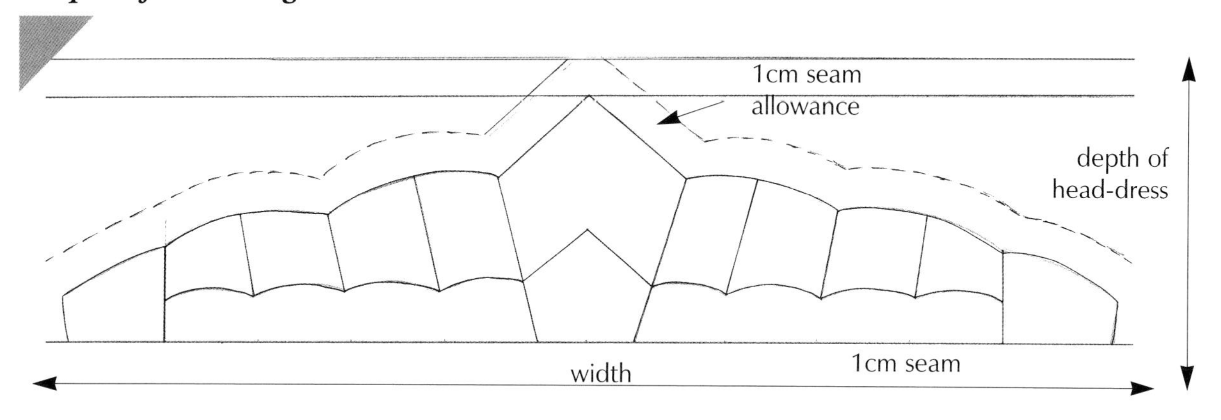

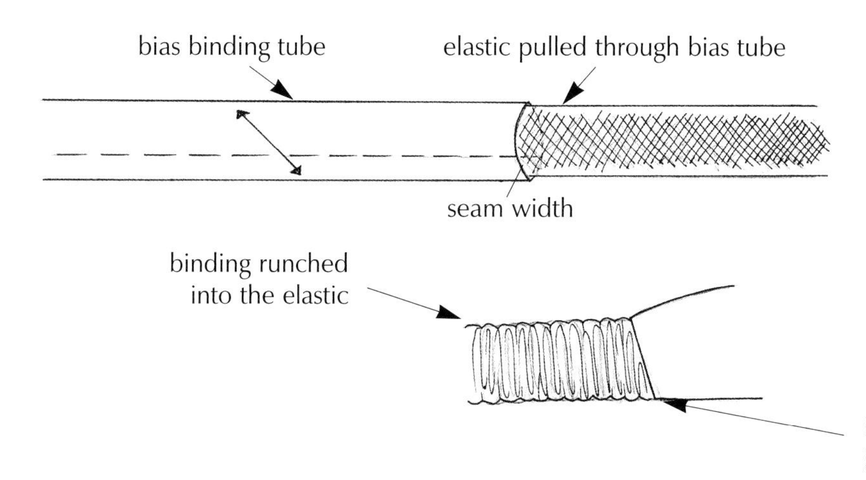

Fig. 4

Appliqué head band

This method, worked out on tracing paper and then transferred to card, makes a flower stencil design in two sizes. These flowers are also used for the petal sleeves in illustration *Fig.6* under Part 5.

The materials used to achieve these shapes are:

- **Tracing paper** and **pencil**, on which the flower designs are worked out
- A **tracing pencil** which becomes invisible on fabric
- A **head band**, prepared in advance and which is slightly padded with wadding and encased with silk dupion
- Two **square pieces of silk** and one piece of interfacing which is fused onto one layer of silk
- Fabric glue to attach the wadding to the plastic head band
- **Spray mount** to weld the two layers of silk together
- **Fabric stiffener** to give the flowers body
- **Decorative trim** to give the design dimension.

Preparing the appliqué: Fig. 5

a. Trace out the shape of the head band on tracing paper and cut to pattern. Use this template to cut a shape for the wadding, which is glued to the top surface of the band. Once dry, wrap a strip of bias-cut silk binding around the wadding to the shape of the band, and hand-stitch each end of the binding once the ends have been tucked in, to secure the raw edges.

b. Decide how big your flower stencils are to be and trace them out.

c. Prepare the fabric for the flowers, by using an iron-on staflex for one layer and spray mount on the second layer and seal them together.

d. When this is dry, trace off the flowers onto the fabric with a tracing pencil. Use a fabric stiffener to seal the raw edges and to increase the firmness of the design.

e. These flowers could look as attractive by using contrasting fabric colours.

f. Before glueing the flowers onto the head band, trim them with beads or sequins. Then arrange them onto the band and glue or stitch where possible onto the fabric underneath.

Fig. 5

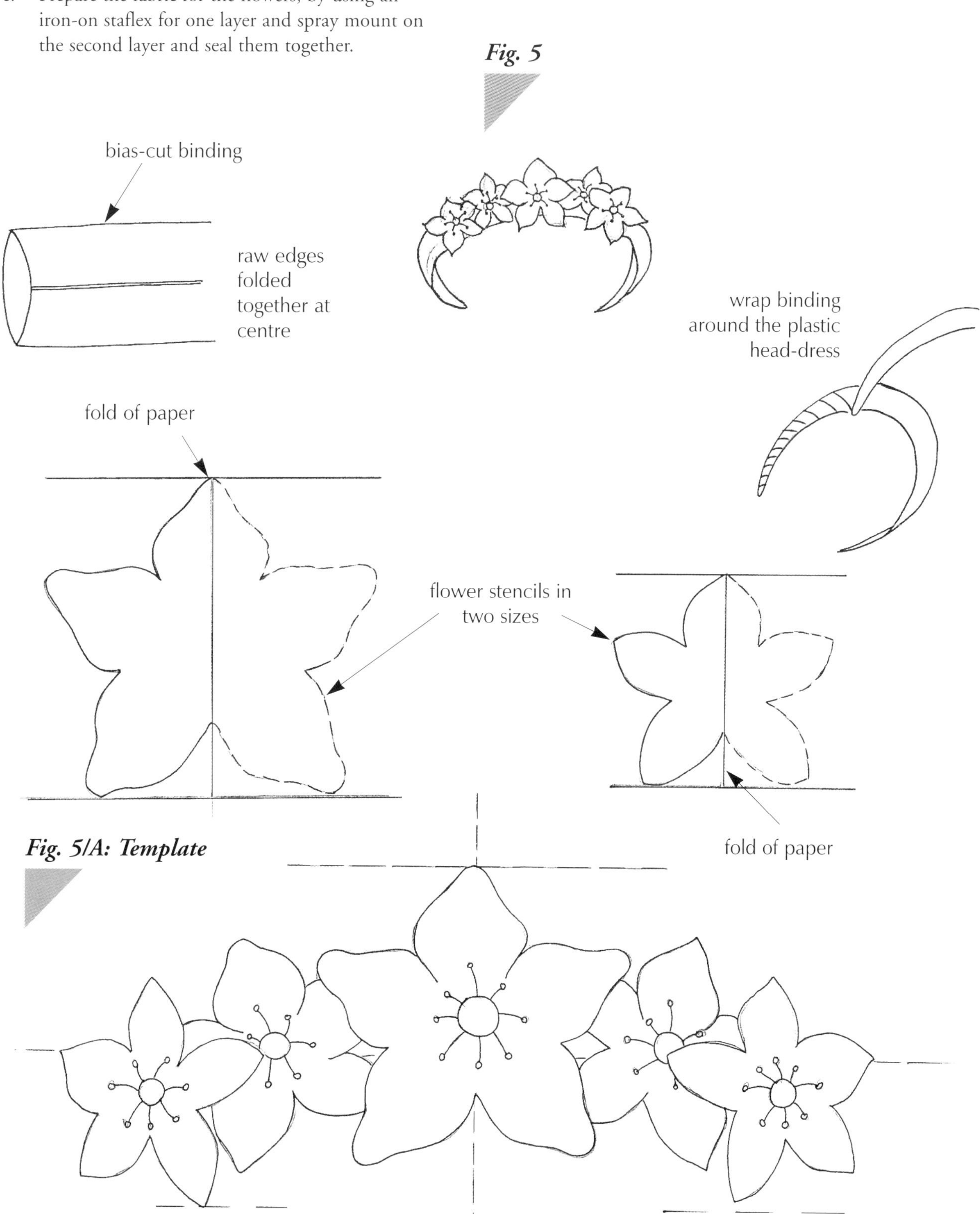

Fig. 5/A: Template

A simple veil: Fig. 6

The veil worn today is mainly seen as a decorative accessory, rather than carrying the implications of many years ago (as discussed under the 'Introduction' and 'Trains'). This simple design is easy to make providing the finished edge is made professionally. Once the head-dress is chosen, the next stage is to make sure the veil ties in with the hair style.

Preparing the veil

a. Most veils start from the crown but some start from the back of the head. Measure from where it is meant to start and to the required length.

b. For accuracy, make a paper pattern or just fold the tulle along its length and mark out a curve at one end.

c. Add approximately half that amount again for the second part, which covers the face and bodice. Then mark out a curve for this end, to match the other end.

d. Decide how wide you want the veil and how much fulness you require, and trim off the excess amount.

e. With the length still folded in half, pin and then tack in the measurement for your gathers, from the front edge to the crown and then towards the hem edge.

f. Trim the edge of the veil with a fine zigzag stitch, pulling out the tulle as you go along. This gives the edge a slightly fluted effect.

g. Sew in two rows of gathers along the position where it is pinned and draw up onto the comb.

Fig. 6: Veil

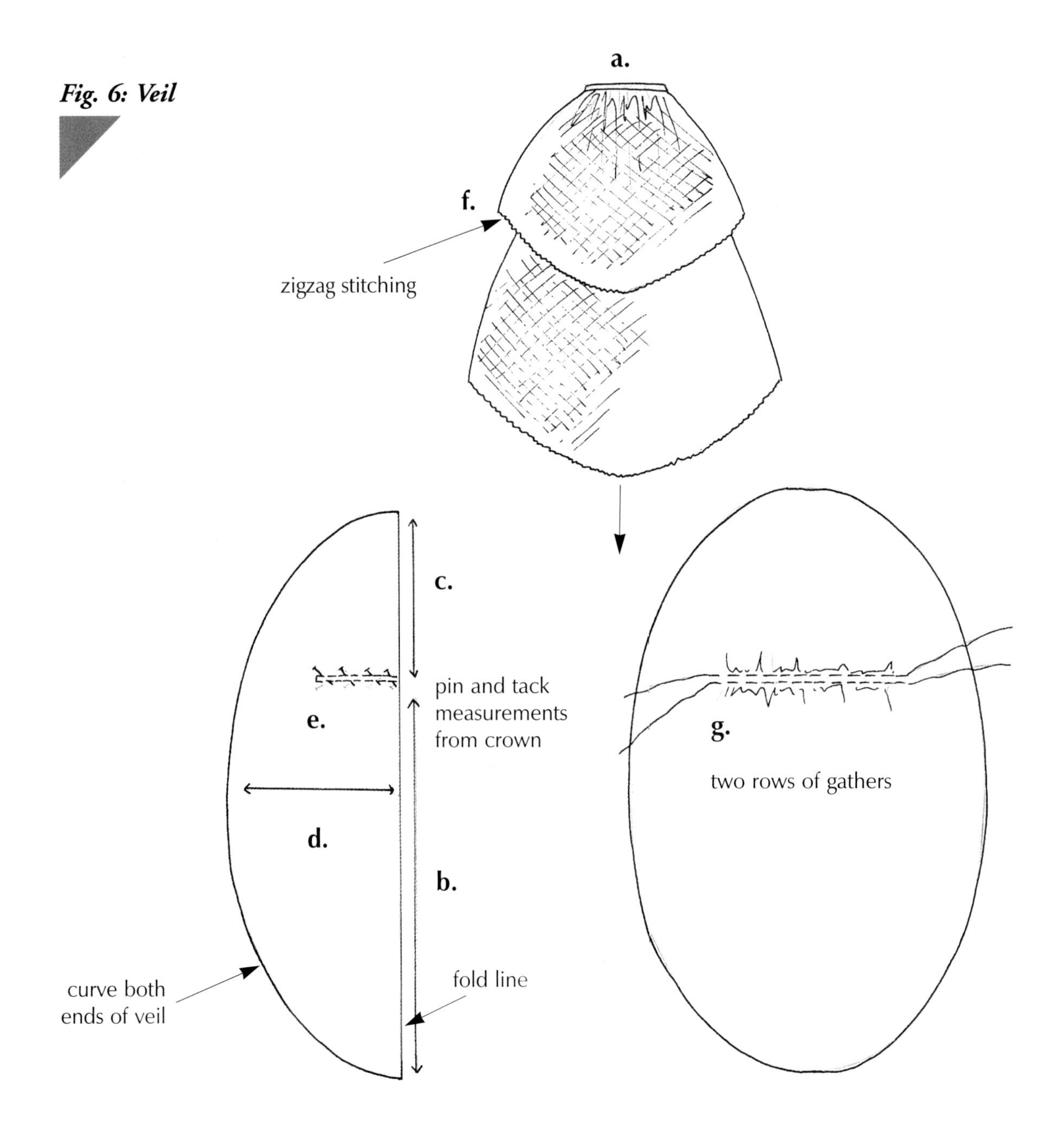

Nettings

Tulle is made from a strong quality nylon and is ideal for overskirting and veiling. It comes in a variety of colours and is approximately 300cm (118")wide. For an elaborate veil that fluffs up and stands away from the head, this quality is the best to use.

Pure silk is the finest quality to use for bridal veiling. It is a light non-stretch quality and comes in several widths 178cm (70") and 267cm (105"). A bobbinet machine net, where the holes are produced on Levers or Pushers: these are the names for the type of machines used for high quality laces and nettings.

Point d'Esprit is a 100% cotton tulle with a width of 132cm(52") made in the same way the silk is produced. The difference in quality is the square or round dots the machine produces at regular intervals. Veils in this quality are normally made without gathers. It sits flat on the crown and extends to the floor. Trimmed with lace or scalloped embroidery, it enhances styles like the 20s wedding gown.

Note
Some nettings are normally heat-sealed when produced, and the risk of dyeing your own is not recommended because the quality of the net creases and becomes difficult to iron out.

Fig. 7: Plain tulles, veils and dress net

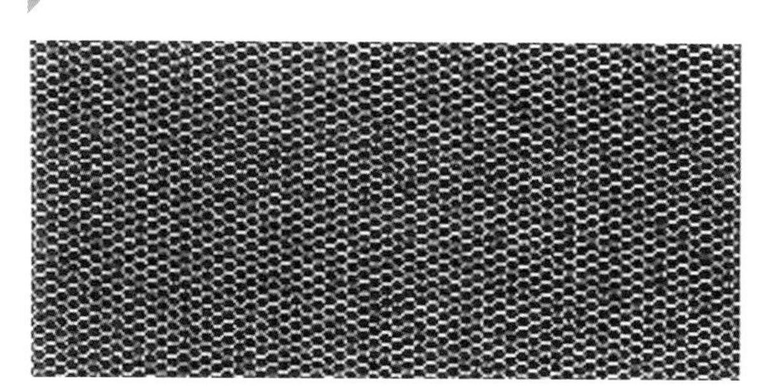

delicate nylon veiling/overskirting

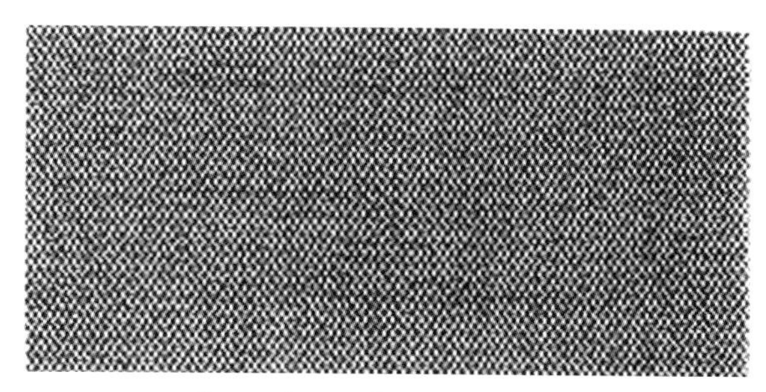

stronger quality nylon tulle in 27 colours

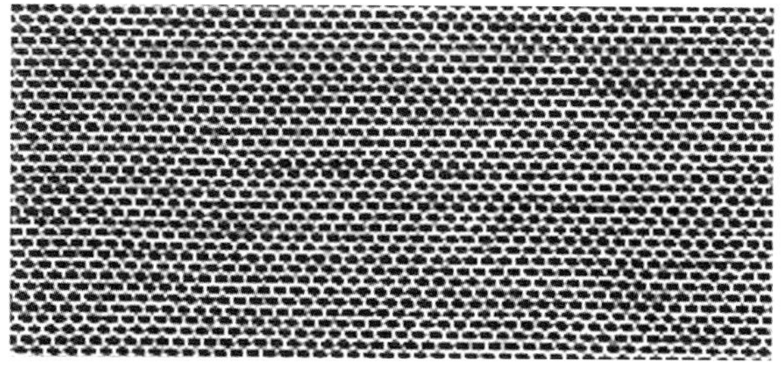

finest quality cotton veiling

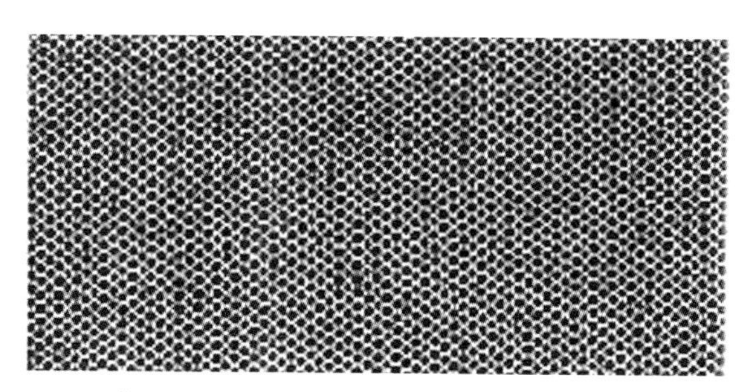

pure silk – the finest and lightest non-stretch quality

point d'esprit 100% cotton tulle

standard petticoat dress net 132-137cm (52-54")

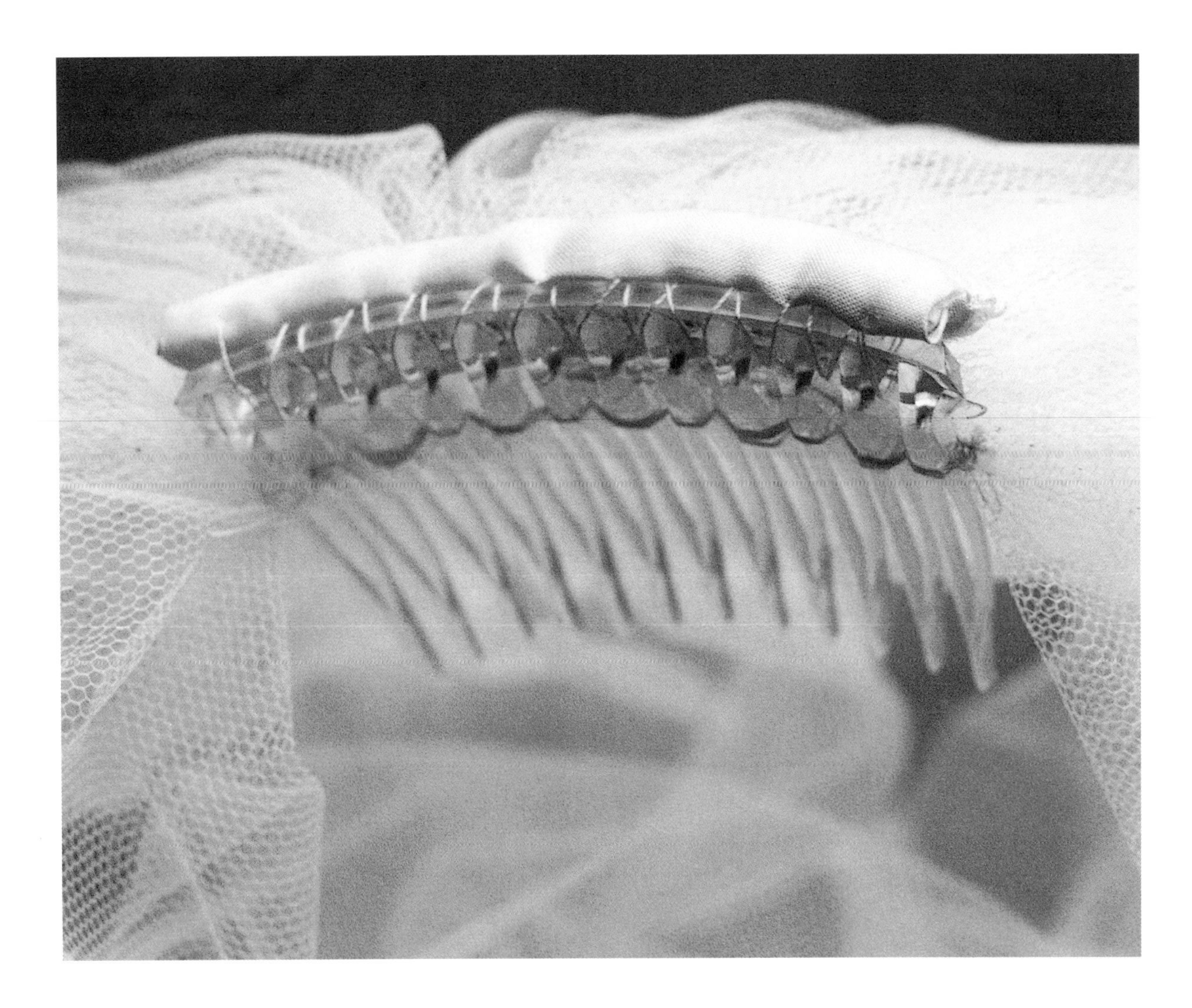

The comb: Fig. 8

Plastic combs can be obtained through any haberdasher. For bridal veils they are usually trimmed with satin to conceal the plastic ridge. To decorate the band of the comb, cut a strip of bias-cut satin of 2cm ($^{3}/_{4}$") and a thin strip of wadding of 1cm ($^{3}/_{8}$"). The satin is wrapped around the wadding to the size of the comb and tacked together, tucking in the raw edges at each end. The seam edge is placed over the ridge of the comb and then stitched down through the teeth for several rows to secure the trim. See illustrations on next page.

Fig. 8: Comb

a.
trimmed with satin binding

b.
2cm bias satin slip

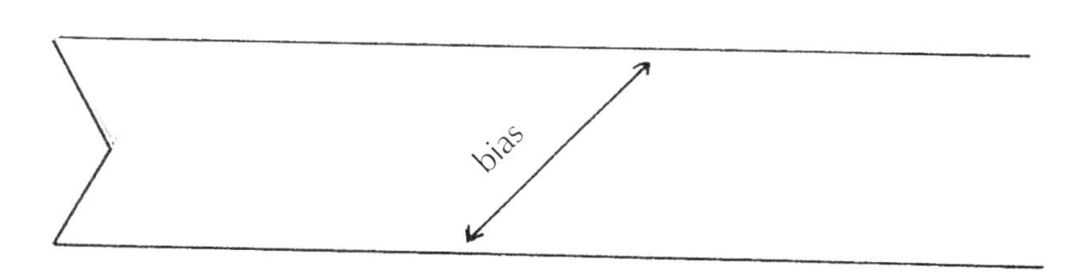

c.
wrap satin over the wad

1cm strip of wadding

d.
stitch wadded satin piece through teeth of comb

A fur hat: Fig. 9

This Russian style hat based on the Kossack, is produced with a mock fur used for the main outer layer and crown (optional). The style is worn for a winter wedding and has a matching muff that wraps around the hands and wrists. The inside layers of both these accessories are lined with a soft but firm quality satin. The head circumference measurement should be taken to allow the hat to fit deep onto the forehead. A tolerance of approximately 1.5cm (5/8") ease should be calculated into the measurement so that there is enough head room after the fur is attached to the base of the hat. For the foundation piece, one could use good quality silk or textured fabric. Line it with a heavyweight interfacing before attaching the lining. The lining pieces are made up separately and are only attached at the base of the crown and where the seam edge is sealed with hat petersham.

Fig. 9

Preparation for a soft hat

There are three parts to this draft: The *foundation piece* that rests against the head; the *crown,* stitched on top and which secures the hat to the foundation; and the *outer layer* which is attached to the base of the foundation piece and turned upwards to lie flat against it.

Fig. 10:

a. Use the head circumference measurement to draw a circle for the crown of the hat.
b. Decide how deep you want the foundation piece to be.
c. Mark out a rectangular shape for both the measurements of the height and length of this pattern.
d. The outer circle is traced from the foundation piece and reshaped by slashing through the top edge at regular intervals.
e. The new curved shape should be approximately 20cm bigger than the foundation pattern, so that it doesn't restrict the shape of the hat when pushed back on itself and rest against the foundation piece.

Note

To stitch the pieces together, cut out the foundation piece in the top layer of silk, an underlayer of heavy weight interfacing and a firm satin for the lining. The crown pattern piece is cut in the same fabric. The outer layer or hat band is cut in fur, with satin for the lining. The mock fur usually has a good quality backing to it and doesn't need an interfacing. The lining pattern pieces are made separately to the top layers of the hat. Attach a width of petersham to the edge of the lining. It is stitched together *only* at the base of the foundation piece. The seam is folded under the petersham and hand-stitched to cover the seam.

Fig. 10

Fig. 10/A

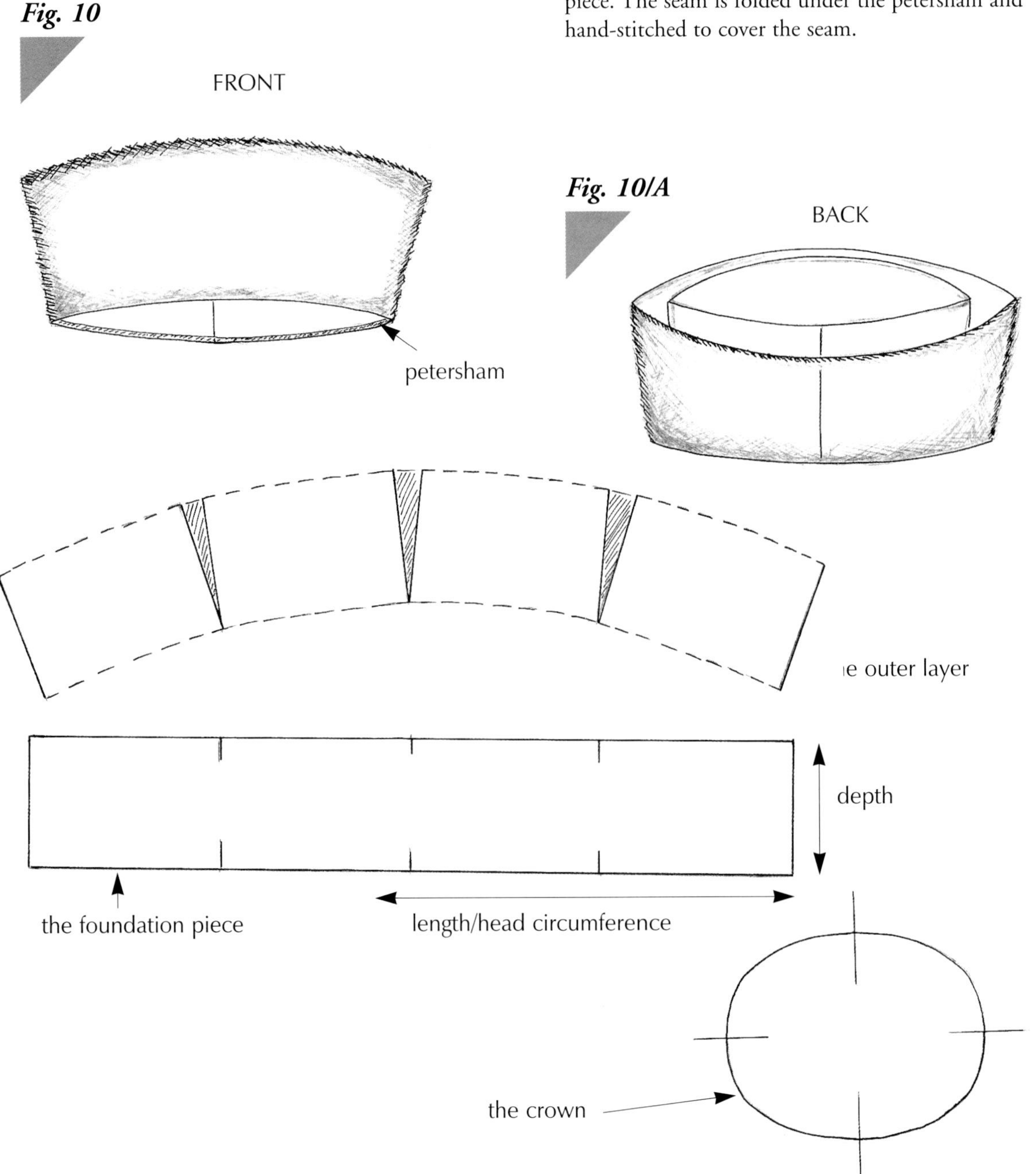

Reading list

The following are a selection of generally reliable and reasonably accessible sources of information on the subject. Many of them include more detailed bibliographies and guides to further sources. The publications should be available from local lending or reference libraries (and if they are not in stock can be obtained through the Inter-Library Loan Service).

Arch, Nigel and Marschner, Joanna — ROYAL WEDDING DRESSES. Sidgwick and Jackson, 1990.

Cunnington, P. and Lucas, C. — COSTUME FOR BIRTHS, MARRIAGES AND DEATHS. A.& C.Black,1972.

Ginsburg, M. — WEDDING DRESS 1740- 1970. H.M.S.O. 1981.

larvis, A. — BRIDES - Wedding Clothes and Customs 1850-1980. Merseyside County Museums, Liverpool, 1983.

Lansdell, A. — WEDDING FASHIONS 1860-1980. Shire Publications, 1983.

Laverack, E. — WITH THIS RING: 100 years of marriage. Elm Tree Books, 1979.

London Museum — ROYAL WEDDING DRESSES. Exhibition Catalogue, H.M.S.O., 1972.

Manchester City Art Galleries — WEDDINGS: Wedding Costume 1735-1970. Manchester City Art Galleries, 1977.

Monsarrat, A. — AND THE BRIDE WORE ... Gentry Books, 1973.

Probert, C. — BRIDES IN VOGUE SINCE 1910. Thames and Hudson, 1984.

Stevenson, P. — BRIDAL FASHIONS. Ian Allan, 1978.

Articles:

Baker, A. — 'Wedding Bouquets' in COSTUME 6, 1972. pp. 53-5.

Staniland, K. — 'H.R.H. Princess Anne's wedding dress' in COSTUME 8, 1974. p. 18.
'Queen Victoria's wedding dress and lace' in COSTUME 17, 1983. pp. 1-32.
'The Wedding Dresses of H.R.H. The Princess of Wales (1981) and H.R.H. The Duchess of York (1986). in COSTUME 21, 1987.

Glossary

Bag-out
When seams are boxed in between a top and an under layer.

Bar-tack
Several short rows of stitching over a particular area.

Bias
Crossway strips cut at an angle of 45% from the straight grain; or the grainline marked at the same angle on a pattern.

Bustle
An artificial appendage fitted to the centre-back skirt of women's clothing, as worn in the 1900s.

CB and CF
the centre back and centre front of a garment or pattern.

Crinolette
A cage-shaped apparatus fastened at the waist and protruding at the centre-back to form a bustle.

Girth
The widest part of an area of the body measured in the round.

Hoop
An oval-shaped petticoat made with a stiff regiline, or with cane threaded through bias strips at the hemline or through tiered seams.

Leg-o'-mutton
A term used in the 1900s for a sleeve shape which took the form of a leg of mutton when gathered at the crown.

Ruching
A form of gathers at the fitting line of a seam, normally created with a tacking stitch.

RS
The right side of a garment.

Silhouette
An outline of a style or the complete design of a garment.

Toile
A calico mock-up made when experimenting on the garment or a part of it, prior to using the correct fabric.

Tolerance or ease
A supplementary measurement allowed in an area where there might be friction.

WR.S
The wrong side of a garment.

Suppliers

Fabric and Haberdashery:

James Hare Silks
Monarch House
P.O. Box 72
Queen Street
Leeds LS1 1LX

McCullock and Wallis Ltd
P.O. Box 3AX
25-26 Dering Street
London W1A 3AX

Nottingham Laces & Trimmings Ltd
Turret E, Harrington Mills
Leopold Street
Long Eaton
Nottingham NG10 4QE

Creative Beadcraft Ltd
Denmark Works
Sheepcote Dell Road
Beamond End
Buckinghamshire HP7 ORX

or

20 Beak Street
SOHO
London W1R 3HA

Flowers by Novelty Ltd
7 Kensington Mall
o ff Kensington Church Street
London W8 4EB

Books & Supplies:

R.D. Franks Ltd
Kent House
Market Place
London W1N 8EJ

Morplan
56 Great Titchfield Street
London W1P 8DX

Patterns: (dressmaking)
Vogue, New Look, Butterick, McCalls,
Simplicity

Reference Libraries:

Museum of Costume and Fashion Research Centre
Bath

Index

Page numbers in italic refer to illustrations